THE WAR THAT DOESN'T SAY ITS NAME

The War That Doesn't Say Its Name

THE UNENDING CONFLICT IN THE CONGO

JASON K. STEARNS

PRINCETON UNIVERSITY PRESS

PRINCETON & OXFORD

Published by Princeton University Press
41 William Street, Princeton, New Jersey 08540
99 Banbury Road, Oxford OX2 6JX

press.princeton.edu

All Rights Reserved

First paperback printing, 2023
Paper ISBN: 978-0-691-22451-0

The Library of Congress has cataloged the cloth edition as follows:

Names: Stearns, Jason K., author.
Title: The war that doesn't say its name : the unending conflict in the Congo / Jason K. Stearns.
Description: 1st. | Princeton : Princeton University Press, 2021. | Includes bibliographical references and index.
Identifiers: LCCN 2021013541 (print) | LCCN 2021013542 (ebook) | ISBN 9780691194080 (hardback) | ISBN 9780691224527 (ebook)
Subjects: LCSH: Civil war—Congo (Democratic Republic) | Congo (Democratic Republic)—History—1997- | Congo (Democratic Republic)—Politics and government—1997-
Classification: LCC DT658.26 .S745 2021 (print) | LCC DT658.26 (ebook) | DDC 967.51034—dc23
LC record available at https://lccn.loc.gov/2021013541
LC ebook record available at https://lccn.loc.gov/2021013542

British Library Cataloging-in-Publication Data is available

Editorial: Bridget Flannery-McCoy and Alena Chekanov
Production Editorial: Natalie Baan
Jacket/Cover Design: Layla Mac Rory
Production: Erin Suydam
Publicity: Kate Hensley and Kathryn Stevens
Copyeditor: Martin Schneider
Map Design: Giovanni Salvaggio

Jacket/Cover image: Northeastern Ituri Province, DRC, February 2020.
© Dieudonne Dirole for Fondation Carmignac

This book has been composed in Arno

For Baye and Masha.

Kupoteya njia ndiyo kujua njia.

CONTENTS

1 Introduction   1

2 The Historical Background   24

3 Explaining the Congolese Conflict   37

4 The Role of the Congolese and Rwandan States   57

5 The Theory: Involution, Fragmentation, and a
   Military Bourgeoisie   91

6 The CNDP and the M23   121

7 The Raia Mutomboki   164

8 Ituri and the UPC   194

9 Peacemaking and the Congo   225

Acknowledgments   259
Notes   261
Bibliography   287
Index   301

THE WAR THAT DOESN'T SAY ITS NAME

1

Introduction

Die ich rief, die Geister, / Werd' ich nun nicht los
(The spirits I called / I cannot drive away)

—JOHANN WOLFGANG VON GOETHE

IN EARLY 2008, I set up my research base at the VIP hotel in downtown Goma, a trade hub in the eastern Congo nestled between the Nyiragongo Volcano and the shores of Lake Kivu. A peace conference was being held close by, and many of its attendees were staying at the hotel, where they also dined. After a year and a half of fighting, the Congolese government had decided to sit down with several dozen armed groups to talk peace.

Expectations ran high. While the main Congo wars, which had lasted from 1996 to 2003, had ended in a comprehensive peace deal, the fighting had escalated to the north of where we sat, displacing hundreds of thousands of people. This time, the peace brokers wanted to go further than just elite pacts and deal with the root causes of the conflict. "For the first time, the sons and daughters of North and South Kivu have come together to speak about peace, security, and development," announced the minister of the interior in his speech. Envoys from the United States, the European Union, and the United Nations rubbed shoulders with armed group commanders, NGO workers, and civil society leaders.

The peace conference was, in many aspects, a positive and cathartic experience. It situated conflict as the historical product of local tensions over land and identity; community leaders were given space and time to express their anger and grief over decades of war, voicing emotions they had never had a chance to put into words in front of their rivals. I met a preacher and peace activist from the Banyamulenge community of South Kivu province who carried in his briefcase a fifty-page-long list—handwritten, on yellowing paper—of all the people from his community who had been killed in the previous fifteen years. "This is why our youths are fighting," he said. Jeannot Muhima, a combatant from just outside of Goma, described to me eloquently, calmly, how his sister had been raped and his younger brother killed by an armed group. He turned his head to show a shiny scar parting his hair on the back of his head. "I barely escaped," he said. "That is why I fight. But it is also why, more than anything, I want peace."[1]

And yet, in the end, despite the best intentions of many of the participants, the Goma Peace Conference became a source of profiteering and accomplished little. Initially, six hundred people were supposed to attend, ranging from civil society leaders to customary chiefs and members of armed groups. However, attracted by per diems of $135, which were even given to people who lived nearby, attendance reportedly swelled to fifteen hundred people. "Peacemaking has become a source of business around here," a friend, a rebel turned human rights activist, cynically remarked, watching armed group commanders walk past the lunch buffet at the VIP hotel, plates piled perilously high with food.[2] In the evening, the bars and nightclubs of Goma were full of delegates to the peace conference; one establishment, having run out of Congolese beer, had to source it from neighboring Rwanda.

As in subsequent peace talks, negotiations also became a tactic, a means of maneuvering. A United Nations official shared confidential reports with me about how both the armed groups and the national government were rearming and recruiting new troops during the truce. "These guys were never serious," she told me. "And we play along with their game." In the end, after months of laborious negotiations, fighting erupted again to the north of Goma, pushing all the way into the outskirts of this town of several hundred thousand people.

How could it be that the violence persisted, when so many of the key actors—soldiers, civilians, diplomats, and members of civil society—wanted it to end? This is the puzzle that this book addresses. Despite billions in international aid, a national army of 130,000 pitted against ragtag rebel groups, and the largest United Nations peacekeeping operation in the world, conflict has simmered on until the present day.

These snapshots from the Goma Peace Conference offer pieces of an answer. While many suffered from the conflict, a slim class of commanders and politicians emerged for whom, plates laden high, the conflict had become a source of survival and profit. These protagonists have had little interest in bringing an end to a conflict that was peripheral for the government but for many combatants had become a livelihood. Conflict, as well as peacemaking, had become an end in itself, the fighting carried forward by its own momentum. Meanwhile, foreign donors and diplomats provided food and urgent health care for millions in need, preventing the Congolese state from collapsing, but were unable to bring about transformational change. "Too big to fail" was a quip I often heard from diplomats, riffing on the financial crisis unfolding in the United States at the time.

Congolese have developed their own, often witty ways to express this sad state of affairs. "No Nkunda No Job," was a popular saying in Goma around this time, referring to the main rebel commander and suggesting that violence had become a source of employment for foreign aid workers and local militia. The epithet "Ebola business" surfaced in 2018, when donors pumped in a billion dollars to stem an epidemic of hemorrhagic fever in northern Congo, creating a cottage industry of Congolese security contractors—some of whom stoked violence so as to increase demand for their services—rental car dealers, and hoteliers. The eccentric Congolese pop star Koffi Olomide put it differently, alluding to the propensity to turn adversity into a source of profit, even pleasure: "Oyo eza système ya lifelo—moto ezopela kasi tozo zika te" (We live in the system of hell—everywhere the fire is raging, but we don't get burned).

What is this *système ya lifelo*? How has it come about? That is the motivation for this book. Drawing on two years of field research, interviews with over three hundred people intimately involved in the conflict, and almost two decades of continuous work in the country, I try to explain why conflict in the Congo has persisted from the time of the 2002 peace deal until the time of writing in 2020, defying international and local efforts to bring about peace.

Congo's Forever War

Serious armed conflict has roiled the Democratic Republic of the Congo, through different permutations, at least since 1996. The early phase of the conflict received considerable media and diplomatic attention. The First Congo War (1996–1997) saw a coalition of neighboring countries band together to overthrow Mobutu Sese Seko, who had ruled the Congo for thirty-two years. His successor, Laurent-Désiré Kabila, then fell out with his foreign backers, triggering the Second Congo War, which split the country into at least four parts and lasted from August 1998 until June 2003.

Under the leadership of the South African government, the United Nations, and the African Union, a peace deal—called the Global and Inclusive Agreement—was negotiated in 2002. All major Congolese belligerents joined a transitional government and merged their troops into a new national army. The former belligerents, together with civil society and members of the political opposition, passed a new constitution and held the country's first democratic elections in over forty years in 2006, bringing an end to the transition. The peace deal, however, did not end the conflict; instead it spawned a more amorphous and fragmented phase of violence—*la guerre qui ne dit pas son nom* ("the war that doesn't say its name"), as Congolese sometimes refer to it.

The conflict became mostly confined to the eastern Kivu region, where it escalated and fragmented, becoming more intractable. Armed groups proliferated to over 120 in 2021, fighting over often intensely local issues. At the time of writing, 5.5 million people were internally displaced in the Congo, more than at any other time and more than in any other country in the world except Syria. Estimates of mortality from the conflict are contested, but it is fairly certain that hundreds of thousands have died from direct violence, with probably between 1 million and 5.4 million people dying due to the humanitarian consequences for the period between 1998 and 2007—less than half the total conflict period between 1996 and today.[3]

While the First and Second Congo Wars received significant international media and diplomatic attention, the subsequent wars seemed less important, in part because they no longer threatened major urban centers and featured a dizzying number of armed factions. This complexity became a challenge for journalists and activists alike—how can you get people to care about a conflict featuring over a hundred different groups, fighting for a host of reasons? Despite its enormous human toll, the Congolese conflict was mentioned only twice on the front page of the *New York Times* in 2017; by contrast, the Syrian conflict was mentioned 240 times. It did not appear at all on US broadcast news, except for a few brief mentions, including George Clooney's charitable work and efforts to protect gorillas.[4]

———

As the Congolese conflict has plodded on inexorably, hindsight makes it easy to think that there was never any hope for peace. This view infuriates my friend Raphael Wakenge, a human rights activist in Bukavu who is locally known as a *mtu matata* (troublemaker) for his propensity to cause controversy. "That's just defeatism," he told me one morning after reading an article—one of many in Western media—arguing that the Congo was unviable and should be broken up.[5] "As if we didn't get into this mess because of decisions that our leaders made. As if there were not other paths that could have been taken, more visionary people who could have taken us there."

Raph was right—at least in part. This did not have to be a forever war. Closer inspection of the morass of the Congolese violence reveals

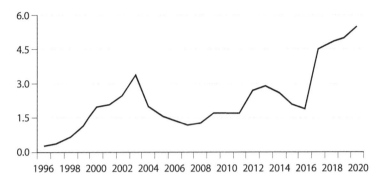

FIGURE 1.1. Internal displacement in the Congo, millions of people, 1996–2020
(Source: various OCHA reports)

patterns and nuances that call into question the inevitability of the conflict. Two particularities stand out.

First, the violence had dramatic peaks and valleys, suggesting that the conflict was susceptible to change. In 2002, with the signing of the Global and Inclusive Agreement between the major belligerents and the formation of a power-sharing government, there was a sharp drop in displacement and violence. Between 2002 and 2007, internal displacement dropped from 3.4 million to 1.2 million people, and 130,000 combatants were demobilized in a national program. Then, abruptly, violence escalated again, reaching levels never before seen in the Congo (see figure 1.1). What happened in 2003 that de-escalated the conflict, and what happened in 2007 to ramp it up again?

Second, there has been striking geographic variation. While conflict in the Kivu provinces has escalated since the end of the transitional government in 2007, it initially declined dramatically in Ituri province, just to the north, once the scene of some of the most gruesome violence in the country. Displacement there declined from 500,000 in 2003 to 146,000 in 2015. What helped stabilize Ituri even as violence in the rest of the eastern Congo persisted?[6]

These questions pose a challenge to conflict scholars. Most of the variables invoked by academics to explain why conflicts last so long— poverty, state weakness, ethnic conflict, the absence of peacekeepers, the abundance of natural resources, and ethnic exclusion—are spread relatively evenly across the eastern Congo and have not changed much over the past twenty years.[7] And yet, we see huge differences, both temporally and geographically, in the intensity of conflict.

Part of this book is an engagement with these broader academic debates. My explanation places much greater emphasis on government elites—in the Congo and Rwanda—than on local actors, in contrast with the "local turn" adopted by some conflict scholars.[8] It is also more focused on the actors, their interests, and their interactions than on material variables, in contrast with literature by conflict scholars that has aimed to detect laws of causation through large datasets with high degrees of abstraction. The story told here is not primarily one of natural resources, a corrupt government, an impoverished population, and a difficult topography—after all, those features are relatively commonplace, while conflict is not—but of the protagonists who animate and interpret these factors.

Explaining the Congolese Conflict

So what explains this persistence of conflict in the Congo? The evidence provided here points to several concurrent dynamics—to be distinguished from "variables" in that they consist of relationships between groups of people, each with its own, contingent interpretation of its political and social context: a lopsided peace deal that pushed one former belligerent back into war; a failed army integration process that created a multitude of new armed groups led by army defectors; and an electoral process that created incentives for politicians to ally with armed groups. All of this occurred against the backdrop of a weak, patrimonial state and a political culture in which armed violence was seen as an acceptable and established means of obtaining power and resources. In chapter 3, I trace these developments and flesh out this analysis. The second part of this book, consisting of chapters 6 through 8, provides further detail to this story by investigating the armed groups that mobilized against the state.

Many of these dynamics were linked to the same peace process that ushered in the democratic transition: it privileged the incumbent president, Joseph Kabila, and allowed an elite that was unaccountable to voters to entrench itself and to resist a democratic reckoning. It also dramatically disfavored one of the strongest but least popular belligerents, the Rassemblement congolais pour la démocratie (RCD). These two factors interacted to spark a new insurgency, the Congrès national pour la défense du peuple (CNDP), which then provoked countermobilizations by dozens of other groups.

Meanwhile, outside actors failed to transform these dynamics. Since 1999, when the peace process officially began, the United Nations has deployed two of its largest and most expensive peacekeeping missions there. Donors have spent over $48 billion on development, stability, and relief projects, and in 2015, 180 different international nonprofits had projects there.[9]

The results have been mixed. International efforts did help broker the 2002 peace deal, reuniting the country and setting up new, democratic institutions. However, in the wake of the 2006 elections, as the conflict became more amorphous and fractal, donors and diplomats adopted a postconflict mindset and became increasingly marginalized. As I explore in chapter 9, donors and diplomats were blinkered by a liberal model of peacemaking that placed too much emphasis on the formal trappings of the peace process, especially the creation of new democratic and regulatory institutions, and on liberalization of the economy. Real power, however, resided in informal, parallel networks largely untouched by these interventions. The government showed little interest in creating strong, impartial state institutions. At the same time, the peace process triggered a fire sale of state assets, in particular mining concessions, which led to a massive influx of money into the ruling elite from multinational corporations—a process encouraged and fostered by the World Bank with little pushback from donors. This further entrenched the new, unaccountable elites in Kinshasa and the provinces.

Inscrutable Congolese, Defiant Rwandans

Why did donors get it wrong? In part, outsiders spent too little time trying to understand the belligerents. This is not surprising; portrayals of the Congo have often dealt in stereotypes. This is how Joseph

Conrad—whose *Heart of Darkness* remains one of the best examples of how compassion, even when conjoined with eloquence and erudition, is not immune to prejudice—described his protagonist's trip up the Congo River:

> The steamer toiled along slowly on the edge of a black and incomprehensible frenzy. The prehistoric man was cursing us, praying to us, welcoming us—who could tell? We were cut off from the comprehension of our surroundings; we glided past like phantoms, wondering and secretly appalled, as sane men would be before an enthusiastic outbreak in a madhouse.[10]

More recent depictions recall Conrad's imaginary Congolese. A *New York Times* journalist, musing about the gruesome rapes, wrote: "No one—doctors, aid workers, Congolese and Western researchers—can explain exactly why this is happening."[11] His colleague, Nicholas Kristof, concurred: "This is a pointless war—now a dozen years old—driven by warlords, greed for minerals, ethnic tensions and complete impunity."[12]

The war was *not* pointless. It was driven by actors with specific interests, steeped in particular institutional and political cultures. Much like Conrad's sailor, donors and diplomats were handicapped by their preconceptions, unable to see or understand these interests and cultures.

For example, after the 2006 elections, donors placed priority on strengthening government institutions, or "the extension of state authority," as it was formulated in the mandate of the UN peacekeeping mission. Belgian, American, French, and South African officers trained the Congolese army, the World Bank launched an overhaul of Congolese administration, and various donors set up a stabilization program in the eastern Congo to build roads, government offices, prisons, and courts.

This approach underestimated the degree to which weakness had become a means of rule, as I discuss in chapter 4, with elites actively colluding in the erosion of state institutions. During this period,

Congolese government rarely showed an interest in strengthening its institutions or bringing an end to a peripheral war that did not threaten the country's capital a thousand miles away. It has favored the maintenance of patronage networks, some linked to its armed opponents, over the security of its citizens and the personal survival of its elites over institutional reform. The challenge here was not so much how to increase administrative efficiency or promote free market reforms but rather how to render political power more accountable and invested in security, rather than conflict.

A second example further elucidates the centrality of political culture in the conflict. For many years, the inability of donors and diplomats to acknowledge Rwandan intervention in the eastern Congo formed a major stumbling block. This was driven both by misguided assumptions about the Rwandan Patriotic Front (RPF) government and by pathologies in the donor bureaucracies. "The Rwandan government has no interest in backing the CNDP. They want a stable eastern Congo," a senior British diplomat insisted to me in 2008.[13] He was not alone. Leaders from former British prime minister Tony Blair to billionaire philanthropist Howard Buffett to former US national security advisor Susan Rice either rejected the mounting proof that Rwanda was involved or justified it by playing up security concerns.

Rwanda played a critical role in the creation of both the CNDP and Mouvement du 23 Mars (M23) rebellions, in 2006 and 2012, respectively, dramatically undermining the stability of its neighbor. It did so even though it had experienced few security threats and—contrary to popular belief in the Congo—stood to lose as much as it could gain economically. To understand why it intervened nonetheless, we must examine how the RPF functioned. Decision-making was dominated by members of the security forces, was rarely the result of open internal debate, and was marked by a deep fear of internal military dissent. Involvement in the eastern Congo reinforced the image of a besieged Rwanda and reminded domestic elites of the RPF's role as defender against genocidal forces, a key legitimizing discourse of the government. All these factors supported belligerency toward the eastern Congo, as I explore further in chapter 4.

The Social Nature of Rebellion

What can these dynamics teach us about conflict more broadly? My argument here, laid out in detail in chapter 5, is staked out in two inter-related realms: structural factors—fragmentation and the rise of a mili-tary bourgeoisie—as well as ideational or cultural ones—phenomena that I call involution and symbiosis. I argue that these trends are being reproduced in other conflicts on the African continent as well, linked to the liberalization of politics and the economy.

Self-interest, to paraphrase Alexander Wendt, is what belligerents make of it. The goals, ambitions, and desires of belligerents are deeply shaped by the worldviews of the main actors and the institutions, norms, ideas, and habits that shape these. The conflict in the Congo has persisted because war has become a means of governing the country; this was increasingly an acceptable and profitable lifestyle for a military bourgeoisie stretching from Kinshasa through the Kivus to Kigali that has matured and flourished through conflict.

Interests, in other words, need to be examined, not assumed. This is hard, as the high stakes of violent conflict create incentives to dissimu-late and obfuscate what belligerents really want and feel. In chapter 4, I draw on dozens of interviews with government officials and security operatives in the Congo and neighboring Rwanda. In both places, elites' attitudes toward conflict have been marked by *involution*, reproducing and intensifying existing patterns of violence, despite the cost to the local population and even though other approaches could be more ben-eficial to these elites.

While in part this involution, this rut in which the conflict is stuck, is driven by naked economic interests, these attitudes have also been driven by the normalization of violence and the essentialization of identity. How else can we understand the apathy—and sometimes complicity—of political and military elites in Kinshasa toward the grinding violence that affects millions to the east? After all, few of these decision-makers derive direct benefits from the conflict, and one could imagine many other ways in which they could extract resources or render themselves popular that do not involve violent conflict. Similarly, Rwanda's dogged intervention cannot be easily explained away by greed or self-defense, as I show in chapters 4 and 6.

The second realm of analysis is structural, perhaps best exemplified by the dramatic fragmentation of armed actors immediately apparent in the maps of the Congolese conflict at the end of this chapter. The riotous splatter painting of roughly 120 armed groups—up from a few dozen in 2008—shows the growing complexity of the conflict (see the maps and accompanying key on pages 16–23). This fragmentation has rendered the conflict less threatening to the central government but also more intractable and devastating for the local population.

At the same time, as hundreds of thousands of combatants have cycled through armed groups and the security forces, a new elite of violent entrepreneurs has emerged—what I call a *military bourgeoisie*—controlling large parts of the economy in the eastern Congo and with deep links to political elites across the country. This bourgeoisie is endowed with engrained habits and vested interests, further entrenching the conflict.

This analysis runs against the grain of the most familiar notion about war—that it is fought between two sides seeking to defeat or compel the other, battering rams going at it until one side wins.[14] Instead, war has become a social condition, an outcome that may not have been the intended objective of any of the protagonists but that has produced its own actors, cultures, and interests.

A Methodological Note

The main argument of this book is that in order to better understand why the Congolese conflict has persisted for so long, and to understand conflict duration in general, we need to have a better understanding of the constituencies of an armed group—the ties between the belligerents and the other groups in society—and the interests and identities of the main actors in the conflict, including the state. This methodological approach relies on a combination of process tracing and comparative analysis, methods that I briefly describe here.

Over a period of two years—and drawing on research and contacts in the region that go back another decade—my research team interviewed 305 people associated with armed groups. The research team interviewed people with direct knowledge regarding the trajectories of armed groups, although we also conducted interviews with experts on the historical context. Of the interviewees, 41 percent were former or current members of armed groups, 21 percent were former or current members of the national security sector (police, army, or intelligence officials), 12 percent were foreign diplomats and United Nations officials, 15 percent were members of civil society or customary chiefs, and the remaining 11 percent were political and economic elites.

In addition, I was able to obtain around three thousand pages of confidential internal reports from the UN peacekeeping mission, whose team would report daily on security dynamics across the country.

My team was made up of researchers whom I knew well and who had deep personal ties with the group in question. For example, one of my research assistants had been a member of the CNDP and had deep family and personal ties with both the CNDP and the M23. Another was a former Congolese intelligence official who had facilitated supplies to armed groups from the government.

The interviews that we conducted took place against the backdrop of a context in which armed groups have ambivalent feelings about foreign observers. After all, a quarter of all the people indicted by the International Criminal Court have been Congolese, and over the past 150 years there have been numerous foreign interventions—often by white men, like myself—that have had sinister consequences for the Congolese state and its citizens. Why should they tell a relative stranger who was financing their movement, who was involved in negotiations with the government, and what the main interests of the group were? My research assistants helped deal with this challenge, but I doubt it can be fully overcome.

Once we had gathered the data, my first step was to establish causation within a particular armed group through process tracing, the "analysis of evidence on processes, sequences, and conjunctures of events within a case for the purposes of either developing or testing hypotheses about causal mechanisms that might causally explain the case."[15]

As opposed to statistical analysis, process tracing is well suited for trying to establish causality within single cases while remaining sensitive to social relations and interests, which are difficult to capture quantitatively. Researchers who deploy process tracing are not simply describing the sequence of events but are developing causal theories, distilling observable implications for these theories, and then applying them to the facts at hand. This is a heuristic device that we can easily grasp intuitively, as it has similarities with medical diagnosis as well as legal detective work. Like process tracing, these disciplines also often employ processes of induction and deduction, confronting them with facts, then adapting the theory and trying it out again on the facts.[16]

The final step, which I employed in my analysis of each armed group, was to elaborate competing hypotheses and their observable implications and to test these out against the facts. This step reverses the order of induction and deduction, beginning with abstractions based on prevailing theories of conflict and studies of the Congo and inferring what the observable implications would be in this specific case—for example, I evaluated whether natural resources and local struggles over power and identity played a role, as some scholars have argued.

Conclusion

I cannot wholly agree with my friend Raph's trademark optimism regarding how malleable the course of the Congolese conflict is. While it could easily have taken a different turn in 2003, or even in 2006, by 2018 parts of the dynamics of violence had become self-perpetuating. The conflict has produced an entire generation of Congolese politicians and military officers. The economy of the Kivus has become deeply militarized, and the fact that a weak Congolese state is now interacting with 120 armed groups means that even the most visionary of governments would be hard-pressed to stabilize the region. It will take at least a generation, probably more, to undo the damage done by the wars, damage that includes the infrastructural and the psychological, the social and the political.

The main thrust of the book is to understand the Congolese conflict as a social phenomenon, with its capillaries reaching deep into society, political culture, and the economy. It will be impossible to find a solution to this kind of conflict without transforming society and politics as a whole. Defeating armed groups requires a more functional army, which in turn requires a shift in the incentives for elites but also a shift in political culture. While there are many ways to produce this, it is impossible to envisage a path out of the violence without some form of accountability for both national and international actors, an element that has been almost completely excised from the peace process. It is also difficult to imagine a transformation away from the political horse-trading and cynical power that elites have embraced without youth movements, political parties, and civil society leaders setting examples of a different kind of politics. Finally, the Congolese economy must be reworked, both in its internal logic as well as in its place in the world. Currently, almost all investment and attention is focused on mining, telecommunications, and banking, leaving only a tiny share of the profits in the Congo, with almost no concern for the agriculture and petty trade that sustain the majority of Congolese.

In the coming years, Congolese, donors, and diplomats will discuss how to move beyond the turmoil in which the country has been embroiled for over twenty years. This book aims to inform that conversation by scrutinizing the roots of the current predicament and the failures of past remedies. As I highlight in chapter 5, I do not think Congo is an anomaly on the African continent—in the fragmentation and involution of the conflict and in the perverse symbiosis between the belligerents and the government, it exemplifies trends occurring more broadly across the continent.

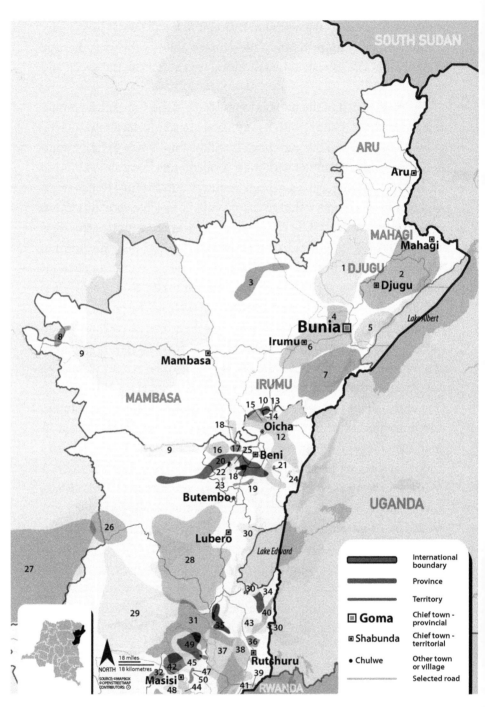

Map 1.1. Armed groups in the eastern Congo in 2020. The numbered key to the groups is on pages 20–23. (Source: Kivu Security Tracker)

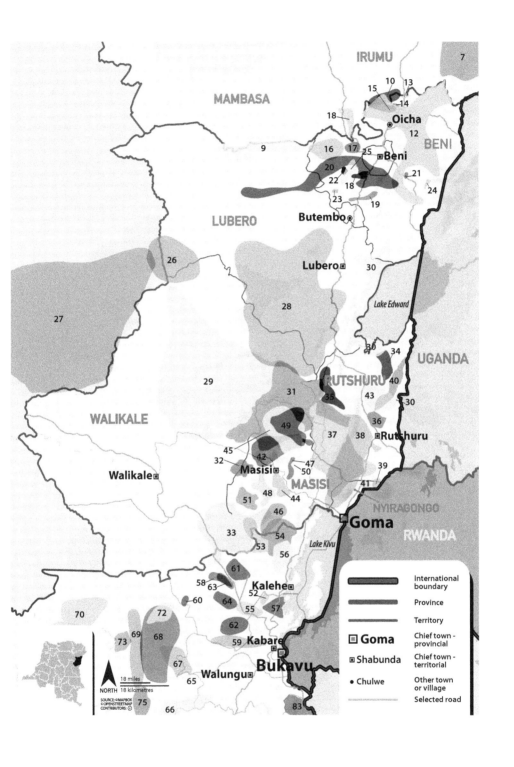

IRUMU

7

MAMBASA

15 10 13
        −14
18   Oicha ◉
          12
          BENI
9   16 17 25 ▫Beni
         20
         22
         18
         23
              19
         Butembo ◉

LUBERO

26
        Lubero ▣   30
27
        28   Lake Edward

29   UGANDA
                  31   30 34
        WALIKALE   RUTSHURU 40
                  35   43
                      36   30
        45 49   37 38 ▫Rutshuru
        32 42
        Masisi ▣ 47
                  50 39
        51 48 MASISI   41
        46   NYIRAGONGO
        33 54   ▣Goma
        53 56 Lake Kivu RWANDA
                  61
        58 63   Kalehe ▣
        60 52
70   64 55 57
        72 62
73 69 68 59 Kabare
        67
65   Bukavu
        75 Walungu ▣
NORTH 18 miles
        18 kilometres
SOURCE: ©MAPBOX
©OPENSTREETMAP
CONTRIBUTORS: ⊙   75
        66   83

	International boundary
	Province
	Territory
▣ Goma	Chief town - provincial
▫ Shabunda	Chief town - territorial
• Chulwe	Other town or village
	Selected road

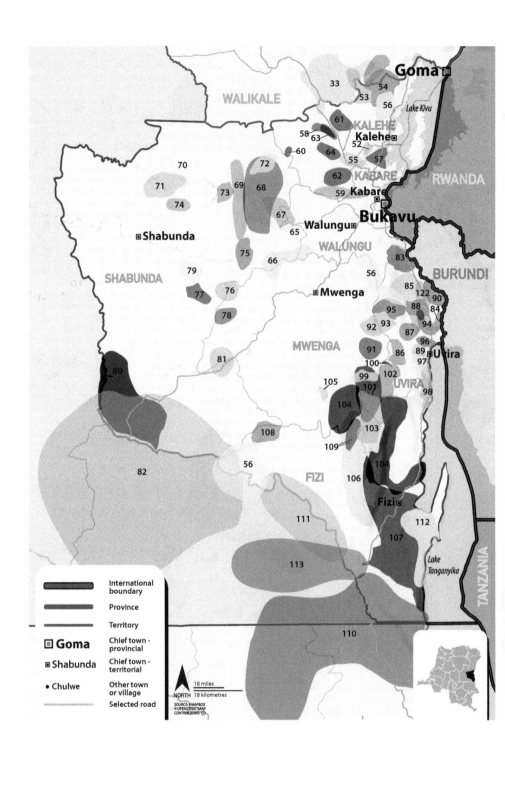

WALIKALE

Goma

33
54
53
56

Lake Kivu

61
KALEHE
58 63
Kalehe
60
52
64
55 57
72
70
62
KABARE
RWANDA
71
69 68
73
59 Kabare
74
67
Bukavu
Shabunda
65
Walungu
75
WALUNGU
83
66
79
56
BURUNDI
85
77 76
Mwenga
122 90
78
88 84
95
94
92 93
87
MWENGA
96
91
86
89 Uvira
81
100
97
105
99 102
UVIRA
107
98
80
104
103
108
109
56
82
113
FIZI
106 104
111
Fizi
112
110
107

Lake
Tanganyika

TANZANIA

International
boundary

Province

Territory

⊡ **Goma**   Chief town -
            provincial

⊡ Shabunda   Chief town -
            territorial

• Chulwe   Other town
            or village

            Selected road

NORTH   18 miles
         18 kilometres

SOURCE: MAPBOX
©OPENSTREETMAP
CONTRIBUTORS

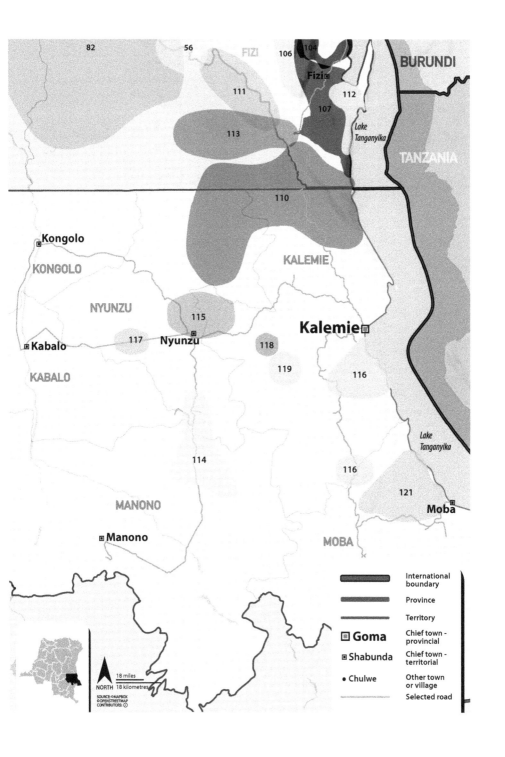

TABLE 1.1. Key to armed groups in the eastern Congo, October 2020

Ituri

1	Zaïre–FPAC
	(Front populaire d'autodéfense en Ituri)
2	CODECO–URDPC
	(Union des Révolutionnaires pour le Développement du Peuple Congolais)
3	CODECO–FCBC
	(Forces contre la balkanisation du Congo)
4	CODECO–BTD
	(Bon Temple de Dieu)
5	CODECO–ALC
	(Armée de Libération du Congo)
6	Chini Ya Kilima–FPIC (Front des Patriotes Intégrationnistes du Congo)
7	FRPI
	(Force de Résistance Patriotique de l'Ituri)
8	Mai-Mai Alaise
9	Mai-Mai Simba Mangalibi
10	Mai-Mai Kyandenga MNLDK
	(Mouvement National pour la Libération Durable du Kongo)
11	Mai-Mai Barcelone

North Kivu

9	Mai-Mai Simba Mangalibi
10	Mai-Mai Kyandenga MNLDK
	(Mouvement National pour la Libération Durable du Kongo)
11	Mai-Mai Barcelone
12	ADF
	(Allied Democratic Forces)
13	FLEC/NG
	(Front de Libération à L'Est du Congo/Nouvelle Génération
14	Mai-Mai Ngolenge
15	Mai-Mai Uhuru OAPB
	(Organisation d'Autodéfense pour la Paix à Beni)
16	Mai-Mai Shingo Pamba
17	Mai-Mai Mandefu
18	Mazembe-APASIKO
	(Alliance des Patriotes pour le Salut Intégral du Kongo)
19	Mai-Mai Léopards
20	Mai-Mai UPLC
	(Union des Patriotes pour la Libération du Congo)
21	APRC
	(Armée du Peuple pour la Reconstruction du Congo)
22	Mai-Mai Ninja
23	FAP
	(Force d'Autodéfense Populaire)
24	APR
	(Armée patriotique de Ruwenzori)

25	RNL
	(Résistance Nationale Lumumbiste aka « Mille tours par seconde »)
26	Mai-Mai Simba UPLD
	(Union des Patriotes pour la Libération et le Développement)
27	Mai-Mai Simba FDS (Forces Divines Simba)
28	Mai-Mai Kabidon FPP/AP
	(Front Populaire pour la Paix Armée du Peuple)
29	NDC-R/Guidon
	(Nduma Defense of Congo–Rénové, Guidon wing)
30	Mai-Mai Jackson FMP
	(Front des mouvements populaires)
31	NDC-R/Bwira
	(Nduma Defense of Congo–Rénové, Bwira wing)
32	MAC, ex-Guides
	(Mouvement d'Action pour Changement)
33	Mai-Mai Kifuafua
34	AFRC
	(Alliance des Forces de Résistance Congolaise)
35	Nyatura FPDH
	(Force de Défense du Peuple Hutu)
36	Amka Jeshi
37	Nyatura CMC
	(Collectif des Mouvements pour le Changement)
38	FDLR-FOCA
	(Forces Démocratiques pour la Libération du Rwanda-Forces Combattantes Abacunguzi)
39	M23
	(Mouvement du 23 Mars)
40	Rassemblement Unité et Démocratie (RUD)-Urunana
41	Nyatura Turarambiwe (Rutshuru)
42	APCLS
	(Alliance des patriotes pour un Congo libre et souverain)
43	Nyatura FPPH (Forces pour la Protection du Peuple Hutu)
44	Nyatura GAV
	(Groupe armé les volontaires)
45	Nyatura APRDC
	(Alliance des Patriotes pour la Restauration de la Démocratie au Congo, APRDC, now Abazungu)
46	Mai-Mai Kifuafua Maachano
47	Nyatura Bagaruza
48	Nyatura Delta FDDH
	(Forces de défense des droits humains)
49	Nyatura Jean-Marie
50	Nyatura Musheku
51	UPDC Kapasi
	(Union des Patriotes pour le Défense du Congo)

Continued on next page

TABLE 1.1. (*continued*)

North Kivu

52	Raia Mutomboki Soleil
53	Mai-Mai Kirikicho
54	Nyatura Kalume

South Kivu

33	Mai-Mai Kifuafua
52	Raia Mutomboki Soleil
53	Mai-Mai Kirikicho
54	Nyatura Kalume
55	Raia Mutomboki Shabani
56	Conseil national pour le renouveau et la démocratie (CNRD)-*Ubwiyunge*
57	Groupe JKK / CCCRD (Coalition Congolaise pour le Changement Radical et la Démocratie)
58	Raia Mutomboki Mungoro
59	Raia Mutomboki Blaise
60	Raia Mutomboki Bralima
61	Raia Mutomboki Butachibera
62	Raia Mutomboki Bipopa
63	Raia Mutomboki Hamakombo
64	Raia Mutomboki Lance
65	Raia Mutomboki Lukoba
66	Raia Mutomboki Ndarumanga
67	Raia Mutomboki Mabala
68	Raia Mutomboki Donat aka FPP
69	Raia Mutomboki Walike
70	Raia Mutomboki Kazimoto
71	Raia Mutomboki Kabazimia
72	Raia Mutomboki Musolwa
73	Raia Mutomboki Charles Quint
74	Raia Mutomboki Kabé
75	Raia Mutomboki 100kg
76	Raia Mutomboki Kimba
77	Rai Mutomboki Kampanga
78	Raia Mutomboki Bozi
79	Raia Mutomboki LeFort
80	Raia Mutomboki Musumbu
81	Mai-Mai Makindu
82	Mai-Mai Malaika
83	Mai-Mai Rasta
84	FNL (Front national de libération)
85	Mai-Mai Buhirwa
86	Mai-Mai Ilunga
87	Mai-Mai Kashumba
88	Mai-Mai Kijangala
89	Mai-Mai Makanaki
90	Mai-Mai Mbulu

91	Mai-Mai Issa Mutoka
92	Mai-Mai Ruma
93	Mai-Mai Mushombe
94	Mai-Mai Nyerere
95	Résistance pour un état de droit (RED)-Tabara
96	Mai-Mai Rushaba
97	Mai-Mai René
98	Mai-Mai Réunion FPLC (Forces pour la libération du Congo)
99	Mai-Mai Ngalyabatu
100	Mai-Mai Mupekenya
101	Twigwaneho
102	AFP–Gutabara (Alliances de fédéralistes patriotes, alias Android and Abakenya)
103	Gumino
104	Mai-Mai Mutetezi FPDC (Forces populaires pour les défenses du Congo)
105	Mai-Mai Bishake
106	Biloze Bishambuke
107	Mai-Mai Yakutumba
108	Mai-Mai Aochi
109	Mai-Mai Shoshi
110	Mai-Mai Apa na Pale
111	Mai-Mai Mulumba
112	Mai-Mai Alida
113	Mai-Mai Brown
114	PERCI Nyumbaisha
115	Mai-Mai Éléments Katadaye
116	Mai-Mai Fimbo na Fimbo
117	PERCI John Majimbo
118	Groupe Mazout
119	PERCI Kaomba
120	PERCI Mpululu
121	Mai-Mai Éléments Mutono
122	Mai-Mai Mwenyemali

Tanganyika

110	Mai-Mai Apa na Pale
114	PERCI Nyumbaisha
115	Mai-Mai Éléments Katadaye
116	Mai-Mai Fimbo na Fimbo
117	PERCI John Majimbo
118	Groupe Mazout
119	PERCI Kaomba
120	PERCI Mpululu
121	Mai-Mai Éléments Mutono

Data from Kivu Security Tracker, https://kivusecurity.org/

2

The Historical Background

THIS BOOK AIMS to explain why violence has persisted in the eastern Democratic Republic of the Congo since the signing of a critical peace deal in 2002.[1] Doing so, however, requires some historical excavation of past episodes of mobilization. After all, this is just the latest episode in a history of violence that dates back to the pre-colonial period. Some leaders of current insurrections participated in rebellions going back to the 1960s; memories of that period have shaped their actions and expectations in the present. And the worldviews of many of the young men and women who came of age in the 2000s are marked by the injustices and folklore of the past insurrections, much like the "rebellious cultures" that scholars have found in Cuba's Oriente Province or in the Chadian Sahel.[2]

This excursion into the past is linked to a core argument of this book: that we need to understand armed groups as embedded in their local societies and histories. Indeed, the mistake of many outside interventions has been to neglect these textured backdrops, leading to missteps and blunders. In particular, we need to invest greater efforts in understanding *who* is fueling these insurgencies—the groups in society that provide recruits and resources—and *why* they are taking up arms and risking their lives. These questions surrounding the constituencies and the interests of belligerents motivate my understanding of the situation in the eastern Congo today.

This exercise also serves to dispel the facade of inevitability that affixes itself to violence in the Congo. Armed mobilization in the region has changed dramatically over the past 150 years and will inevitably continue morphing.

The Rise of Political Agitation and
the *Pax Mobutuensis*

There was ample armed mobilization before independence from Belgium in 1960, ranging from peasant protests against colonization to bands of slave raiders marauding across the Kivu provinces around the turn of the century.[3] However, it is to the period around independence that the armed groups studied here can trace their immediate antecedents.

These uprisings were largely the result of Congolese independence on June 30, 1960. Almost immediately, the country was engulfed in turmoil as political parties, which had been legalized only in 1957, became the primary vessels for collective action, initially peacefully and then through violence. Under colonialism, groups mobilized on a narrow basis, often in ethnic terms and almost invariably against the local colonial government. After independence, the scale of violence grew dramatically as rebellions engulfed large parts of the country, aiming either at seceding from the state or at overthrowing the government.

The opening of the political arena and the holding of elections pushed new actors to the forefront of violence: a new multiethnic intelligentsia made up of a newly empowered class of workers, soldiers, teachers, and bureaucrats, mostly educated in Catholic missions and schools. Drawing on their pan-Africanist peers, they articulated a bold new nationalism; the idea of "the Congo" became a positive, uplifting ideal. Figures such as Patrice Lumumba, Joseph Kasavubu, Jason Sendwe, Cléophas Kamitatu, Justin Bomboko, and Mobutu Sese Seko are examples of this pantheon of new leaders.

The main new actor—in the streets, in the halls of power—was the urban bourgeoisie, members of which channeled their ambitions and grievances through the new political parties that emerged almost overnight throughout the country. It is astounding how within a short period of time these political identities became salient even in rural areas, crystallizing around the divide between those allied with the old colonial order (customary chiefs, police, state officials) and the new radical elite. Almost all of the main armed group leaders during this period had benefited from a relatively high degree of education and affluence, including Laurent-Désiré Kabila, Louis Bidalira, Christophe Gbenye, Gaston Soumialot, Nicholas Olenga, Musa Marandura, and Pierre Mulele.

This new elite captivated the Congolese imagination with its promise of liberation and emancipation, not just from colonialism but also from rigid customary social hierarchies. The Belgian colonial state had co-opted and reshaped the customary elites, creating deep tensions between the population and local rulers. In 1910, the colonial government issued a decree recognizing chieftaincies and making them subservient to Belgian administrative officials and their military forces, entrenching ethnic divisions and identities.[4] The colony thus empowered chiefs and at the same time rendered them less accountable to the traditional checks on their authority, making them "decentralized despots," in the words of political scholar Mahmood Mamdani.[5] Ethnicity, so often depicted an atavistic, immutable identity, was in fact deeply shaped—in the case of the large Songye, Ngala, Luba, and Tetela groups, either forging them altogether or radically shifting which populations were included—by colonial rule.[6]

The nation's first parliamentary elections were held on May 22, 1960, leading to a fragmented national assembly. Patrice Lumumba's Mouvement national congolais-Lumumba (MNC-L; Congolese National Movement-Lumumba) won around a third of the seats, with the remainder shared between twenty-six other parties. While Lumumba's party was the only one with truly national scope and several other important parties shared his anticolonial effervescence, personal and ideological tensions made the formation of a government difficult. Lumumba, who became prime minister, was finally able to cobble together a broad, shaky alliance, which appointed Joseph Kasavubu as president. That government eventually collapsed due to internal disputes and pressure from the US and Belgian governments, after only months in power.

Lumumba was arrested and assassinated, and many of his sympathizers fled, eventually joining with other nationalist leaders and rebels to form the Conseil national de libération. It was the CNL that, despite internal divisions, helped coordinate much of the massive armed mobilization, the Simba rebellion, that took over large parts of the eastern Congo between 1963 and 1965. Working with local leaders, who were outraged at Lumumba's assassination and deeply opposed to the Belgian government and its Congolese allies, the Simbas eventually folded under the weight of their own internal contradictions, succumbing to a Congolese army offensive, once again backed by the US and Belgian governments.

During this period, armed mobilization took place along the main political cleavages of the time: the struggle of moderates against radicals but also complex local agendas, often expressed in ethnic terms. These ethnic tensions were particularly salient, and most violent, in areas with large migrant communities. This was the case in South Kivu, where several waves of immigration from Burundi and Rwanda since at least the nineteenth century had created the Barundi community in the Rusizi Plain and the Banyamulenge community in the highlands overlooking Lake Tanganyika.[7]

In North Kivu, immigration was more recent, much larger, and the direct result of colonial policy. Here, the sparsely populated and fertile highlands of Masisi, Lubero, and Rutshuru attracted large numbers of European settlers in the early decades of the twentieth century. As the number of ranchers and mining companies increased, so did the demand for labor from neighboring Rwanda, where famine and population density made migration attractive. The Belgian government embarked on a massive migration plan, the Mission d'immigration des Banyarwanda (MiB). The lack of reliable data makes it difficult to know how many were involved in this relocation, but estimates range from 150,000 to 300,000 people.[8] In large parts of the highlands of what today are the Masisi, Rutshuru, Walikale, and Lubero territories, these immigrants became the demographic majority.

By the time armed conflict erupted in earnest in South Kivu in 1964, the nature of mobilization had changed. During the colonial period, resistance was confined to local concerns, but now it was framed in the language of nationalism and Cold War ideologies. The new political parties played a crucial role as constituencies and mobilizing structures, providing most of the leadership, the ideology, and the channels for recruitment. Most of the leaders of the rebellion on the ground had been cadres of the MNC-Lumumba[9] or the affiliated CNL political parties. For some of these parties, inspired by anticolonial struggles elsewhere after the assassination of Lumumba, armed violence became an acceptable, even necessary means to their ends.

Despite their brutality, it is striking that these uprisings around independence were shorter lived than the current conflicts. Although the Simba rebellion engulfed almost half the country, its main phase lasted only a little more than a year, and the Kwilu uprising in western Congo was even shorter.

In 1965, enjoying the backing of Western governments motivated by Cold War rivalries, Joseph-Désiré Mobutu, as he was then called, overthrew the elected government with the help of foreign mercenaries. Granting himself exceptional powers, he successfully suppressed the violent competition for elected office in the Kivus. While sporadic resistance continued, especially the remote parts of Fizi territory and the Ruwenzori mountains, armed repression and the creation of Mobutu's party-state— he abolished political parties in 1967 and founded the Mouvement populaire de la révolution (MPR), of which all Congolese became members at birth—quelled most armed mobilization for several decades.

This abrupt end to rebellion, a *pax Mobutuensis*, provides insights into what had been driving the violence. On the political level, by abolishing elections, getting rid of political parties, and deploying security forces and mercenaries, Mobutu could tamp down both the events that triggered and the social infrastructure that facilitated armed mobilization. He also clamped down on local causes of unrest by suppressing the discourse of ethnicity in political debate—although he would reverse course sharply in the twilight of his regime—and by alternately coopting and dismantling customary structures.[10] The economy aided him dramatically: in the first thirteen years of his rule, income per capita in the Congo almost tripled, buoyed by exports of raw minerals and agricultural production. This provided employment, infrastructure development, and resources for considerable patronage to potential rivals.

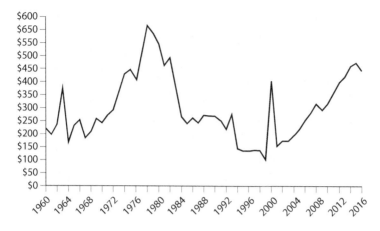

FIGURE 2.1. GDP per capita in Congo (Zaire), 1960–2016

The Congo Wars: The Confluence of Regional, Local, and National Trends

For much of the 1970s and 1980s, there was little armed group activity in the eastern Congo, although there were brief, sizable rebellions further south, in Katanga province.[11] It was not until Mobutu began to lose his grip on power and the country began to democratize that conflict bubbled up again. In 1990, financially crippled, under pressure from his former Cold War allies, and facing domestic opposition, a teary Mobutu declared an end to single-party rule on national television and promised democracy. The prospect of elections brought cynical manipulations of ethnicity by the central government that pushed the issue of citizenship for descendants of Rwandan immigrants back into the limelight.[12]

Over the previous two decades, Mobutu had alternately empowered and then undermined these communities. In 1971, he had promulgated a law that granted blanket citizenship to all Rwandans and Burundians who had been in the Congo since 1960, as he sought to curry favor and cultivate loyalty among these relatively affluent communities. When Mobutu expropriated all foreign businesses in 1973 during a nationalization campaign, many Tutsi in North Kivu benefited. Barthélémy Bisengimana, his powerful chief of staff who had been born in Rwanda before emigrating to the Congo, was instrumental is empowering key members of the Congolese Tutsi community during his time in power, between 1969 and 1977. Then, in 1981, seeking to mobilize nationalist sentiment, Mobutu reversed this decree, legislating that citizenship could be obtained only on an individual basis and was available only for those who could trace their Congolese ancestry back to 1885. In theory, this not only stripped many Hutu and Tutsi in North Kivu of their citizenship but also expropriated much of their property, since under the new law only Congolese citizens could own such large concessions. Although this latter law was never really enforced, for the "immigrants" this legal back and forth underlined how tenuous their status was.

Several government initiatives accentuated antagonism against both Hutu and Tutsi immigrants: an "identification of citizenship" census sparked outrage and riots from these communities in 1991; a parliamentary resolution in 1995 called for all "Rwandan refugees" to leave the country, explicitly including Banyamulenge, who had been in South Kivu for generations; and several decrees were issued to identify property owned by "refugees and immigrants," categories that were interpreted to apply to all Tutsi.[13] Following these leads, the commissioner of Uvira territory in South Kivu went so far as to say he would expel all Tutsi by the end of 1995 and then helped to organize gangs of youths to harass Banyamulenge.

Triggered by the "citizenship census" and the anticipation of elections in which ethnicity promised to be a key mobilizer, violence began in earnest on the border between the Masisi and Walikale territories in March 1993, then spread across the southern part of North Kivu. The Tembo, Nyanga, and Hunde communities mobilized to push Hutu out of their homelands, while Hutu formed militia to protect themselves. This "Guerre de Masisi" lasted for most of the year, killing thousands in the largest outbreak of violence in the Congo since the turmoil of independence.[14]

This mobilization differed in important ways from that of the 1960s. In the 1960s, the issue of *autochtonie*—which involved definitions of who was a "son of the soil"[15] or an indigenous Congolese—had been important in the Kanyarwanda war that took place in the southern part of what is today North Kivu and, to a lesser extent, in the armed mobilization in the Fizi territory but in general had taken a back seat to the split between those allied with Mobutu—and perceived to be close to the Belgians—and the Lumumbists, who saw themselves as the true nationalists. For example, in the 1960s Laurent-Désiré Kabila led a rebellion that featured members of various communities, including Rwandan Tutsi exiles, against Mobutu's government, which in turn allied with the Banyamulenge.

In the 1990s, *autochtonie* became the central focus of armed groups, but ethnicity was still expressed in very local terms, motivated by concrete communal grievances. This was the case for the Mai-Mai, self-defense groups that recruited largely along ethnic lines and drew on traditional rites and potions that they believed made them invincible to bullets.

The bloody conflict, which was only in its infancy, was about to be dramatically transformed by a massive influx of foreign fighters into the country. One of the key features of the recent Congolese conflict has been that armed mobilization has never been sustained or grown to become a national threat without outside backing. It was civil wars in neighboring countries that brought an influx of weapons, rebel refugees, and eventually foreign invasions. In 1993, tens of thousands of Burundian refugees arrived in the eastern Congo following the assassination of President Melchior Ndadaye, and for the next ten years Burundian Hutu rebels would maintain rear bases in South Kivu. Then, in 1994, following the Rwandan genocide, over forty thousand militiamen and soldiers and a million civilian refugees crossed into eastern Congo from Rwanda. At the same time, hundreds of Ugandan rebels from the West Nile Bank Front and the Alliance of Democratic Forces–National Army for the Liberation of Uganda (ADF-NALU) began to put down roots on the Congolese side of the Ruwenzori Mountains.

By 1996, the Congo had become a haven for rebel groups from at least four neighboring countries. These groups used these rear bases to destabilize their home countries. This, coupled with Mobutu's physical and political deterioration, paved the way for the regional wars that were to follow.

One of the main protagonists in these wars was the Rwandan Patriotic Front (RPF), led by Paul Kagame, which had overthrown the government of Juvénal Habyarimana in 1994 after a bloody civil war that had culminated in a genocide against Tutsi, alongside the killing of many moderate Hutu. The forces that carried out the slaughter of up to eight hundred thousand Tutsi, Habyarimana's former Forces armées rwandaises (FAR) and various militia, then fled into the eastern Congo, where they were housed in refugee camps run by the United Nations High Commission for Refugees (UNHCR).

In 1996, the new RPF government, alongside its Ugandan ally that sought to root out its own armed rebellions in its neighbor, launched an invasion of the eastern Congo, ostensibly to dismantle the Rwandan refugee camps. To mask their involvement, they created a rebel fig leaf, the Alliance des forces démocratiques pour la libération du Congo-Zaire (AFDL), which eventually came to be led by the veteran and mercurial rebel Laurent-Désiré Kabila. The Angolan army joined this regional coalition, and many other African countries, dismayed with Mobutu's corruption and abuse, provided support as well.[16]

Congolese Tutsi from North Kivu and Banyamulenge from South Kivu featured prominently in this rebellion, some having joined the RPF during its bush war in Rwanda, while others took up arms as violence escalated in their home communities in 1994–1996. Separately, thousands of youths from other communities in the Kivu region, known in Swahili as *kadogos* (small ones), joined the AFDL, eager to liberate their country and to join a rebellion that could empower them socially and economically. Even today, while there is no public regional breakdown, the national army into which many of those rebels integrated is disproportionately from the eastern Congo.[17]

Shifts in economic and social structures contributed to this mobilization. By the early 1990s, the state monopoly on mining had been broken as parastatal companies crumbled and artisanal mining began to flourish. This created large numbers of young migrant men from the eastern Congo who tapped into a lucrative and often illegal transnational trade. When armed groups proliferated following the Rwandan refugee crisis and the subsequent AFDL invasion, they became involved in illegal taxation, smuggling, and racketeering, creating a new war economy.

The foreign invasions radically changed how armed groups perceived themselves and their objectives. As one militia commander remembered, "Before 1996, it was about this village, this community. With the AFDL, it was about 'Us Congolese,' it was us against the Rwandans."[18] Thus the parochial communal feuds of the early 1990s started to be overshadowed by, or combined with, a renewed feeling of nationalism in defense against foreign aggression. This is how Mai-Mai self-defense militias expressed themselves, especially in areas with a history of armed insurrection like Masisi, Bunyakiri, Ruwenzori, and Fizi. This nationalism was increasingly expressed in ethnic terms—"Tutsi aggression" became a dominant trope for many Mai-Mai, while Tutsi and Banyamulenge groups developed a rhetoric of victimhood—even as many Congolese Tutsi took leading roles in the various rebellions—often linking the experiences of their communities with the genocide in Rwanda.

The AFDL war lasted for nine months, from September 1996 to May 1997, sweeping Laurent-Désiré Kabila to power in the capital Kinshasa. His position, however, was extremely tenuous, as he had to contend with the influence of the Rwandan army, which dominated his security services and army. Seeking to emancipate himself, Kabila asked the Rwandans to leave and began reaching out to their archnemeses, Habyarimana's ex-FAR. This triggered another invasion of Rwandan troops in the eastern Congo, leading to the much longer and deadlier Second Congo War (1998–2003) that split the country into several parts. The Rwandans backed the Rassemblement congolais pour la démocratie (RCD) rebellion, while the Ugandans supported the Mouvement de libération du Congo (MLC). Meanwhile, Kabila received critical backing from the Angolan, Zimbabwean, and Namibian governments.

It was during this Second Congo War that armed groups in the Kivus began to flourish with the help of outside backing and collaboration. For the RCD and the local militias that it partnered with,[19] support came from Rwanda, while for the dozen or so Mai-Mai factions, backing came from Kinshasa and from alliances with Rwandan and Burundian rebellions.[20] This proxy warfare was exacerbated following the Lusaka

Ceasefire Agreement of 1999; Kinshasa rarely fought directly with the Rwandan, Ugandan, and Burundian armies, instead funneling support to its allies behind the front lines.

Over time, the Congo Wars transformed society in the eastern Congo, leading to the creation of the military bourgeoisie that I describe in chapter 5. The rise of regional rebellions deeply involved in local administration, especially the RCD, further eroded the established structures of authority and social cohesion. While the first wave of militias that had formed in the 1990s strongly relied on support from customary chiefs and local communities, those ties weakened when military leaders started to build up autonomous bases of revenue and support through links to the Kabila government in Kinshasa, foreign armed groups, and trans-boundary trade networks. Customary chiefs were also intimidated, assassinated, or replaced by the various rebel groups active in the eastern Congo, undermining that institution. At the same time, the large-scale recruitment of youths created a militarized generation that became increasingly detached from customary chiefs, village elders, and their parents.[21]

Several factors precipitated the end of the Second Congo War and the signing of the Global and Inclusive Agreement in December 2002 by all major belligerents. Congolese civil society, along with the international community—led by the United Nations, South Africa, and key Western powers—pushed for an end to the fighting, which was one of the most devastating conflicts in the world at the time. Their pressure had a particular impact on the Rwandan and Ugandan governments, which were deeply dependent on donor funding, while the Zimbabwean government scaled down its involvement due to economic and political troubles at home. On top of this, Laurent-Désiré Kabila, the bellicose Congolese president, was assassinated in his office in January 2001, leaving power in the hands of his young and reclusive son, Joseph Kabila, who was more inclined to seek a political resolution to the conflict.

On June 30, 2003, the belligerents formed a transitional government, based in the capital, Kinshasa. The country was unified, and all armed groups were merged into a new national army, the Forces armées de la

République démocratique du Congo (FARDC). In due course a new constitution was drafted; the country's Third Republic had begun.

Conclusion

The purpose of this chapter was to set the stage for the current conflict that affects the Congo but also to reach into the Congolese past to explain the history of armed mobilization, particularly in the east of the country. By grappling with the dynamics of conflict of the past, we can glean insights into the drivers of conflict today. Throughout this chapter, I focus on the main actors behind mobilization as well as their interests.

Over the past 60 years, we have seen a shifting cast of protagonists in violent protests taking place in the Congo. In the 1960s, mobilization—sometimes peaceful, sometimes not—was a vehicle for emancipation. While it had a variety of participants with diverse motives, the armed mobilization that followed the assassination of Patrice Lumumba trumpeted a rhetoric of liberation and was driven by a new urban bourgeoisie that was eager to challenge customary and state power.

After a lull imposed by the dictatorship—what I call the *Pax Mobutuensis*—armed mobilization once again emerged in the eastern Congo in 1993. While the conflict was expressed largely in ethnic terms, there is no doubt that part of the impetus came from marginalized peasants and youth. The regionalization of the crisis since the AFDL war of 1996 then poured enormous resources into the conflict, creating a large class of young men with an expertise in deadly conflict, many of them unmoored from the social structures out of which they emerged. Over time, these conflict entrepreneurs came to constitute a relatively independent social class.

What about the interests driving these more recent waves of mobilization? The early days of the AFDL rebellion, as many combatants still recall today, were marked by a deep nationalism as armed mobilization became a means of seizing power. Since then, however, armed groups have lost much of the emancipatory impulse that was so obvious throughout the colonial period and then into the 1960s—impulses to free their fighters from colonial rule, to reform the state, to rid themselves of the confines of customary rule. Similarly, the state—still called *Bula Matari*, the Breaker of Rocks, by many Congolese, referring to the repressive colonial state—which sought to stamp out all dissidence during the colonial era and the early years of Mobutu's rule, gradually developed an interest in cultivating violence and disorder on the periphery of the state as a means of dividing the opposition and providing patronage to the security services. This eventually led to the involution of interests, as belligerents became invested in perpetuating this system of violent governance.

This historical account paves the path for the next chapter, which tackles the most recent phase of conflict in the Congo, which occurred between 2002 and 2019. It is not difficult to see why an approach to solving the conflict that was fundamentally focused on brokering a deal between the government and its opponents did not bring an end to the fighting. If the dynamics driving conflict are rooted in the nature of the state and if violence is not a means to an end but also an end in itself, then a formal settlement will only serve to transform, but not eradicate the conflict.

3

Explaining the Congolese Conflict

THE PEACE DEAL USHERED in the "postconflict" era with new institutions and the promise of democracy and stability. However, as the quotation marks suggest, this period was anything but peaceful. Conflict escalated, albeit in a different form, to levels at least as high as during the great Congo wars that came before.

Why did that peace deal, which had fostered so much hope, not bring an end to the conflict? And what is the nature of this not-war-not-peace hybrid in which the country has been languishing since 2003?

I argue that the peace process *transformed* the conflict but did not end it. In fact, the peace deal, while successful on many fronts, carried within it the seeds for this new round of violence: it pushed one of the most powerful belligerents back into war; a failed army integration process created a multitude of new armed groups led by army defectors; and an electoral process created incentives for politicians to ally with armed groups. In this chapter I address these proximate causes of violence. In the next chapter, I then scrutinize the structural, permissive causes: the backdrop of a weak, patrimonial state and a political culture in both Kigali and Kinshasa in which armed violence was seen as an acceptable and established means of obtaining power and resources.

TABLE 3.1. Chronology of major events since 1990

1990	Mobutu disbands single-party rule, announces multiparty electons
1991–1992	National Sovereign Conference in Kinshasa decides on new constitution and prime minister, backs 1981 citizenship law
1993	Run-up to local elections turns violent in North Kivu; 6,000–15,000 die in communal violence
1994	Rwandan genocide sends perpetrators and close to one million refugees into eastern Congo
1996	First Congo War. AFDL rebellion is created in Kigali, backed by pan-African coalition to break up refugee camps and topple Mobutu
1997	AFDL topples Mobutu's government, puts Laurent Kabila in power
1998	Second Congo War. Kabila falls out with Rwandan and Ugandan allies
1999	Lusaka Ceasefire Agreement signed by major belligerents, creates UN peacekeeping mission (MONUC)
2001	Laurent Kabila is assassinated by a bodyguard, is replaced by his son Joseph Kabila
2002	Accord global et inclusif is signed by major belligerents
2003–2006	Transitional government of former belligerents
2006	Presidential, legislative, and provincial elections; Kabila elected president
2006–2008	CNDP rebellion in North Kivu
2008	Goma Peace Conference
2009	Integration of CNDP and other armed groups into national army
2009	Launch of joint Congolese-Rwandan Umoja Wetu operations against FDLR and other armed groups
2010	MONUC becomes a stabilization mission (MONUSCO)
2011	Presidential and legislative elections; Kabila reelected president
2012	Defection of ex-CNDP officers creates M23 rebellion
2013	Defeat of M23 rebellion
2014	Launch of Sukola I operations against ADF, provokes widespread massacres around Beni
2015	Launch of Sukola II operations against FDLR and other armed groups
2016	Kabila postpones presidential elections, extending his own term and prompting protests
2018	Presidential and legislative elections are held but become mired in controversy; Félix Tshisekedi is named winner, forms alliance with Kabila

The Political Conflicts Created by the Peace Process:
The CNDP and the Mai-Mai

The initial days of the transition were heady, especially for political elites and their foreign partners. The 2002 peace deal, the Accord global et inclusif, reunified the country after five years of brutal war and shared positions in the new government, parliament, and other state institutions among the various signatories of peace deal. The armed forces of most belligerents were integrated into a new national army, the FARDC, and 130,000 soldiers—including 30,000 children—were demobilized within four years.[1]

It is almost difficult to remember now, given the subsequent failures of peacebuilding, but this was a period of optimism and dramatic change, the high-water mark of international intervention in the conflict. A new constitution was signed, enshrining the rights of citizens as never before, creating democratic institutions and decentralizing power to the provinces, inaugurating the Congo's Third Republic. A national assembly and provincial assemblies were set up, as were the following bodies: an election commission, a state auditor general, a media regulation body, a human rights observatory, and an anticorruption commission.

The signatories of the peace deal had great incentive to take up their new positions in Kinshasa, as the peace process brought a huge influx of donor money and foreign investment. The streets of Kinshasa were crowded with new cars—Hummers were favorites with many politicians—and restaurants popped up to host the *nouveaux riches* and expats. The peace process encouraged both donors and investors to open their pocketbooks; the World Bank and the IMF, often considered bellwethers of financial stability and political acceptability, launched new loan and grant programs in 2001 and 2002, respectively.[2] Other donors followed suit, as did private investors, leading the revenue of the central government to almost triple between 2003 and 2006.

This appeared to be the logic of the peace deal, in line with the tenets of liberal peacebuilding: entice all belligerents to join a national transitional government in which they will all gain in prestige and wealth, then create an environment—a new constitution, a thriving economy, a new army—that will make it difficult for them to defect back to the bush when some of them lose elections in 2006.[3] One Western diplomat based in Kinshasa at the time told me as much: "How do you get rebels to put down their weapons and trust in this peace process? A government car, salary, and access to state coffers. Peace first, good governance

TABLE 3.2. DRC national revenues and grants, 2003–2008 (millions of USD)

	2003	2004	2005	2006	2007	2008
Government revenue (excluding grants)	436.58	623.12	820.58	1129.69	1474.78	2140.83
Grants (excluding humanitarian aid)	114.82	129.03	371.18	701.93	147.31	215.77
Overall budget	551.41	752.15	1191.76	1831.63	1622.09	2356.61

later."[4] In a country where 94 percent of the population made less than $1.90 per day, the monthly salary for a minister during the transition was around $4,000 (while some directors of state-run companies earned $25,000 per month), and opportunities for illegal enrichment were also plentiful.[5]

This approach had some notable successes. By 2006, the number of internally displaced in the Congo had declined to 1.2 million, a third of what it had been just three years earlier. Since displacement is correlated with higher mortality rates, these security improvements almost certainly saved thousands of lives.[6] Only around a dozen significant Congolese armed groups remained active, clustered in the Fizi, Uvira, and Lubero territories in the eastern Congo. They did not have much financial or military heft and had only weak links to national politics. These successes, however, were eventually overshadowed by the failures. By 2011, displacement had more than doubled, and by 2018 it had reached levels higher than even during the war.

The main challenge to the transition came from a narrow military elite backed by the Rwandan government, which contested the new order. Over the next few years, first the former RCD rebels, then the Mai-Mai, would launch a series of insurgencies and counterinsurgencies in the east of the country, triggering a vicious cycle of violence. The timing of this crisis determined the government's response, as it struggled to balance the competing imperatives of keeping the shaky ruling coalition together and creating strong institutions that could defend their country. In the end, the fractious ruling class opted for the former, engaging in patronage-based politics, encouraging military officers to become involved in local racketeering and politicians to support armed groups at the expense of investing in strong institutions. Contrary to the maxim proffered by the diplomat cited above, it became clear that, since conflict became closely enmeshed with patronage politics, you could not cement peace until governance was radically reformed.

A Failed Political Compromise: The Birth of the CNDP

The core of any peace process is a political compromise—a deal in which former belligerents will commit to further their interests through the political process, not on the battlefield. Invariably, however, some signatories will lose out and become marginalized, especially when—as in the Congolese case—the deal was scheduled to culminate in elections where some of them, inevitably, would lose. This was the main failing of the peace process: that it failed to predict these dynamics and then take appropriate measures.

The main challenge to the process came from the RCD. It was one of the strongest belligerents but was extremely unpopular, due to its abuses and Rwandan support, and stood to lose much of its power in the upcoming elections. It was this mismatch between their military prowess (which stemmed in considerable part from Rwandan backing) and their popularity that eventually produced a series of new rebellions. The straitjacket of the peace deal could not contain the contradictory interests of its signatories.

The marginalization felt by the RCD was particularly acute within the Tutsi community, a demographically small community that occupied many senior roles within the RCD rebellion. The community was broadly resented—and was the target of ethnic vitriol—due to long-standing communal conflicts over land and power, but also because of the many abuses of the RCD, including several large-scale massacres of civilians. Polling in both 2005 and 2016 suggested that only about a quarter of Congolese thought that Hutu and Tutsi could be Congolese.[7]

The RCD's fears eventually came true. The former rebellion lost much of its power in the elections that took place in 2006, going from controlling a third of the country to holding about 4 percent representation in elected institutions.[8] The RCD presidential candidate, Azarias

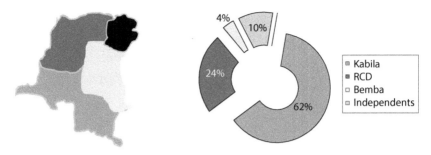

FIGURE 3.1. Comparison of territory controlled by armed groups in 2002 and representation in national parliament after the 2006 elections

Ruberwa, got a paltry 1.69 percent of the vote. In addition, with the end of the transition came also an end to the RCD's right to influence nominations and promotions within the security apparatus, state administration, and foreign service.

Both the clientelist nature of the Congolese state and the influence of the Rwandan regime, which I discuss in depth in the following chapter, accentuated the RCD's fears. On paper, the peace process had forged an arrangement that required Kabila to share power with four vice presidents. It also distributed positions in parliament, state-run enterprises, the administration, and the security services among six different belligerents, the political opposition, and civil society.

In practice, however, the main spaces of decision-making and accumulation of resources in the Congolese state were managed informally. Kabila exercised disproportionate power through informal chains of command, maintained control over key economic assets, and blocked the integration of key parts of the security service and state-run companies. Even in institutions in which power was supposed to be shared, the president was able to control key positions. For example, the head of the election commission was supposed to be named by the religious component of civil society; the Catholic Church, however, disavowed Apollinaire Malu Malu, the priest who was named, a close collaborator of President Kabila.

Kabila's dominance of these informal networks of power frustrated RCD members who were excluded from these favors.[9] "We were being asked not to share power in government, but rather to integrate into a system controlled by Kabila," Azarias Ruberwa, then secretary-general of the RCD, later told me.[10]

The Rwandan government also played a critical role in fomenting the new crisis. The ruling party, Rwandan Patriotic Front (RPF), had long seen the eastern Congo as an area critical for its national security, and many of its leaders had personal and economic ties with this region. It also had the means of influencing developments there: many RCD officers from the Tutsi community had passed through the ranks of the Rwandan army and maintained family and business relations with RPF members. As I explain in chapter 6, RPF leaders encouraged a small clique of RCD commanders, mostly from the Congolese Tutsi community, to launch a new rebellion. Without Rwandan support, it is difficult to imagine that the ensuing crisis would have reached anything like the scale it did.

In addition, two related dynamics accentuated the RCD's sense of vulnerability. A local power struggle in their North Kivu bastion made the threat of losing political power more acute. The province was split demographically between the northern region, "le Grand Nord," populated largely by the Nande ethnic community, and the southern region in which the Banyarwanda community was politically and economically dominant (see figure 6.1). The two parts of the province had been separated by the war but were now due to be reunited. Here, again, the RCD's fears would come true: the 2006 elections produced a Nande governor and a Nande majority in the provincial assembly as well as dominance by Kabila's coalition.

Internal divisions also plagued the RCD, exacerbating their predicament. Spurred by the RCD's unpopularity and Kabila's desire to neutralize his most powerful rivals, many RCD leaders jumped ship, leading the remaining leaders to panic. Eugène Serufuli, the governor of North Kivu and the party's most important Hutu leader, was courted by Kinshasa and switched allegiance to Kabila in 2005, eventually being named chairman of the board of the state electricity company in 2007. Other RCD leaders, realizing that they would need to curry favor with Kabila to obtain important positions in Kinshasa, also defected.[11] As one former RCD leader said, "The transition wouldn't have been so fatal for us

TABLE 3.3. Key administrative positions in Goma, 2004

Position	Name	Ethnic origin
Governor, North Kivu	Eugène Serufuli	Hutu
Vice Governor	Bakungu Mithondeke	Hunde
Vice Governor	Kayisavera Mbake	Nande
Administrator, Masisi	Paul Sebihogo	Tutsi
Administrator, Rutshuru	Oscar Ntambiye	Tutsi
Mayor, Goma	Xavier Nzabara	Hutu
Security		
Commander, 8th Military Region	General Gabriel Amisi	Kusu
Commander, 11th Brigade	Colonel Bonané Habarugira	Tutsi
Commander, 12th Brigade	Colonel Smith Gihanga	Hutu
Commander, 5th Brigade	Colonel Mayanga wa Gishuba	Hutu
Commander of Police, North Kivu	General Jean-Marie Ndaki	?
Commander of Police, Goma	Major Ntawavuka	Hutu
Coordinator, Agence nationale de renseignements (national intelligence agency)	Gillain Birate	Hutu
Coordinator, Direction générale de migration (immigration agency)	Albert Semana	Tutsi
Economy		
Director, OFIDA (customs agency)	Déo Rugwiza	Tutsi
Director, SNEL (electric company)	Léon Muheto	Tutsi
Director, REGIDESO (water company)	Vincent Mihatano	Hutu
Director, OCC (customs quality control agency)	Oswald Mukingi	Hutu
Director, land registry	Dieudonné Birate	Hutu
Director, Direction générale des impôts (tax agency)	Robert Mbarushimana	Hutu
Director, SEPCONGO (state petroleum company)	Débat Muzo	Tutsi

if we had been united. We could have kept control of North Kivu and negotiated with Kabila from a position of relative strength."[12]

This was the somber outlook for the RCD in 2003: it was marginalized nationally, under attack locally, and divided internally. It was to this backdrop that the Congrès national pour la défense du peuple (CNDP) emerged, as a means for a faction of the RCD and the Rwandan government to defend their interests in the eastern Congo.

The key figure in this sequence of events was General Laurent Nkunda, a charismatic and temperamental Tutsi RCD commander.

Nkunda, a notorious figure in the RCD army, was worried that he would be arrested for a large massacre of civilians that had taken place under his watch in Kisangani in May 2002.[13]

Shortly before the transitional government was inaugurated, the Rwandan government pushed for the promotion of a number of RCD commanders and officials in the eastern Congo who were worried that they would be arrested if they went to Kinshasa. This represented a significant obstacle for the peace process. Several of these officials, including the governor of South Kivu province, were alleged to have planned the assassination of Laurent-Désiré Kabila, the president's father. Nkunda was another wrench in the works of the peace process, named commander of North Kivu province, despite his dismal human rights record. Rwanda then mounted a persuasion campaign for these RCD officials: according to one officer who took part in these discussions: "The Rwandans told us: 'If you go to Kinshasa, you will come back in coffins.'"[14]

In the end, three ex-RCD brigades in North Kivu province refused to join the new national army, receiving significant clandestine support from the Rwandan government. As we shall see in chapter 6, the CNDP would grow to become one of the most powerful armed groups in the country between 2004 and 2009, controlling much of the southern part of North Kivu province.[15]

Nkunda's insurgency became the linchpin of this new bout of conflict in the Kivus, prompting countermobilization by at least a dozen other groups, some of them with backing from Kinshasa. Coming at a time when the new national army was being formed out of disparate armed groups and tens of thousands of combatants were demobilizing, the CNDP dramatically undermined the creation of fledgling institutions.

The Mai-Mai and the Perverse Incentives of Elections and Army Reform

Nkunda was not the only one mobilizing. Much like the RCD, many Mai-Mai groups felt deeply marginalized within the transitional government and army, although in a very different way. Their disillusionment had more to do with the realities of the army integration and demobilization processes. The government failed to provide sufficient opportunities for many Mai-Mai, either by providing them alternative sources of income or by appointing them to satisfactory positions within the security forces. To make matters worse, when some of these Mai-Mai then returned to the bush, the army supported some of them in operations against the CNDP.

During the 2003–2006 transition, the most important Mai-Mai groups in North and South Kivu had joined the national army. At the time, I was working for the UN peacekeeping mission, traveling throughout South Kivu with the new FARDC commander of the province. While there were some holdouts in Uvira and Fizi territories, some of the most important Mai-Mai leaders obtained positions in the national army and administration, including Padiri Bulenda, Sikuli Lafontaine, Fabien Mudohu, Akilimali Shemondo, and Baudouin Nakabaka.

The new war against the CNDP brought an end to this positive trend, leading to defections within the army and increased armed mobilization. When Nkunda launched his rebellion, it triggered a massive countermobilization by Mai-Mai and other smaller armed groups.[16]

There were several reasons for this. During the war, Mai-Mai groups had largely sided with the Kinshasa government, and a shaky coalition of Mai-Mai sent a delegation to the peace talks at the Inter-Congolese Dialogue, obtaining a quota for representation in the transitional government. Nonetheless, the emergence of the CNDP led many Mai-Mai groups to remobilize, as local communities sought to protect themselves and entrepreneurial commanders seized on a new opportunity. The most important ones were the Coalition des patriotes résistants congolais (PARECO) (Masisi and Lubero territories) and the Mai-Mai Yakutumba (Fizi and Uvira territories), but several smaller groups also mobilized between 2004—when Nkunda launched his first major offensive—and 2009, when Nkunda was arrested.

While the CNDP provided the main trigger for this mobilization, the clientelistic nature of the Congolese government was, once again, an important factor. Despite a progressive constitution that fostered new, democratic institutions, the transitional government was based largely on the sharing of spoils. Here, a fateful decision was made, or perhaps a non-decision, by leaders of the government and army. Faced with a newly formed army riven with competing networks of former belligerents, the senior leadership failed to step in to enforce a unified chain of command and discipline.

One senior officer, a colonel with Kabila's army during the Second Congo War, told me: "The strategy was to absorb all the armed groups, to bring them in. We didn't have the capacity to crack down on thugs and indisciplined officers. The strategy was to be a sponge, not a stick [*tukuwe éponge, hapana fimbo*]."[17] Officers were allowed to use their personal connections, both within the army as well as with local armed groups, to manage military operations and to carry out illegal racketeering. For example, FARDC commanders siphoned off salaries and logistical funds through kickbacks with their subordinate commanders—the notorious *opérations retour*—and worked with local militia to obtain or tax gold, tin, and tantalum mines in the eastern Congo. This approach to security deeply militarized local society and undermined demobilization efforts.

The various Mai-Mai commanders who balked at integration[18] often lacked the elite connections that would have allowed them to benefit from this patronage and thus did not obtain high-ranking positions in the national army. Many had only rudimentary military education; some lacked basic literacy, further reducing their chances for promotion.[19] To make matters worse for them, armed groups were already extremely "top-heavy"—they had a very high ratio of officers to soldiers. According to one analyst in 2009, 25 percent of the FARDC were officers and 37 percent non-commissioned officers.[20] Many of those officers were unlikely to find suitable positions and remuneration in the national army.

My own observations bear this out. In late 2003, I traveled across South Kivu with General Prosper Nabyolwa, the newly deployed FARDC commander, to integrate Mai-Mai groups into the new national army. On a soccer field in Mwenga town, the general asked one Mai-Mai group led by the self-styled "Colonel" Nyakiliba to line up their troops by rank. The group of officers was almost twice as large as the foot soldiers, to the disbelief of General Nabyolwa. Outraged that Nyakiliba, who must have been in his early thirties, was calling himself a colonel, he tore Nyakiliba's epaulettes off and threw them on the ground.

Poor cohesion within the Mai-Mai also fed into the fragmentation. The few Mai-Mai commanders who did obtain positions of importance, like General Padiri Bulenda, often used nominations to reward members of their own ethnic community or family, sidelining many of their former fellow commanders. Of the Mai-Mai delegates to the peace talks in South Africa, the two representing the largest groups—Anselme Enerunga, of Padiri Bulenda's movement, and Kosco Swedy, representing the Dunia group—were eventually repudiated by their commanders in the field for having been bought off by Kabila's people.

A similar situation existed the political realm, where Mai-Mai groups from across the eastern Congo were given thirteen seats in the transitional parliament, four ministerial positions, and one provincial governor position. One Mai-Mai officer described the way these positions were shared as follows: "Our delegates got to Kinshasa and then began selling the positions we had a claim to. People who had nothing to do with the Mai-Mai could buy one of the military or political positions that belonged to us. It was our own internal weakness that allowed them to do this."[21] Thus Kisula Ngoy, who had only marginal links to Mai-Mai, became governor of Katanga, while Mushi Bonane, a lawyer based in Kinshasa, claimed a Mai-Mai parliamentary seat.

The introduction of democratic elections at various levels also contributed to this mobilization. Politicians who had previously obtained power through networking and patronage now had to prove themselves at the ballot box. For some, armed mobilization was an easy way to curry favor, play to ethnic stereotypes, and intimidate opponents. Elections also created losers, some of whom then resorted to violence. With few safeguards to prevent armed groups from stepping into the electoral arena, some candidates—a small but important minority—sought alliances with them to bolster their stature and intimidate opponents. One parliamentary candidate summed it up like this: "Elections changed a lot about how violence is linked to politicians. The average voter has no understanding of the legislative machinery in Kinshasa. Even if they did, what we vote on rarely makes a difference for the average Congolese. So we have to show them that we matter and that we are powerful. For some of my colleagues, [backing] armed groups is a good way of doing this."[22]

Strongmen emerged in North and South Kivu who specialized in combining armed force with political popularity. Figures such as Eugène Serufuli, Justin Bitakwira (Uvira territory), Jemsi Mulengwa (Fizi), Antipas Mbusa Nyamwisi (Beni and Lubero), and Robert Seninga (Masisi) leveraged their influence among armed groups into political power on the provincial and national stage.[23] Congolese colloquially referred to this as the *phenomène pompier-pyromane* (firefighter-pyromaniac phenomenon) or *maladie auto-immune* (autoimmune disease): strongmen starting a fire so that the government has to negotiate with them to put it out, or state officials backing militia that challenge their own government. While violence had been used as a bargaining tactic between the government and its enemies in the run-up to the transitional government, starting in 2003 violence was also used as a means of bargaining *among* members of the same government.

While the CNDP was critical in the escalation of armed conflict, by the time it was dismantled in early 2009, most Mai-Mai and other local armed groups had developed their own momentum. They were deeply rooted in the local society and economy, whereas various exit doors had closed: the national demobilization program was winding down, and many combatants had become skeptical about joining a national army that was seen as abusive and indigent. Insurrection became an open-ended endeavor, a lifestyle, in contrast with the 1996–1997 and 1998–2003 wars, which had concrete objectives.

This new phase of violence thus introduced new actors as well as new interests and dynamics. Conflict went from a relatively centralized affair anchored by governments in Kinshasa, Kigali, and Kampala to a fragmented dynamic among many semiautonomous armed groups. The number of armed groups grew from around 15 in 2005 to 80 in 2015 and 130 in 2018. Meanwhile, the goal of insurrection was transformed from an antagonistic rivalry to a symbiotic interplay of armed groups, all of whom had a vested interest in continuing the conflict.

The Post-CNDP: Neither Peace nor War

While the Congolese army eventually succeeded in dismantling the CNDP, the period that followed was not more peaceful. As described in chapter 6, a successor movement to the CNDP, the M23, would eventually emerge, once again challenging the stability of the eastern Congo. The nature of the violence, however, changed. As Rwanda's influence began to dwindle, conflict became integrated into the governance strategy of the government in Kinshasa. This can be seen in my interviews with combatants, which I detail in the coming chapter. The great emancipatory project of liberating the Congo, whose prominence had been dwindling since the end of the AFDL war, took a distinct back seat in the belligerents' rhetoric to more mundane, parochial objectives: survival, individual self-affirmation, and local conflicts over land and power.

Armed conflict became a sticky status quo, benefiting the military leadership and providing income to hundreds of thousands of people inside armed groups or affiliated to them. The proliferation of armed groups and the fragmentation of the government also made it more difficult to reach a settlement as the number of actors and potential spoilers increased.

The military operations against the CNDP ebbed and flowed between 2004 and 2008. Then, after several humiliating defeats, President Kabila decided in late 2008 to negotiate directly with the Rwandan government, which in turn was also increasingly looking for a way out of the conflict due to pressure from Western donors. In January 2009, the parameters of a peace deal became known: the CNDP's leader Laurent Nkunda was arrested by the Rwandan army, which was then allowed to deploy troops to the Kivus to hunt down the FDLR in joint operations with the FARDC. Two months later, an agreement was signed, stipulating that the CNDP should be transformed into a political party and its troops integrated into the Congolese army. Refusing to be redeployed across the country, many CNDP officers stayed in the Kivus, where they formed an influential network within the FARDC.

The 2009 deal also provoked widespread resentment among other armed groups, which accused the government of providing excessively generous terms to their enemies and of keeping most ex-CNDP units deployed in the Kivus. These grievances were amplified when the national army, now including many ex-CNDP officers among its leaders, launched a brutal counterinsurgency campaign against the FDLR and other armed groups, leading to the displacement of hundreds of thousands in the Kivus. The Congolese government had solved the CNDP problem, perhaps, but in doing so had created several others. These developments also coincided with a slow shift in the perception of Joseph Kabila himself, from being seen by many as the bulwark against Rwandan aggression prior to 2006 to becoming complicit with the much-decried "balkanization" of the Congo.

Similar to previous periods, the government often resorted to subterfuge—buying off armed group leaders or pitting them against each other—instead of coercion to deal with insurgents. This displaced conflict but did not solve it. For example, an army restructuring process called *régimentation*, launched in 2011 and intended to dismantle ex-CNDP networks within the military hierarchy, produced a military vacuum in rural areas of the Kivus. This created local security dilemmas as the FDLR moved in to occupy positions deserted by the FARDC, provoking further mobilization—in particular the Raia Mutomboki, a cluster of local militias described in detail in chapter 7. At the same time, discontent about the distribution of positions in the newly formed regiments prompted defections, with some deserters launching new armed groups.

Much like in 2006, the 2011 general elections further intensified armed mobilization. Politicians sometimes fell back on armed groups to obtain electoral support and, when unsuccessful at the polls, to maintain influence. For example, in Fizi territory, parliamentary candidates like Jemsi Mulengwa supported the Mai-Mai Yakutumba, while the *mwami* (customary chief) of the Fulero community in Uvira, who also ran for parliament, mobilized his personal self-defense militia, the Forces d'autodéfense locales et légitimes (FALL), for his campaign.[24]

The M23 and After (2012–2018)

Finally, in early 2012, the Congolese government decided to move more forcefully to dismantle the ex-CNDP networks that controlled large parts of the FARDC in the eastern Congo. The trigger for this was the flawed 2011 elections, which many observers deemed to be rigged, thus undermining Kabila's domestic legitimacy. By cracking down on the ex-CNDP networks, Kabila hoped to distract from that debacle and regain international support. This move was met with resistance, and in April 2012 a group of ex-CNDP officers launched a new rebellion, the M23. With heavy Rwandan backing, the M23 took over the major trade hub of Goma in November 2012 before retreating under international pressure.

As with previous waves of mobilization, the M23 crisis triggered a wave of mobilization by local armed groups, some allied with and some in opposition to the new rebellion.[25] These local initiatives were often backed by marginalized politicians seeking greater relevance and political clout. In the north of North Kivu, Antipas Mbusa Nyamwisi, a former foreign minister, organized significant political support and military supplies for a group allied with the M23.[26] In South Kivu, the failed parliamentary candidate Gustave Bagayamukwe spearheaded the creation of another M23 ally, the Union des forces révolutionnaires du Congo (UFRC).[27] Meanwhile, Mai-Mai groups and Rwandan FDLR rebels mobilized against the M23 and often received backing from FARDC.

In November 2013, the Congolese army, backed by special South African, Malawian, and Tanzanian contingents within the UN peacekeeping force, defeated the M23. Following this success, the government launched new operations against foreign armed groups—Sukola I and Sukola II. These first targeted the Allied Democratic Forces (ADF) insurgency around Beni and then the FDLR in North and South Kivu. The operations against both groups quickly revealed how deeply embedded they were in local society. In Beni, the ADF collaborated with local armed groups in carrying out a series of massacres in retaliation to the FARDC offensive.[28] During their campaign against the FDLR, the army allied with local militias, while the FDLR did the same with a variety of Nyatura groups.[29]

Since the defeat of the M23, several new trends in the conflict have emerged.[30] If the initial phase of the conflict after the peace deal (2003–2013) was dominated by the regional dimension of the conflict—especially a proxy war pitting the government in Kigali against the one in Kinshasa—in this new period new arenas of mobilization opened up. For the first time in seventeen years, the Rwandan and Ugandan governments did not have serious military allies on Congolese soil. While several foreign rebel groups persist—the Ugandan Alliance of Democratic Forces (ADF) and Rwandan Democratic Forces for the Liberation of Rwanda (FDLR) are the most notable—they are mostly a threat to local civilians, not regional stability.

Second, armed violence became more tied up in national political struggles, in particular President Joseph Kabila's succession struggle. Barred by the constitution from seeking a third elected term, Kabila delayed the 2016 elections, a strategy known as *glissement* (slippage). Many armed groups, expecting the crisis to provide new opportunities, ramped up mobilization. They went on the offensive against the government, attacking army camps, prisons, UN peacekeepers, and police stations, especially in the Beni and Lubero territories. For example, on December 19, 2016, the day President Kabila was originally supposed to leave office, the Coalition nationale pour le peuple et la souveraineté du Congo (CNPSC) armed group announced that it would fight to "liberate" the Congo, while in North Kivu the day was marked by an attack on Butembo's police station by Mai-Mai Kilalo. In January 2018, Mbusa Nyamwisi, a veteran of opposition and rebel politics, declared, "There will not be elections. So, we need to use the same means as Kabila and the opposition knows this."[31]

Both of these dynamics—the drop in regional interference along with the focus on elections—led to a shift in rhetoric from armed groups. Kabila had lost the Kivus in the 2011 elections, and subsequent polling suggested that opposition candidates would win a large majority. It was no surprise, then, that a virulent anti-government tone emerged, for instance among the Raia Mutomboki, de-emphasizing anti-Rwandan themes in their rhetoric, a striking turn for armed groups. Statements critical of the government were also made by other groups, including Mai-Mai groups in Lubero and Nyatura coalitions in Rutshuru.

Finally, the conflict began to be fueled by its own momentum. Here, the path-dependent nature of the conflict came to the fore: the initial impetus for the conflict faded away as groups sprang up in competition with each other, often fueled by local security dilemmas. This also contributed to the fragmentation of armed groups, which I will explore further in chapter 5. Whereas there were probably twenty to thirty armed groups active in the Kivus in 2008, by 2018 there were around 130.[32] This proliferation of groups was a symptom of the broader geopolitical context. Prior to the 2002 peace deal, the deployment of large armies in the Congo required local armed groups to be cohesive so that they could muster greater force on the battlefield and wield greater influence in negotiations. During the transition, a large number of former rebels with inflated ranks but little formal training had to vie for power within one national army. Defecting from the army and mounting new insurgencies became a means of bargaining. For Kinshasa, in turn, the creation of new armed groups, many of which had ties to senior officers, served as a means of enforcing protection rackets and of developing proxies to fight groups like the CNDP and the M23.

Around 2011, however, the Congolese government suspended the wholesale integration of armed groups into the army in exchange for ranks and positions. Meanwhile, several demobilization programs had limited success, and a new one proposed in 2015 was never fully implemented. These developments effectively shut down exit options for armed groups, leaving few options other than continued rebellion. Given the lack of cohesion within these groups and the limited military operations against them, this led to a proliferation of belligerents.

Conclusion

The Congolese conflict persisted because the peace deal failed to produce a stable settlement among the belligerents, instead transforming the conflict through an escalation with the CNDP at its center. This new wave of violence then metastasized when a host of other armed groups dropped out of the army integration process, at times receiving support from the Congolese army.

The explanation offered here emphasizes actors, their relationships, and their interests as opposed to material variables that are relatively homogeneous in time and space. The Congo war persisted after 2003 because major protagonists in the conflict—first the RCD and Rwanda, then local armed groups, and finally the Congolese government itself— did not find it in their interest to put down their arms. We will see in later chapters that their interests were complex constructions containing a mix of material concerns—economic gain or physical survival— and norms, ideas, and identities.

This account does not necessarily contradict other theories of conflict duration found in the academic literature, but those are not sufficient to explain the violence. For example, the participation of many different players in the conflict certainly made it more difficult to resolve.[33] The country's size, difficult topography, and abundance of natural resources made it easier to sustain a rebellion.[34] Ethnic divisionism was a key factor in the mobilization of armed groups.[35] However, most of these factors were present both in Ituri and in the Kivus, whereas conflict declined precipitously in the former and escalated in the latter.

More than a rebuttal of those theories, my argument points to an epistemological difference in approach from quantitative studies of conflict. While analyses of the correlations of variables can estimate their impact, it cannot unravel the mechanisms, processes, or norms that drive conflict. There is not one factor that has produced violence in the eastern Congo, and even the variables that are important were mediated by the agents, structures, and networks through which they found expression. It is on this political context and process that this study focuses, not to neglect important factors like natural resources, local conflicts, or state weakness but to infuse them with the context and history that makes them relevant.

This chapter has emphasized proximate causation: the mechanisms and process that explain escalation of conflict. The next chapter scrutinizes the nature—the structure and the interests—of the two most important parties to the violence, arguing that the neopatrimonialism of an economically emboldened Congolese state and the aggressive attitude of the Rwandan leadership furthered this escalation, either wittingly or through inaction. Chapter 5 then distills the theoretical lessons of this analysis.

4

The Role of the Congolese
and Rwandan States

If you want to steal, steal a little in a nice way. But if you steal too much
to become rich overnight, you'll be caught.

Mutu na mutu abongisa. [Everyone has to manage for himself.]

Everything is for sale, anything can be bought in our country. And in
this flow, he who holds the slightest cover of public authority uses it
illegally to acquire money, goods, prestige or to avoid obligations.

—MOBUTU SESE SEKO[1]

THE PREVIOUS CHAPTER DESCRIBES the dynamics behind the persistence of conflict in the eastern Congo following the 2002 peace deal. It could be simplified thus: the peace process created losers, who then launched new rebellions. In a nutshell, this describes the defection of the CNDP and Mai-Mai groups during the transition. This is not dissimilar to the academic research focusing on spoilers in peace process, kindled by the seminal work of Stephen Stedman.[2]

However, this stratospheric account is not satisfactory. It leaves unpacked the key question: Why? Why are these spoilers taking up arms again? What are their interests and how are these constituted? In this chapter, I use this lens to focus on the most important actors in these dynamics: the Congolese and Rwandan governments. The behavior of both seems, at first blush, counterintuitive. In the case of the former, the puzzle lies in its apathy, and at times even its direct complicity, with the escalation of violence. In the case of the latter, it is the opposite tendency that baffles: Rwanda's excessive belligerency, interfering in its neighbor even when it seemed against its interests to do so.

The Congolese State

Many scholars of civil war depict conflict as a confrontation between the state and its adversaries. Most popular depictions of war in the media and film echo this dichotomous depiction of conflict, with tank regiments rolling across trenches or US marines fighting door to door in Fallujah. What could be more oppositional than war? The German philosopher Carl Schmitt even famously held that it is in the potential of war that the distinction between friend and enemy crystallizes; that distinction, Schmitt held, is the definition of the political realm itself.[3]

There is another, more sociological aspect of war, often highlighted by academics: the relationship between governments and elites.[4] "It is a truism," sociologist Jack Goldstone states, "that fiscally and military sound states that enjoy the support of united elites are largely invulnerable to revolution from below."[5] Governments wage war against their domestic opponents, and if the elites that prop up and constitute the government are united, they will be successful.

The Congo goes against the grain of both of these arguments. Between 2003 and 2013, it was often the social connections *between* armed groups and the government that brought more opportunities for insurgency. And, paradoxically, it was precisely the deep fragmentation of the elite and the insurgency that enabled both the government to survive and the rebellion to persist.

This analysis motivates a sharper focus on what the Congolese state is, what its interests are, and how it makes decisions. Perhaps it does not want to win? Perhaps the Congolese state is not one actor but an unruly gaggle of people and interest groups pulling in different directions? Perhaps the belligerents are not rivals at all but partners locked in a perverse symbiotic dance?

Drawing on past studies of the Congolese state, I evaluate its structure and interests. The two aspects interact powerfully, with the structure shaping the interests of the state and its leaders, whose interests, in turn, influence the structure that the state takes.

The Structure of the Congolese State

The structure of the Congolese state is characterized by high degrees of informalization of power and fragmentation of decision-makers. It is also, despite its ubiquity, limited in its capabilities and hemmed in by actors in civil society. Together, this renders it more difficult to credibly guarantee peace deals, enforce the law, and coordinate effective policy. However, this kind of plural society also harbors a kind of dynamism that can serve to constrain autocrats and innovate new forms of order and prosperity.

THE INFORMALIZATION OF POWER

Much political power in the Congo resides in informal networks. Decisions regarding the allocation of state resources and extraction of rents often take place outside of formal institutions, often circumventing or in violation of laws and regulations.[6] Informal relations and networks of power have played an important role in the Congolese state since independence. Joseph Kabila reinforced this informalization after he was forced into the 2003 power-sharing agreement in order to preserve his power, particularly in the security and mining sectors. This allowed him to maintain control over the most important levers of power, despite having to initially share power. This informality persisted even after the transition, as it allowed Kabila to preserve his influence despite the poor cohesion within his political coalition.

Until he stepped down as president in January 2019, Kabila maintained ultimate control over the attribution of major contracts in mining, oil, telecommunications, and state procurement, all of which should be controlled by the respective minister under the supervision of the prime minister. Government ministers often had little say in decisions regarding national security, important financial matters, and foreign affairs. Instead, the president and a rotating group of advisors—some of whom had no official title—dictated policy. For a long time, the person many considered the most powerful in the country after Kabila was Augustin Katumba Mwanke, who did not have an official position in government between 2004 and his death in 2012.[7]

The impact this informality had on conflict could clearly be seen in the security sector, where promotions, bonuses, and deployments in the army depended considerably on their "protectors" within the institutional hierarchy—in the first years of the transition, up to two-thirds of all salaries were paid to fictitious soldiers and thus embezzled.[8]

The FARDC was the product of the peace process, producing an amalgam of competing and overlapping patronage networks.[9] Here, loyalty, support, and the provision of certain services are exchanged for access to resources and protection. As one officer explained, "In this army, you need to have an 'umbrella,' someone who can look after you, secure promotions and lucrative deployments. Nothing works on merit alone."[10] Subordinates were required to kick back regular amounts to superiors, often referred to as *operation retour* (return operation), *rapportage* ("bringing in")—or, as many Congolese soldiers put it, "feeding the horse so the horse feeds you."[11] *Rapportage* works as an instrument of control: those failing to satisfy the requirement of their superiors can be redeployed or relegated to the barracks.

The networks that riddle the FARDC, which are overlapping, are organized based on geography, ethnicity, education, or prior membership in an armed group or military unit. For example, some former Forces Armées Zaïroises (FAZ) officers collaborate due to their common experiences under Mobutu—often contrasting their own professional training with that of the poorly trained post-1996 recruits. Since 2003, the overall commanders of the armed forces have been ex-FAZ officers, and until 2014 this was the case for more than half of the eleven regional military commanders.

A similar network, which over time began to fray, was made up of RCD officers from the east who were integrated into the army in 2003. By 2011, more than half of the command positions in North and South

Kivu were held by officers from this group.[12] Some of the most prominent of these maintained their positions thanks to General Gabriel Amisi, a former RCD officer and commander of the land forces between 2006 and 2012.

Divided and privatized loyalties strongly affected combat performance, as evidenced by the FARDC's mixed record against the M23. Many officers complained that they were ordered by the high command *not* to pursue the M23, just as they gained the upper hand during the defense of Kibumba, 30 kilometers north of Goma. One FARDC officer said: "Suddenly we received the order to stop. It didn't make sense; it just gave them the chance to regroup and pull together a force that went on to take Goma."[13] The foreign-trained commando battalions were also "sabotaged," according to one of their trainers: the 391st Battalion was deployed in the Virunga National Park without reconnaissance, got lost, and was ambushed by enemy forces.[14] According to officers I interviewed, this was because senior FARDC officers, including the head of the land forces, General Gabriel Amisi, were close to the M23 and Rwanda. While this is difficult to prove, it is consistent with observations made by the UN peacekeeping mission,[15] and these beliefs were deeply held by many FARDC officers.

Appointments based on connections rather than merit further diminished the FARDC's fighting capabilities. Subordinates lost respect for incompetent commanders, leading to insubordination and the refusal to obey orders. In addition, the disorganization created by parallel chains of command and the embezzlement of military funds and equipment undermined operational effectiveness. Troops often found themselves on the front line without food, ammunition, medical supplies, or adequate communications equipment. This was reflected in the military operations against the M23 before the fall of Goma in November 2012, when troops rapidly ran out of supplies.

This informalization of the security apparatus also aggravated commitment problems during negotiations. The proliferation of secretive parallel networks of decision-makers made it difficult to know where the real power resided and how to hold it accountable. One M23 combatant told me, "You can tear up any agreement the government signs.

It's worth nothing, as they can renege on it tomorrow."[16] It also made it more difficult for the government itself to reach decisions about and make compromises with armed groups, for it was never clear who the relevant authorities are and which chain of command should be followed. One M23 leader said: "It's never clear who we are negotiating with. We make a deal with one presidential envoy, who is then contradicted by another."[17]

THE FRAGMENTATION OF POLITICAL ELITES

The second structural characteristic is the dispersion of power among different individuals and groups across the country. As with the informalization of power, fragmentation fostered uncertainty and made it more difficult to reach consensus and compromise.

This tendency toward fragmentation, and in particular the use of division and state weakness as a political resource, goes back to the late Mobutu period. During the first part of his reign, from 1965 to 1974, Mobutu embarked on a nation-building exercise, centralizing power and patronage networks, but also forging strong horizontal networks out of trade unionists, army officers, administrators, and intellectuals.[18] This strategy, along with high copper prices, allowed Mobutu to increase revenue and expand social services; it also marginalized the importance of the customary authorities and of ethnicity in general in public life.

The turning point came in the early 1970s, when a confluence of high oil prices, plummeting copper prices, and catastrophic economic management prompted a change in political strategy. Faced with limited resources and becoming increasingly paranoid, Mobutu resorted to fragmentation, orchestrating the proliferation of ethnicity-based vertical networks throughout the state. Fearing dissent in the army, he arrested or replaced dozens of officers based on their ethnicity and his suspicions of insubordination, promoting officers from his Équateur region of origin. He then allowed security services to proliferate, often in competition with each other. This fragmentation was exacerbated by the World Bank–led structural adjustment program, which began in

1983, as well as a rising challenge from democracy activists. While this "divide and rule" strategy was relatively successful in allowing Mobutu and his MPR party to survive, by the end of the 1980s patronage had been decentralized and the state administration hollowed out.

The process of fragmentation under Joseph Kabila proceeded with a different logic, although Mobutu's precedent served as a sort of blue-print. Kabila arrived in power with extremely poor cohesion within the ruling elite, as his father and predecessor had never been able to forge strong cohesion and trust within the government or in the government's relationships with the business class and with civil society.

This fragmentation increased during the peace process—the creation of a national assembly and senate in 2003, the establishment of an elec-toral system with large districts and proportional representation, and the proliferation of civil society organizations all produced a dizzying carousel of actors. There were 428 political parties in the Congo in 2011—602 in 2018—66 of which were represented in the 2006–2011 na-tional assembly, which also had 63 independent parliamentarians.[19] In the 2011 elections, the number of political parties in the lower chamber increased to 98.

Much as with Mobutu, this proliferation of competing networks was used as a political tool. According to three different presidential advi-sors, their 2011 electoral strategy was to purposely fragment the political elite through the creation of new political parties to prevent potential challengers from emerging the so-called partis mosaiques.[20] However, as a result, President Kabila himself often complained that his coalition in power was so unruly that he had to allocate significant resources to bribing his own parliamentarians to pass legislation.[21]

Perhaps most important, even within the executive branch Kabila often appeared to have little control over the numerous competing pa-tronage networks. A former minister put it this way in 2016, as the ruling party was deciding on a new cabinet:

> Kabila's basic attitude is to let people fight it out and only to step in as the ultimate arbiter. You have Boshab [the interior minister], who hates Matata [the prime minister]; then you have Yuma [the head of

Gécamines, the largest state mining company] fighting with Ekanga [the head of economic cooperation with China] and Yav [minister of finance] over the economic portfolios. It's plots, intrigues, rumor-mongering. It's very Louis XIV.[22]

In an interview in 2009, Kabila himself said: "Sometimes I feel over-whelmed. . . . You don't need a thousand people to transform a coun-try. No, you need 3, 4, 10, 15 people with the necessary convictions, determined and resolute. Do I have those 15 people? Probably 5, 6, 7, not yet 15."[23]

This fragmentation was further accentuated by the decentralization of authority that was enabled by the new constitution. The country is divided into twenty-six provinces as well as the capital Kinshasa,[24] each with its own legislature and governor; each should, in theory, retain 40 percent of national taxes gathered in their provinces.

THE LIMITS OF STATE POWER

Finally, the Congolese state, despite its ubiquity, is relatively limited in its power. A far cry from the *Bula Matari* ("Breaker of Rocks"), as the state was called in its colonial form, the contemporary state is impover-ished, with a budget that since 2011 has hovered around $5 to $6 billion—smaller than that of New York University, or of Seattle, a city of 650,000 people—with one of the lowest rates of revenue extraction from its citizens in Africa. It ends up spending most of its budget on salaries and the day-to-day operations of the government. In 2019, the amount spent on salaries, servicing public debt, and the functioning of institutions was 77 percent of the total budget, leaving less than $1 bil-lion for everything else the government was supposed to do.

This reality—"*on contrôle tout, on ne contrôle rien*" (we control every-thing, we control nothing) is how one permanent secretary in a minis-try put it—results in a deep rift between the state and the population.[25] The state is seen everywhere as extracting resources, but much of the service provision is organized by nonprofits, churches, and foreign do-nors. Two examples: while the government is mandated by the constitution to provide free primary education, in reality 72 percent of its cost is paid by parents and a further 6 percent by foreign donors.[26] Meanwhile, 63 percent of primary school students attend schools managed by religious networks—in particular the Catholic Church. While the budgets of these *écoles conventionnées* are paid for by the same mix of parental, donor, and public funding, the schools are run and supervised by the churches.

Similarly, in 2011 the government only footed 11 percent of the bill for health care—40 percent was paid for by consumers and 49 percent by foreign donors and NGOs in a system in a large part run by churches.[27] Only 20 percent of Congolese have access to electricity, which is in the process of being privatized and is relatively expensive and unpredictable where it is available. Other public services are also provided at a cost— almost every road in the rural sections of the Kivus features a roadblock, often with several different government agencies present, and often imposing taxes that are at times legal but most often are just crude extortion. One NGO counted 798 roadblocks in North and South Kivu in 2017. Another study on the Congo River showed that boat operators had to pay illegal "taxes" to more than twenty different authorities at ten different places in downstream journeys toward Kinshasa; each boat paid an average of 14 percent of the cost of the trip to authorities.[28]

This reality contains in it a kernel of hope. The weak and fragmented state—which contrasts deeply with the more hierarchical and party-dominated states of Angola or Rwanda and with the more intrusive, bureaucratic states of Kenya or Senegal—is hemmed in by civil society actors, who have a large impact on government policy. Since the democratic transition began under Mobutu in 1990, civil society, often in coordination with the political opposition and the Catholic Church, has been able to maintain pressure on the government through street protests, media appearances, and reporting. The fragmentation, however, is present in this sphere too, leading to factionalism and the cooptation of many members of civil society and the opposition by the successive governments. In other words, civil society has served to prevent a drift toward authoritarianism, but it has also not been able to bring about transformational reform.

This fragmentation, which prevails in the security sector as well, has also made it more difficult for the army to impose itself as it has in other African countries. This could be seen during the transition between Joseph Kabila and Félix Tshisekedi, which began in 2019. The latter came to power in what most observers deem to have been a rigged election, concluding a deal with his predecessor. This *"compromis à l'africaine"*—in the deplorable terms of the French foreign minister—handed the presidency to Tshisekedi but left the national and provincial parliaments, and therefore also their governments, in the hands of Kabila's coalition. However, because this coalition was so diffuse and Kabila was relatively unpopular, it was possible for Tshisekedi by mid-2020 to begin chipping away at it, eventually constituting a new parliamentary majority and pushing Kabila into the opposition. At least by the time of this writing, the various competing patronage networks within the army seemed more interested in currying favor with the new president than in defending their former boss.

The Interests of the Congolese State

State weakness and violence are not merely the result of the colonial legacy, of historic structures that the current political class has inherited. These features of the state have become part of a mode of governance, a contested set of ideas, norms, and practices that are constantly being reshaped. I emphasize the dynamic and systemic aspects of governance through and in violence to distinguish my theory from depictions of violence that are mostly instrumental—the influential book *Disorder as a Political Instrument* by Patrick Chabal and Jean-Pascal Daloz is one such example. Nor can violence be understood only in terms of material extraction, as suggested by activists' use of the term "violent kleptocracy."[29]

Images in popular culture illustrate this normalization of political violence. For example, the widespread expression, familiar to most Congolese, of *pompier-pyromane* (firefighter-pyromaniac): you set fires in order to be the one called upon to put them out. Chéri Chérin's 2009 painting "Demoncratie" visualizes these cynical politics. In it, the "train of democracy"—as the United Nations mission used to call the electoral process—is beset by mobs of stone-wielding protestors, devils stuff ballot boxes, and rats beat cheetahs in the electoral race.

Congolese author In Koli Jean Bofane explores this culture of *antivaleurs*, unethical behavior, in his novel *Mathématiques congolaises*. The protagonist, a mathematical savant, makes use of his skills to uncover the hidden logic of Congolese politics. Having grown up in poverty, he puts his creativity to use for a powerful government minister, only to discover that his boss was staging false-flag protests, a tactic often invoked by Congolese political analysts and conspiracy theorists alike, in order to manipulate public opinion and crack down on his opponents.

This normalization operates on several levels: by creating new templates for social action that become readily available to actors; by rendering violent behavior acceptable according to prevailing norms and practices; and by dehumanizing or rendering invisible the victims of violence.

For example, thousands of Congolese are killed each year due to conflict, and there is little time devoted to this problem, either among Congolese elites or among those abroad who are intrinsically linked to the Congo through colonial history, geopolitics, or international trade; this apathy is structured and maintained by power. As Judith Butler writes, media representations and political discourse render people invisible by differentiating between "the cries we can hear from those we cannot, the sights we can see from those we cannot, and likewise at the level of touch and even smell."[30]

In this chapter, I describe the nature of the interests of the main Congolese actors as well as their transformation over time. I turn to the international actors in chapter 9.

INTERESTS AMONG LEADING GOVERNMENT OFFICIALS

Drawing on lengthy interviews with twenty-five senior members of the Congolese security services and civilian security officials, I argue that the capture of the state by private interests during the transition became entwined with violent conflict, together constituting a mode of governance.[31]

There is little evidence, as some argue, of a sadistic conspiracy to kill Congolese that sees Joseph Kabila as a stooge of Rwandan president Paul Kagame in a plot underwritten by the United States and Europe. This argument is relatively widespread, especially in the Congolese diaspora, and has been articulated by the French-Cameroonian pundit Charles Onana or Mobutu's former advisor Honoré Ngbanda. Instead, violence has become systemic in the sense that is has been normalized and that those who produce it often do so unwittingly, as a side effect of a generalized attempt by the political elite to extract resources from the state. This system has largely normalized and excluded from the public sphere and in political discourse—with certain exceptions around elections—the extreme violence that Congolese suffer .

One might think that the government should have an interest in controlling the eastern Congo; rationalizing revenue collection; building infrastructure to access gold, tantalum, and tin mines; and securing a monopoly on legitimate violence. After all, not only do elites in Kinshasa forgo economic opportunities by allowing low-grade violence to persist in the eastern Congo, they create deep resentment among the population as well as within the army.

Instead, political elites' approach to the conflict has been a mixture of apathy, helplessness, and opportunism. Many of the political leaders I interviewed, even some of those from the East, expressed little knowledge about or engagement with the situation there. "Those people have always been at war," one parliamentarian from Kinshasa told me. "Nothing we can do will change that."[32] When asked why the government had not rooted out corruption and mismanagement within the army, a vice minister replied: "We are aware of the problems, but these conflicts were created by the international community—they let the Rwandan refugees in here in 1994, they allowed Rwanda to invade and kill our brothers and sisters."[33]

While some politicians may be influenced by stereotypes surrounding the violence, others are well informed of government complicity and yet do little to change things, as it would be risky for them to do so. The main reason for this stems from the importance of the military during the period following the transitional government of the 2003–2006 period. Political elites in Kinshasa were more worried about military dissent within the army than about the grievances of the local population. The war in the eastern Congo was extremely peripheral to their survival—politicians were not punished at the polls for their neglect of the East, nor was the fighting there a security threat to the country's capital a thousand miles away. "When I campaign in my constituency in Kinshasa, no one ever asks me about violence in the eastern Congo," one MP told me.[34] Elected officials from Équateur, Kasaï, and Bandundu provinces reported similar dynamics.[35] Another advisor to Kabila said: "It was not until LUCHA started their #Beni campaign that this became an issue. That was then injected into the noise around the 2018 elections, that is when violence in the East became an issue as part of a general perception that Kabila was bad, was corrupt, was Rwandan. But even then, the violence was not as important as the corruption scandals, the poverty."[36]

By deploying most of the army to the East, keeping officers' salaries low but their discretionary allowances and bonuses high, and giving them a free hand in racketeering, political elites protected themselves from possible coups and enriched themselves through kickback schemes. President Kabila himself, while apparently well informed about the violence, often privileged loyalty over accountability, allowing corruption and patronage rackets to persist within the national army.

Together, Human Rights Watch, the United Nations High Commissioner for Human Rights, and the UN Group of Experts have compiled information regarding serious human rights abuses and racketeering committed by over a hundred Congolese military officers. "Almost none of these people have been prosecuted, or even investigated," Ida Sawyer, the senior researcher on the Congo for Human Rights Watch, told me. "That shows that this is not a priority for the government."[37]

Why did this elite decide to use fragmentation and violence to consolidate its power? In part, path dependence explains why the Congo has bucked the expectations of academics. The power-sharing agreement of the transition reinforced Kabila's tendency to shift real power from official institutions to the shadow parallel networks that he controlled. The windfall in mining investments that came in the 2005–2012 period then cemented the strength of the shadowy inner circle around Kabila, encouraging him to invest not in public goods but rather in private patronage. Finally, the rise of the CNDP triggered an entrenchment of the conflict as a way to manage military patronage networks that has been extended since then. These developments were consistent with economic self-interest: a new elite partnership received so much revenue from other sources—in particular major investments by large multinationals—that they did not feel the need to extract rents from the restive East or to bring enough stability and infrastructure to attract large foreign investments there. At the same time, it saw greater risks from trying to impose discipline inside its own security forces than from allowing patronage and racketeering networks to proliferate.

This lack of priority regarding discipline is probably not surprising. The terms of the peace deal required Kabila to integrate his army, bringing his former enemies into the senior ranks of the new FARDC and raising the possibility that they could overthrow him. After all, his father was killed in office by his own bodyguard, and Kabila was said to be worried about his personal safety, wearing bulletproof vests in public. However, it is clear that the threat came not just from his former enemies but also from so-called loyalists. In 2004, Eric Lenge, a major in the Republic Guard, attempted to overthrow the government, briefly occupying the national radio and television station before fleeing. According to several sources, he was protected, perhaps even encouraged, by General John Numbi, one of Kabila's most senior generals.[38] Numbi was not arrested or questioned. This reluctance to crack down on insubordination was apparently not unusual. According to a senior security official in the UN peacekeeping mission, General Dieudonné Banze, the commander of the Republican Guard, sometimes hired out entire units of the presidential guard to work for a private security company in South Africa, unbeknownst to President Kabila.[39]

Perhaps the most notorious example of this type of behavior was General Gabriel "Tango 4" Amisi's complicity with the CNDP. As commander of North Kivu in 2006, Amisi abetted the CNDP, paying out salaries to a roster of CNDP soldiers that had been inflated by fictitious names. During the failed offensive against the M23 in 2012, Amisi—then commander of all FARDC land forces—allegedly gave orders to prevent the FARDC from advancing on the enemy, even when it was obviously in their interest to do so. Despite this complicity, which senior FARDC officers raged about in private,[40] President Kabila kept Amisi in high-ranking positions, prioritizing his personal connection to the president and ability to control a solid network of senior officers.[41] "Kabila cares more about making sure his officers are weak than making sure they are loyal or good at their jobs," one senior FARDC officer complained.[42] This has allowed these officers to cultivate their own patronage networks, thereby proliferating chains of command. "Keep the troublemakers close to you, even if it means alienating the population," advised one senior military officer.[43]

While it is true that the security forces were already fragmented and riddled with patronage networks when Joseph Kabila came into office, he did little to strengthen his control, instead reinforcing those networks and pitting them against each other. Jean Omasombo, a Congolese political scientist, argues: "According to his logic of rule, Kabila does not have to be popular or strong. He just has to make sure everyone else is weaker. This is why he has undermined state institutions and not done much about the conflict in the East."[44] In other words, fragmentation is not just an accident of history and society: it has become part of a strategy of rule.

This system of fragmentation and clientelism has been baked into the organization of the state, rendering it invested in the persistence of conflict. It can, for example, be observed in how members of the security services are compensated—payment is structured in such a way that officers struggle to prosper in the absence of armed conflict. In 2014, up to more than 90 percent of officers' remuneration depended on legal or extralegal payments directly linked to military operations. For example, officers in command positions often received a *prime de commandement* worth up to $1,000 a month, and intelligence officers sometimes received a *fond secret de renseignement* worth several hundred dollars a month, but only if they were conducting military operations. These payments were not statutory and were made at the discretion of military officers, which reinforced their individual loyalty to them.

In addition, military operations come with opportunities for pillage, extortion, and embezzlement of funds. These sums dwarf officers' salaries, which in 2018 peaked at around $150 a month for the highest ranks. In contrast, officers awaiting deployment are *à la disposition de la région militaire*—colloquially known as "dispo"—a label associated with indigence and humiliation. "The only way to make money in the army is to be deployed in military operations or to control the deployment of soldiers in the East," one officer said.[45]

This perception of the Congolese state as a source of profit and survival—and not as a means of guaranteeing health care, security, education, or development—can also be seen in the civil service, where the government, seeing increasing revenues, expanded its ranks from 600,000 to almost 1,300,000 between 2007 and 2017, even though in some ministries over two-thirds of employees were not paid.[46] Much as in the security sector, up to 95 percent of a civil servant's income can come from bonuses and salary supplements, which come at the discretion of his or her superiors.[47] Illegal patronage is thus made possible by administrative decisions on how to organize payroll. In this system, the population ends up paying directly for access to "public" services, and a large part of the civil service ends up sourcing much of its income outside of its irregularly paid salaries.

Both the fragmentation of actors and these interests produce what I describe in the next chapter as involution, drawing on Clifford Geertz's famous study of rice agriculture. In this case, Congolese government officials and army commanders reproduce the same patterns of governance, albeit improvising and creating more intricate systems of extraction. Due to the multiplicity of players and the shadowy nature of these networks, each actor finds it difficult to imagine another logic, let alone take concrete actions to reform, even though almost every actor within the current system finds it reprehensible, a *système ya lifelo*.

INTERESTS AMONG THE COMBATANTS

In order to understand how members of the army and armed groups conceive of their interests, I conducted semi-structured, individual interviews with forty-three lower-ranking members of the Congolese security services (22) and armed groups (21) between 2012 and 2014. During these interviews, which often involved several sessions, the shifts in the political culture of the conflict between 1996 and 2018 became apparent. In particular, after the end of the Second Congo War in 2003, according to their own portrayals of their motives, the interests of individual combatants became more self-regarding, more focused on material benefits, and more targeted at local instead of national objectives.

Almost all the interviewees were young men—there were only four women among them—who took up arms between 1993 and 1998. While reading perceptions and interest back into time is problematic, almost all combatants felt that their objectives and motivations had shifted clearly over time.

For those who participated in the AFDL rebellion, especially the young *kadogo* (child soldiers) of the Kivus, their memories of these early days reverberate with the promise of liberation, the notion that they were on the verge of large, fundamental change. "We had enough of humiliation, we wanted to create a new world," one former combatant who had been 15 when he joined in 1996 remembered.[48] The mood was revolutionary, infused with utopian, often masculine, visions of liberation. Another former combatant said: "All our lives, in church and in the movies, we had heard stories of heroes, men who got rid of the bad guys and changed their lives. We looked around and just saw bad guys ruling us. We needed to change this. It was like a movie. It was like David and Goliath."[49] While all interviewees also spoke of their economic motives, most recollections of this period were colored with this revolutionary spirit.

The outlier in this trend were former soldiers of Mobutu's army, many of whom had joined before the 1996 war. Of the eleven of these soldiers that we interviewed, most of them, predominantly men from the western provinces, said they had joined "as a job," seeking employment during the economic stagnation of the early 1990s.

For all combatants, but especially for the recruits from the eastern Congo, the objective during this period seemed well defined: military victory. "I remember when I was kid, I used to wonder what I would do with my life. Everything seemed to be suffering, struggle [*kuteseka, kujidébrouiller*]. Then Kabila came, and I saw a purpose: kick out Mobutu!"[50] This sentiment persisted into the Second Congo War.

It was during this second war (1998–2003) that cynicism creeped into combatants' worldview, although notions of national liberation lingered. "After Mobutu was gone and the Rwandans attacked us, we realized that we had not yet achieved our liberation, so we rolled up our sleeves again," remembered a combatant who had been a junior officer in Kabila's Forces armées congolaises (FAC) at the time.[51] One of the soldiers in the Rwandan-backed RCD, however, said: "When they started the RCD, we really didn't see the purpose. We fought, but we lost the taste [*tulipoteza goût*] for war." In general, the interviewees expressed mixed feelings. Almost all soldiers expressed their disillusionment with their leadership during this time. "During the AFDL, we were paid, they looked after us. When we fought against the RCD, we didn't have even soap to wash. But our commanders were making money! That war was not serious, it was too political."[52]

This creeping cynicism could be seen in many interviews, from all sides of the conflict. For many, it seemed to be linked to their poor treatment as well as the rampant abuse that they witnessed and at times participated in. One former RCD combatant said: "[Our commanders] treated us like dirt. I remember my best friend dying because they didn't get him to a doctor quickly enough. That's when I realized it was a worthless war [*vita ya bure*]."[53] A former soldier in Kabila's army remembered: "We told the population we were protecting them, but then how did we treat them? Stealing manioc off the plates of the population. Forcing them to carry our boxes of ammunition."[54]

This trend continued. Speaking of the period following the transition and through the CNDP war, soldiers in the national army spoke more frequently, and more disparagingly, of the cynical motivations of their commanders. Violence appeared to no longer be just a way to resist an enemy; it also became a tool of groups to negotiate for better positions and ranks and to obtain access to resources. While members of newly formed armed groups were more upbeat, apparently caught up in the élan of their initial formation, those who had been fighting for more than two years were almost as cynical as the FARDC soldiers. One former combatant expressed this clearly: "When we fought in 1996, we fought to free the country. Now, they fight to make money, to show the government they are strong so they can get a big house, a big position in Kinshasa."[55]

When asked why they were fighting during this period, only around half of our interviewees responded immediately that it was to defeat the enemy. Others said that it was a mixture of profiteering and inertia or simply that they didn't know. "*Tufanye nini yengine*" (what else should we do?), "*hii vita ni faranga tu*" (this war is all about money), and "*kuko siasa mbaya hapa, shiye bakurutu hatujui akili ya bakubwa*" (there are some bad politics here, us foot soldiers don't know what our bosses want) were typical answers. Combatants themselves also stated that they were driven by material self-interest. In response to the question, "Why did you continue fighting during this period?" almost all FARDC soldiers answered that they did so for economic reasons, as did over half of the armed group combatants.[56]

These self-regarding interests of combatants and their disappointment with their commanders and living conditions did not change during the next period, between the M23 rebellion of 2012–2013 and the Kabila succession crisis of 2016–2018. However, the perceived objective of armed groups shifted, from seeking access to the state to local struggles over land and extortion rackets. "We once thought our goal was to become a soldier in the army," a Raia Mutomboki soldier said, "but then we saw how they lived: in dirt and disease, robbing from the population. From then on, we decided to protect our communities but not to join the FARDC."[57] For many, violence became an end in itself.

At the same time, the rhetoric of armed groups shifted slightly away from Rwanda and the Congolese Tutsi community—which had distanced itself considerably from Rwanda—toward a condemnation of

Kinshasa's corrupt and abusive rule. As described in chapter 2, armed group declarations from 2003 to 2006 point to an almost ubiquitous language of opposition to the Rwandan government, sometimes expressed in ethnic stereotypes against the Tutsi community (or the "Hima Empire") that they presume to be in power in Rwanda and Uganda. While this language did not disappear, by 2016 many groups were much more concerned about their own abusive government. For instance, during the 2016–2018 period, in the run-up to national elections, many Raia Mutomboki shifted away from anti-Rwandan rhetoric to emphasize the corruption of the government, a striking turn for armed groups that were previously much more concerned about local issues. Mai-Mai groups in Lubero, the CNPSC in Fizi, and Nyatura coalitions in Rutshuru also made anti-government statements during this period.

This shift in emphasis could also be seen in the alliances struck up by armed groups, sometimes in direct contradiction to their official ideology. For example, despite their anti-rwandophone rhetoric, the NDC-R and the UCPC—two large armed groups in North Kivu— allied with the Rwandan army or its M23 proxy, while the APCLS collaborated with the FDLR, and several Mai-Mai groups in Fizi and Uvira territories worked with the Burundian army.[58]

The Rwandan State

"The Rwandan government has no interest in backing the CNDP. They want a stable eastern Congo," a senior British diplomat insisted to me in 2008 as I presented evidence of that exact kind of support to a group of diplomats in Kigali.[59] It is not difficult to see why the Rwandan government would, in theory, want a stable eastern Congo. The Congo is Rwanda's largest export market, consuming over 30 percent of the goods produced in Rwanda, according to a World Bank database.[60] Stability in the Congo could result in that market growing and could bring in foreign investment in mining and other sectors, which in turn would almost certainly drive growth in Rwanda.

And yet, Rwanda continued to intervene in the eastern Congo, under-mining instead of forging stability. How did it understand its interests?

Culture, history, and the way decision-making is conducted within the RPF had a huge impact on decision-making within the Rwandan govern-ment. Much as scholars have argued about decision-making in the US government during the Cuban missile crisis,[61] the Rwandan government should not be seen as a cohesive actor with transparent interests. As else-where in the world, foreign policy decisions in Rwanda are warped by domestic conflicts, organizational dysfunctions, and skewed perceptions of what the interests of the nation or regime are.[62]

The Structure of the Rwandan State

It is impossible to speak of the Rwandan state in isolation from the RPF government. While it has obviously drawn on decades of state tradi-tions, norms, and habits, the RPF party has permeated every level of government and society. In order to understand why the Rwandan gov-ernment has engaged in the eastern Congo, we must therefore grapple with the nature of the RPF.

The RPF worldview and organization remain deeply marked by its past. The party was formed in 1987 by exiles and refugees as a political-military movement that spent its formative years preparing for and fighting an insurgency against the regime of Juvénal Habyarimana. When it came to power, it took over a country in ruins that few of the rebels knew very well. It had to remake the economy, reconstitute the civil service, and gain the trust of a population that saw the RPF as a foreign, conquering force.

I do not propose here a comprehensive analysis of the decision-making process within the Rwandan government; other scholars have made heroic efforts, given the relative opacity of the RPF.[63] Here I focus more narrowly on how decisions regarding interventions in the Congo are made, with the caveat that it is extremely difficult to draw conclu-sions about the internal functioning of the RPF, in light of its opacity. Three structural aspects stand out: the dominance of the security establishment when it comes to making policy about the eastern Congo, the divisions within the ruling elite, and the highly secretive process. These structural aspects reinforce a bias toward belligerency.

The first feature of this decision-making process is its military nature. "It is striking to see that, despite the potential economic opportunities there, discussions about intervention in the Congo only take place among senior officials of the army and intelligence," one foreign diplomat commented.[64] This point was echoed by two Rwandan businessmen I spoke with who were eager to invest in the eastern Congo; their efforts had been stymied by security officials.[65]

Another diplomat based in Kigali said: "The Congo is what keeps these security agencies relevant. It is the only real threat to the country."[66] The RPF came into existence as an armed rebellion, and the backbone of the organization was forged during the bush war of 1990–1994. When it came to power, it had to balance the competing imperatives of rendering the military apolitical and keeping senior army officers content. "The war in the Congo is a source of patronage and status for the army. It helps keep them happy and justifies repression at home," said a former senior RCD officer with many friends in the RDF.[67]

A second feature is the highly charged divisions within the ruling elite, which encumbered the decision-making process. Since the RPF was formed in 1987, many senior RPF politicians and military commanders have defected from the government or have been arrested, including the former army commander, the head of external intelligence, a special advisor to the president, and Kagame's chief of staff.[68] A scholar compiled a list of the thirty-two Rwandan commanders who were part of the Ugandan army, which served as an incubator for the initial RPF leadership; as of this writing, only four are still in senior positions in government.[69] Few of the peers of Paul Kagame alongside whom he fought in the bush war are still in positions where they would be able to contradict him.

Divisions within the Rwandan military reached a fever pitch in the run-up to the Rwandan elections of 2010. Senior members of the security establishment in Rwanda had begun to dissent and express their own ambitions. In 2007, the former head of intelligence, Colonel Patrick Karegeya, left for exile in South Africa, where he was joined in 2010 by General Kayumba Nyamwasa, the former army commander. In 2011 and 2012, around the beginning of the M23 rebellion, a series of high-ranking army commanders was arrested for dissent.

An attempt on Nyamwasa's life was made in 2010, and Karegeya was assassinated in a hotel room in South Africa in 2015; both acts were likely ordered by the Rwandan government. The brazen nature of these attacks—the attack against Nyamwasa took place just two days before South Africa hosted the soccer World Cup, the largest sporting event in the country's history—suggests how seriously the Rwandan government perceived this dissent.

According to two former CNDP officers, such divisions fueled support to the M23 in two ways.[70] First, they created distrust and tension among the senior officer corps of the RPF, heightening pressure for them to prove their loyalty. "Everyone was looking over their shoulder, trying to be the most hardline of them all. So when Kagame asked: 'Should we [back the M23]?' no one dared question him."[71] In contrast to civilian matters of government, where officials have to sign performance contracts and are often rigorously evaluated, military matters are outside of the realm of public debate and even in private are not subjected to rigorous, reasoned debate. As a businessman told one of my sources, "We knew that backing the M23 was the wrong choice. But we couldn't say anything. Then it took [Kagame] eighteen months to walk back that decision."[72]

Second, it created a security imperative for intervention. Nyamwasa was suspected of trying to stage an anti-Kigali rebellion based in the eastern Congo. He had links to officers within the CNDP, some of whom he had commanded in the Rwandan army between 1990 and 1996. Following Nkunda's arrest, he got in touch with Nkunda's former officers, including Makenga and those in the FPLC, allegedly with a view toward setting up a rebel alliance.[73] It is unlikely that he planned on taking power in Rwanda through a military invasion. It is more likely that he was trying to foment internal rifts with the ruling RPF that could provoke a coup.[74]

The Interests of the Rwandan State

Since 2002, when the Rwandan army officially withdrew from the eastern Congo, Rwandan involvement has been clandestine. This has complicated attempts to understand the motives behind it. It is not discussed in public, and because the Rwandan Patriotic Front is a cohesive, disciplined, and sometimes violent organization, most of those involved do not speak frankly, even in private.[75]

There are, nonetheless, several ways to assess Rwandan interests. The first is simple deduction—applying hypotheses to Rwandan behavior to see which fits the facts. In addition, there are testimonies from privileged sources. Many Congolese troops have worked with or for the Rwandan security services, as have foreign diplomats, and often have important insights into their mindset, although one has to take care to check the reliability of such sources. Finally, members of the Rwandan government sometimes do leak information, defect from the government, or speak frankly about their involvement in the Congo. I have drawn on interviews with a total of seventeen such sources for this section.

These sources support the argument that economic factors alone play less of a role than is often claimed. Instead, we need to see Rwandan attitudes as shaped by a complex of interests, steeped in a security-driven culture of control, and warped by pathologies in the way the RPF makes decisions.

SECURITY THREATS

People close to the Rwandan government often mention security as the overriding imperative, and the FDLR, centered around Hutu officers and militias who fled into the Congo after carrying out genocide in Rwanda, remains a symbol of that security threat. A Western ambassador in Kigali analyzed Rwandan support to the M23 as follows: "This is really about the FDLR. The Rwandan government just doesn't trust the Congolese government and sees security as paramount."[76] One Rwandan security official who did admit in retrospect to backing the CNDP said, "The RDF didn't care about Makenga or Nkunda or any of these guys. We supported the CNDP because of the FDLR."[77] One officer used the Swahili analogy: *"Ulinzi unafanya nje ya lupango"* (To defend a house, you have to stand outside) to stress their need for a buffer zone.[78] An American military official based in Kigali, confirming and condoning Rwandan backing of the M23, likened this to the "strategic depth" that drives Pakistani backing of the Taliban.[79] In January 2020, General Mugangu Mubarak, the RDF commander of Kigali and the eastern region, said in a speech to his troops, "If you want us to start in Mont-Kigali, Rebero, Jali [neighborhoods of Kigali], that would be like fighting in your own living room. Children and women could suffer. Pray that your army can carry out its duties over there [in the Congo]."[80]

However, the FDLR threat needs to be seen in its historical and political context to understand what these officials meant. While for Rwanda the FDLR was undoubtedly a reason for backing the CNDP between 2004 and 2009, the Rwandan rebels had been dramatically weakened by the time the M23 rebellion broke out in 2012. The last major incursion by the FDLR into Rwanda took place in 2001, although there have been many smaller incursions since then that resulted in civilian fatalities. Between 2009 and 2012, over 4,500 FDLR combatants were repatriated to Rwanda by the UN, which may have been over 70 percent of all their troops. By 2012, the FDLR may have had as few as 1,500 troops.

Nonetheless, given the central place the genocide still plays in Rwandan memory and politics, the FDLR remained a powerful symbolic threat. This is quite distinct, however, from a purely security issue. Much of the narrative underpinning the legitimacy of the RPF is tied up in the genocide and in the protection of the nation. The threat of the FDLR bolsters the notion that there is a greater good, a security imperative that justifies the repression of the opposition and restrictions on civil liberties, hallmarks of the RPF rule. Genocide ideology—and by proxy also the FDLR—forms the raison d'être of the RPF, bolstering its legitimacy as the force that ended the genocide; it continues to shield the population from genocide even as it tries to exorcise the ideology behind it from the population.[81] In some cases, genocide ideology has

become a pretext for the RPF to repress dissent;[82] in others, RPF officials are motivated by genuine concern. These twin impulses—the desire to preserve the RPF and the drive to extirpate genocide ideology—
have become deeply, perhaps inextricably, entangled.

The Congo expedition thus served to focus the RPF and its domestic
audience on an external enemy in the run-up to the 2010 elections, when
internal divisions threatened the survival of the party. According to a
senior ex-CNDP officer with many contacts inside the army, "The RDF
is a military organization. It needs to fight. Once it stops fighting outsiders, they will start fighting each other."[83]

This perception of security threats was amplified by the decision-
making process described above, what one ambassador in Kigali called "a
bunker mentality in the RPF. They believe they can't trust anyone in the
international community, that they are the victims of an international
conspiracy."[84] This attitude derives from the RPF's history of self-reliance
during the guerrilla struggle as well as the long history of victimization of
the Rwandan Tutsi community, memories of which were particularly
strong in the Ugandan refugee camps out of which the RPF's main leaders
emerged in the 1980s. As Phil Clark has argued:

> The RPF's desire for internal cohesion has made it suspicious of criti-
> cal voices within and outside of the party—a feature compounded
> by Rwanda's fraught experience of multiparty democracy in the early
> 1990s, which saw the rise of ethnically driven extremist parties and
> helped to create an environment conducive to genocide. The RPF's
> singular focus on rebuilding the nation and facilitating the return of
> refugees means it has often viewed dissent as an unaffordable
> distraction.[85]

Self-reliance and security threats fueled a propensity for control,
accentuating a tendency toward belligerency.[86] "The RPF does not
like to leave anything to chance," one foreign diplomat in Kigali said.
"There is a culture of control here that permeates every aspect of life,
especially security."[87] The impact this had on assessing security threats
in the eastern Congo can be judged through this quote from one of
Rwanda's top security officials: "What would the United States do if

Al Qaeda had a cell operating in Tijuana? It would send troops in and take no hostages."[88] An American security official had a similar analysis, referring to former vice president Dick Cheney's "one percent doctrine": "They think if there's a one percent chance that FDLR can attack them from the Congo, they have to treat it as a certainty in terms of our response."[89]

ECONOMIC INTERESTS

The economic interests of the Rwandan government are just as controversial and ambiguous as the military ones. The economic benefits that Rwanda has derived from its involvement in the Congo have changed over time, both in scale and in kind. During the AFDL and the initial phase of RCD (1996–1999) most profits were made through pillage. Between November 1998 and April 1999, the Rwandan army and its RCD allies removed between 2,000 and 3,000 tons of tin ore and up to 1,500 tons of coltan worth between $10 and $20 million, depending on the grade of the ore, from the warehouses of SOMINKI (Société minière et industrielle du Kivu), a state-run mining company active in the Kivus.[90] In another example of plundering, a Congolese commander of RCD troops, Jean-Pierre Ondekane, brazenly entered the Central Bank offices in Kisangani and seized between $1 million and $8 million in Congolese francs, which he then dispatched to Kigali.[91]

During the subsequent phase of RCD occupation, the Rwandan government and its RCD allies institutionalized extraction. Traders had to give a portion of their profits to the Rwandan ruling party in exchange for access to lucrative trade routes and mining sites.[92] Companies created by the Rwandan Patriotic Front, including some operated by the Ministry of Defence, were provided with preferential access to mining areas. This sector became particularly lucrative between June 2000 and July 2001, when the world market price for tantalum, a derivative of coltan, shot from $10 to $380 per kilogram. Some researchers estimate that net profits made by Rwandan companies from coltan alone could have been as high as $150 million during this period,[93] while other researchers estimate total profits from the minerals trade at $250 million per annum throughout the occupation.[94] While it is difficult to calculate a precise figure for this kind of clandestine activity, it is clear that for Rwanda, whose entire annual budget was $380 million around this time, such income made its expensive involvement in the Congo possible. President Kagame himself described his government's involvement in the Congo as "self-sustaining."[95]

Profiteering was confirmed by virtually all of my interviews with local Congolese businessmen in Goma and Bukavu. "The Rwandans made a lot of money off the business here because, ultimately, they were in control. The RCD wasn't well organized," said one.[96] Another said: "Individual RCD officials made money from the Kivus, but as an organization they were always struggling financially. It was Rwanda that benefited."[97] A former RCD vice governor of South Kivu lamented that they never had much money because business was controlled by Rwanda and that all their funds were used to pay for military operations.[98]

This state of affairs changed dramatically during the 2003–2006 transition. In most of the territory formerly controlled by the RCD, these erstwhile business networks were eroded and reoriented toward new patronage networks that were often linked to Kinshasa. In 2011, the owner of a transport company in South Kivu told me: "Rwanda has lost everything [in South Kivu]. Why would anyone pay money to Kigali to get business done here? The people who control things here are the FARDC and the local officials. Those are the people you have to pay off."[99] This decrease in influence by Rwanda and the former RCD went hand in hand with the dismantling of their military and political networks in Orientale, Katanga, Kasaï, and Maniema provinces.

A partial exception was the southern part of North Kivu, which, under the terms of the transitional government, remained under the control of ex-RCD officials. But even there, political power slowly shifted. During 2006, as the transition came to an end and Governor Eugène Serufuli threw his lot in with Kabila's government, new officials were appointed in customs, police, and other state agencies. One businessman in Goma put it this way: "Rwanda's main asset in Goma today is their border. They can influence smuggling, especially since taxes there are much lower than here. But they no longer control Goma's administration."[100] By 2012, according to interviews with local businessmen, members of the Rwandan government still had interests in various mineral-buying houses in Goma but no longer controlled the political or security apparatus.[101]

Nonetheless, the Rwandan government continued to benefit from the Congolese economy, albeit in a different way. During this period smuggling became one of the most lucrative illegal activities. Given its clandestine nature, it is difficult to know how high the profits were, but according to sources within the Rwandan mining community contacted in 2013, the Rwandan mineral sector grew dramatically from $70 million in exports in 2007 to around $226 million in 2011, becoming the country's largest earner of foreign exchange. While much of this growth was due to an increase in domestic production, two industry insiders said that in 2013 between 10 and 30 percent of their official tin and tantalum exports consisted of smuggled Congolese re-exports.[102] In 2010, Global Witness estimated that Congolese-sourced minerals might constitute 75 to 80 percent of Rwandan exports.[103] Several years later, the United Nations estimated that $400 million in gold was smuggled out of the eastern Congo each year—although the majority of that trade passes through Uganda and Burundi, not Rwanda.[104]

It is clear that the Rwandan economy continued to benefit from illegal trade with its neighbor. However, the extent to which this trade was linked to support of the CNDP and the M23 is not clear. While both armed groups smuggled minerals into Rwanda,[105] the dramatic growth in Rwanda's mineral exports appeared to be relatively unaffected by the fate of their rebel allies in the eastern Congo. Mineral exports rose steadily from around $60 million in 2007 to $167 million in 2016, and fluctuations in export figures during this time appear more closely linked to world prices than to Congolese rebellions.[106] In 2019, a gold refinery opened in Rwanda, reportedly a joint operation between the Rwandan government and the businessman Alain Goetz. Gold exports from Rwanda picked up dramatically—in the first nine months of 2020, Goetz's company Aldango exported $522 million of gold.[107] In previous years, the United Nations had reported that much of Rwanda's gold had been smuggled there from the Congo.[108] According to conversations with gold traders and foreign experts following this trade, Rwanda did not need to have its troops physically present in the eastern Congo— although some units were during this time—to benefit from the gold trade. Rather, it was able to leverage its lower taxes and arrangements with Congolese traders. In other words, it benefited not so much from conflict in the Congo but from disorder. It was that country's inability to properly regulate and tax its mining industry that became a boon for Rwanda.

At the same time, the Congo grew as an export market for Rwandan goods. According to the World Bank, Rwandan exports to the Congo increased from 13 percent of its total exports in 2008 to 31 percent in 2016.[109] A year later, 80 percent of Rwanda's exports to the surrounding region went to the Congo.[110]

Rwandan involvement in its neighbor's affairs also incurred serious economic costs. Following revelations of support to the M23, donors suspended $240 million in aid, contributing to a drop in GDP growth of around 3 percent compared with the previous year. Rwanda's brand, arguably its greatest asset, also took a beating. Given the deep involvement of the RPF in many sectors of the Rwandan economy—including real estate, mining, consumer products, and construction—it is clear that the party suffered financially as well.[111]

The tensions among these different economic incentives were highlighted in the early days of the M23 crisis. When the fighting first began in April 2012, President Kagame invited Rwandan business leaders to debate the merits of intervention. According to one participant, many of the business leaders advised against it, for they feared it could be detrimental to the economy. The businessman who attended lamented: "Unless Rwanda succeeds at legally annexing the eastern Congo— which is almost impossible—the economic activity privileged by these rebellions is all underground. Which means it is controlled by the security services, and it leads to aid cuts. That's good for a few members of the RPF, but bad for most of us businessmen."[112]

This discussion within the RPF represented a latent tension within the party. Its survival has relied on its ability both to provide substantial economic growth and reforms and to maintain cohesion in its top military staff. Intervention in the eastern Congo had allowed the RPF to provide economic opportunities to some of its members and had focused the military minds of its top brass on an external enemy but did not bring about large net economic gains.

WHAT ABOUT ETHNIC SOLIDARITY?

What about solidarity between Rwandan and Congolese Tutsi as a possible driver? Several diplomatic officials have suggested that ethnic solidarity played an important role in Rwandan decision-making, and many media reports highlighted the fact that the leaders of the M23 and of the RPF are Tutsi.[113] However, it is unclear what explanatory value their ethnicity has, if any.

Certainly, during the early days of the M23 rebellion, Rwandan officials spoke of the plight of Congolese Tutsi, citing numerous allegations of atrocities that human rights groups and the United Nations were unable to corroborate. And there is no doubt that some Rwandan officials felt that they have a historic right to the southern part of North Kivu province, which they believed belonged to the greater Rwandan kingdom—a view expressed in a meeting at the United Nations by Foreign Minister Louise Mushikiwabo in 2012.[114] This view was also expressed in the past by officials, including Prime Minister Pasteur Bizimungu in 1996.[115]

However, imperial nostalgia is not necessarily linked to ethnic solidarity. The relationship between the RPF and Congolese Tutsi is complicated. Congolese Tutsi are often proud of their distinctive heritage and of their independence from the Rwandan polity. In part, this is because of their history. Many Banyarwanda and Banyamulenge have been living outside of the borders of Rwanda since pre-colonial times, and in the case of the Banyamulenge, their presence in the eastern Congo may be due to the flight of their ancestors from wars in Rwanda. There are important distinctions between the customs, worldviews, and even dialects of these communities and those prevalent in Rwanda.

More generally, the wide expanses of the eastern Congo with its loose governance structures stand in stark contrast to densely populated and rigidly controlled Rwanda.

This narrative of ethnic solidarity is also contradicted by experiences of Congolese Tutsi officers who were members of the M23, the CNDP, and—at least for some of them—the Rwandan rebellion that brought the RPF to power in 1994. Many of them speak of subtle discrimination within the Rwandan army, of having been passed over for promotions and command positions because of their origin, and having been teased for being "Congolese peasants," as one officer put it.[116] These tensions came to a head after the end of the First Congo War when Rwanda decided to withdraw most of its troops from the Democratic Republic of the Congo. It ordered most Congolese Tutsi to leave with them, saying they belonged to the Rwandan army. Many Congolese Tutsi officers in both North and South Kivu refused, saying they were Congolese and had only fought for Rwanda to liberate their country.

In Goma, a mutiny broke out, led by a Lieutenant Murekezi, a Tutsi from Masisi who opposed leaving for Rwanda. Crucially, many future senior CNDP and M23 officers were among those who either participated in or sympathized with this mutiny, including Christian Pay-Pay, Faustin Muhindo, Baudouin Ngaruye, Claude Micho, and Wilson Nsengiyumva. The standoff ended when, at a military assembly in Goma in early November 1997, a commanding Rwandan officer shot Murekezi in the head, killing him. Several others were killed or injured, and the survivors were tied up and thrown on a truck. They were taken to Rwanda, where many were imprisoned on Iwawa Island before being redeployed— demoted and demoralized—back to the Democratic Republic of the Congo.[117] A similar mutiny took place just a few months later in South Kivu, led by Banyamulenge officers there.

One ex-CNDP officer lamented: "Don't believe for one second that Rwanda supported us because they were our friends, or that they sympathized with Congolese Tutsi. They supported us because they needed us. And when they no longer needed us, they turned on us."[118]

Much like natural resources, ethnicity became a permissive enabler of the conflict. There is no doubt that it is an easily recognizable organizing principle for all armed rebellions in the eastern Congo. The CNDP and the M23 are no different—of the ten Tutsi ex-CNDP or ex-M23 officers interviewed for this book, all argued that they felt compelled to take up arms to protect their community.

However, Tutsi identity is not homogeneous—there are significant internal tensions between Congolese Tutsi, Banyamulenge, and Rwandan Tutsi. There are also cross-cutting cleavages, like sub-ethnic groups (sometimes referred to as clans) that can be found in both the Congo and Rwanda, or past military service in the Rwandan army. Ethnicity was a relatively plastic, constantly contested factor in armed mobilization.

One can find just as many Congolese Tutsi who joined the national army or even armed groups opposing the Rwandan government, rather than the CNDP or M23. For those who did join those groups, there is little evidence to show that there was an uptick in ethnic prejudice prior to their joining and considerable evidence to show that they abused members of their own community. In addition, there is even some evidence that the M23 collaborated with former members of the FDLR, suggesting an opportunism in their use of ethnicity. For example, Bosco Ntaganda gave a certain Commander Mandevu, a Hutu former FDLR officer who led his own militia in the Virunga National Park, some weapons in mid-2012, when the latter emerged as a key M23 ally in controlling the wilderness behind Nyiragongo Volcano.

Conclusion

This chapter has depicted a sad marriage of interests: a Congolese government for whom conflict has become part of a mode of governance through a combination of apathy among political elites and direct complicity among military leaders and a Rwandan government whose interests were shaped by political culture that pushed it toward greater belligerency. Of course, in all of this, the interests of the Congolese population of the Kivus was not taken into account.

This kind of ethnography of state actors is not a perfect science. In the case of Rwanda, information about such an extremely centralized process was extremely difficult to obtain; in the Congolese case many were willing to talk but only had part of the picture. I don't presume to have provided the definitive summary of Congolese and Rwandan military decision-making—as Clifford Geertz reminds us about ethnography, it is "marked less by a perfection of consensus than by a refinement of debate. What gets better is the precision with which we vex each other."[119] It is only through repeated research that we can approximate the real dynamics that were in play.

The interests of another important group of decision-makers have not been discussed here: the donors, multinational corporations, and diplomats who, to a considerable degree, funded both governments during this period. It would be a critical fallacy to conclude that the main belligerents, just because they are the most visible actors, would be also the most powerful. Outside actors, despite their purported neutrality, were often enablers and silent participants in the conflict. I turn my attention to them in chapter 9.

5

The Theory

INVOLUTION, FRAGMENTATION, AND THE MILITARY BOURGEOISIE

"THIS WAR IS not what you think it is," Colonel Pierre Masudi told me.[1] It was June 2014, and we were sitting in Nganda la Quatrième, a bar made out of plywood and decorated with Christmas tinsel, a stone's throw from the Colonel Tshatshi Military Camp in Kinshasa. I had met Pierre, an officer in the Congolese army, for the first time five years earlier on the front lines of a military offensive in the eastern Congo. Now Pierre was in the capital Kinshasa, staying with family and making a daily trip to the État major général, the armed forces headquarters, to lobby his superiors to get a deployment back to the front lines.

The "war is not what it is" was a common refrain in our almost weekly meetings at La Quatrième (named, the owner told me, after the constitutional sequence in the Congo—there had been three constitutional regimes since independence; surely after this one we would realize that a bar was about as good a governance arrangement as Congolese could hope for). Pierre had grown up in a good family in Kinshasa; his father had been a senior civil servant under Mobutu Sese Seko, and Pierre had gone to private schools, with one memorable trip to Paris when he was eleven. They had a TV at home, and in the 1980s he had watched a lot of Hollywood war movies on VHS tape. "For me, the army was discipline, dying for your country, coming home to confetti parades. You know, honor and pride."

This was obviously not his current experience. He wanted to go back to the front lines not out of patriotism but because that was how you made money. "My monthly salary, when it comes, is 83,000 Congolese francs [90 USD]. My rent alone here in Kinshasa is 200 dollars. That's officialized corruption." This was a typical refrain from soldiers: keep us poor so you can buy our loyalty. "There is no way I can make a living without being on the front line—without stealing."

As detailed in chapter 3, the bulk of money officers received was through hazard pay and bonuses; skimming from salaries, food, logistics, and medical allowances of their troops; setting up local protection rackets; and extorting money from the local population and traders. Few of these perks were available if you were based in Kinshasa, or even worse, if you were *mis à la disposition de l'hierarchie militaire* ("dispo")—waiting for an active deployment.

The Congolese army was, essentially, a tax farming operation. Pierre told me: *Kila mtu anapata sehemu yake.* Everybody gets his or her cut. Indeed, "sehemu yake," Swahili for "his/her cut," had become slang for widespread kickback schemes, allegedly derived from President Kabila's own insistence on getting a percentage. "Those guys I'm seeing in Ngaliema," the leafy neighborhood where the army headquarters is located, "they calculate how much money I can earn in a particular place—you know, taxing, trading, and so on—and then give me my deployment, expecting a monthly kickback in return." As research has shown, this kind of tax farming principle holds for the Congolese police force as well.[2]

As described in chapter 4, this scheme produces an army that is structurally invested in the persistence of conflict, in which officers are often not given the resources necessary to defeat their enemies and instead are encouraged to extract resources from the local population, in which the hustle has become an art form.

It has also changed the worldview of the protagonists of the conflict. "I remember *The Guns of Navarone*, for example"—Pierre's father had had a penchant for World War II movies, I found out—"it was like a blood pact, you fight until the last man. Here, our bosses do not want the war to end. You don't fight to win. You fight to fight, that's it." When I asked him what would happen if he did not get his frontline deployment, he sucked his teeth and shook his head. "A life in the barracks! *Quelle cauchemar!*"

The Argument

As Colonel Pierre describes, Congolese state and society have undergone a structural transformation that has produced new classes of actors—both domestic and foreign—with new interests. These trends have served to lock the conflict into a pernicious, intractable equilibrium, a low-scale conflict stuck between war and peace. As we shall see in chapter 9, both foreign and domestic actors, ranging from belligerents to donors, have fed into these dynamics.

In this chapter, I provide a theoretical understanding of some of the main features of the Congolese conflict, building on scholars from a variety of disciplines and methodological approaches. I highlight four trends: fragmentation, the rise of the military bourgeoisie, the involution of interests, and the symbiosis of belligerents. Together, this analysis underscores the endogenous nature of conflict and how it is carried forward through its own momentum, transforming social structures, identities, and interests.

The first two trends are structural. First, fragmentation. Decades of conflict and peacemaking have transformed society, producing a startling proliferation of belligerents. This has rendered the conflict less threatening to the central government but also more intractable and devastating for the local population. At the same time—and this is the second trend—the war has produced a military bourgeoisie that controls large parts of the economy in the eastern Congo and has deep links with political elites across the country.

The other two developments, related to the political culture of the violence, have also contributed to this stasis. The conflict has become involuted, stuck in the same fundamental pattern as the protagonists of the conflict have become more invested and habituated in maintaining the status quo. It has also become symbiotic. The most perverse manifestation of this are cases in which members of the Congolese army have provided weapons or intelligence to their rivals on the battlefield, at times leading to the defeat of their own troops. This symbiosis does not require a grand conspiracy to work. In many instances, belligerents have a vested interest in furthering the conflict, thereby feeding the same system while remaining adversaries on the battlefield.

In sum, this analysis runs against the grain of the familiar notion about war—that it is fought between two sides seeking to defeat or compel the other.[3] That kind of theorizing, which conceptualizes violence as an instrument in the search of dominance, has a long lineage in modern political theory, running from Clausewitz through Toynbee to most game theoretical approaches of war. In contrast, I draw on theories of war and disorder that highlight their functions, suggesting that conflict can emerge as a logic of governance in response to a particular historical and political context. As authors such as David Keen, Patrick Chabal and Jean-Pascal Daloz, and William Reno have pointed out, that particular context was the end of the Cold War and the liberalization of political and economic systems, which put pressure on patronage networks and created incentives to invest in disorder.[4]

In other words, violence in the Congo and elsewhere on the continent is not the tragic aberration that some scholars have pointed to, a prisoners' dilemma that is the result of information asymmetries and commitment problems, arguing that both sides could have come to a mutually better solution without violence.[5] At times, fighting persists because both parties stand more to gain from fighting than peace.

There are, however, also contrasts between my theory and the functionalist arguments of scholars like Chabal and Daloz. The conditions they highlight obtain across much of Africa, whereas protracted violent conflict has been rare, which results in the false impression that violent armed conflict is inherent to African politics. I point to the particularities of the Congo, in particular its political and social fragmentation, the emergence of a military bourgeoisie, the acceptability of violence, and the discourse of autochthony. I also argue that conflict should not be seen as merely strategic and instrumental but above all as systemic, exceeding the intentions of any individual actors and forging habits and norms. War has become a social condition, an outcome that may not have been the intended objective of any of the protagonists but that has produced its own actors, cultures, and interests.

In a final section of this chapter I point to similar dynamics taking place across the African continent and make an argument for what could be driving these trends.

The Structural Impediments to Peace

There is a growing understanding that conflicts reshape society, highlighting their endogenous nature.[6] Sarah Daly, working on the Colombian conflict, highlights the role that previous episodes of armed mobilization played, arguing that armed groups are much more likely to emerge where there are "receptacles of collective action: the organizational legacies of war."[7] Specifically, she argues that material endowments and opportunities do not explain rebellion, but rather that areas with a past history of insurgency are six times more likely to experience a recurrence of armed mobilization due to the social networks and identities created by previous episodes of conflict. Similarly, Gina Bateson documents the changes wrought on Guatemalan society by civil war, arguing that violence during the civil war forged networks and perceptions that led to the creation of vigilante organizations after the war.[8]

I build on these insights of how structural changes in society can influence conflict, which then in turn changes society. Two such changes in particular have rendered conflict intractable: the emergence of a military elite with a vested interest in violence and the fragmentation of belligerents on all sides. In contrast with the above-mentioned theorists, I focus on social networks that are embedded both in the state and local communities, and I highlight not just their nature but also the number of belligerents involved.

The Rise of the Military Bourgeoisie

Armed rebellion is not the privilege of any particular social stratum. Whereas Marx and Engels proclaimed that the proletariat is the revolutionary class, some scholars have found that the agricultural export sector has been particularly prone to revolutionary movements,[9] while still others cite landowning "middle peasantry,"[10] ethnic age associations,[11] and networks of military officers.[12] There is no one particular class that has dominated armed mobilization in the Congo. I argue, however, that a military bourgeoisie—spanning the national security forces and armed groups—has taken on a critical role in the perpetuation of conflict.

This bourgeoisie emerged, albeit slowly, during the latter part of Mobutu's reign, when he created competing military branches that were more concerned with pitting potential rivals against each other, and in keeping the civilian population in check, than in protecting its citizens. This created a class of affluent commanders who used their control over men and women in uniform to extract resources from the population. Then, during the recent Congo wars, this class was dramatically inflated, probably doubling in size.

Those who joined the existing Mobutist military elite came from two social classes. Beginning with the major mobilizations of armed groups in 1993 during the democratization period, many armed groups in the eastern Congo had deep roots in rural communities, initially driven by local concerns of self-defense and competition over land and power. Then, with the AFDL rebellion that began in 1996, urban youths, mostly from the Kivu and Katanga provinces, began joining what would become one the largest rebellions in Congolese history.

The mobilization of rural, marginalized youths has continued until the time of writing. During the main period studied here—2003 to 2018—the leaders of most armed groups in the eastern Congo came from this class, in contrast with a previous generation of rebel leaders in the Congo and across Africa—prominent examples include Amilcar Cabral, Samora Machel, Meles Zenawi, and Yoweri Museveni—who came from an urban intellectual elite.[13]

TABLE 5.1. Estimate of military forces in Congo, 1993–2015 (approx.)

Year	Members of armed forces	Members of police/ gendarmerie	Members of armed groups	Total
1993	60,000	60,000	N/A	120,000
2003	250,000–260,000	107,000	20,000–25,000	377,000–392,000
2018	130,000	110,000	11,000–15,000	251,000–255,000

Sources: Meditz and Merill, *Zaire*; Multi-Country Demobilization and Reintegration Program, "MDRP Final Report," 24, 26; Wondo, *Les Armées au Congo-Kinshasa*; Ministère de la Défense Nationale et des Anciens Combattants, *Plan Global De Desarmement Demobilisation et Reintegration (DDRI II)*.

These recruits into the army and armed groups slowly became un-moored from the social structures out of which they emerged, consti-tuting a relatively independent social class, generating their own income and systems of value. When asked what their strongest identity was—ethnic, religious, geographic, or professional—almost all of the fifty-five army soldiers and officers we interviewed referred to themselves as sol-diers first and foremost, sometimes aggressively drawing a distinction with civilians.[14] Even for many armed groups this is the case, as chap-ters 6 and 8, on the CNDP and UPC, respectively, make clear. Both groups emerged ostensibly to defend their ethnic community—the Tutsi and the Hema, respectively—but eventually distanced themselves from these, in some cases abusing their own fellow co-ethnics.

Since the beginning of the war in 1996, close to half a million people have probably passed through the ranks of the national army, the po-lice, intelligence forces, or other armed groups,[15] producing a military bourgeoisie with expertise and a vested interest in violence. In addition to its importance as a class in itself, it has also transformed the econ-omy and society. The United Nations Group of Experts and other re-searchers have documented the involvement of both the national army and armed groups in the trade of minerals, the farming and trade of cannabis, the production of charcoal, cross-border smuggling, and poaching.[16] This military bourgeoisie is not large. Of the estimated 255,000 men and women in the security services and armed groups in 2018, there were probably only several thousand who have amassed significant wealth. However, the exploitative system over which this elite presides includes hundreds of thousands of soldiers, intelligence agents, police, businesspeople, and politicians, all of whom have a stake in this structure.

I should clarify that I apply the term *military* to members of armed groups as well, as there has been a high degree of cycling in and out between armed groups and the national army and police. The use of the term *bourgeoisie* also requires an explanation. It is substantially different from the bankers, factory owners, and traders that Marx described. These are not industrial or financial capitalists but rather military capitalists. They use violence in order to extract value, both from the state as well as from the population. While this group has little self-consciousness or internal solidarity, it can nonetheless be perceived as a class, understood as a category people with similar economic motivations and opportunities.[17]

This military elite is similar to the concept of "state bourgeoisie" that has frequently been used to describe the bureaucrats and politicians who populated the echelons of government and who made up much of the middle and upper classes in the first decades of post-independence Africa.[18] Clémence Pinaud has documented a similar phenomenon in South Sudan, arguing that the civil war had produced a "military aristocracy" through the accumulation of resources during the fighting, ranging from taxing relief aid to cattle trade to the capture of oil rents once the main Sudan People's Liberation Army (SPLA) rebellion shared state power through the 2005 Comprehensive Peace Agreement.[19] I prefer the term *bourgeoisie,* as it places more of an emphasis on the processes of extraction and accumulation and less on the status and hereditary nature of aristocracy.

The nature and role of these military elites vary across the continent. The military leadership of the Sudan People's Liberation Movement (SPLM) in South Sudan has become the dominant force within the government and economy, centralizing rents and—until oil revenues came to an abrupt halt in 2012—spending a considerable amount to keep the various military and militia forces loyal. This logic was only reinforced during the subsequent civil war that engulfed South Sudan, as government revenues plummeted but the threat of rebellions increased.

In contrast, the Congolese military elite seems strikingly uninterested in consolidating control of the state and—in contrast with Rwanda, Uganda, and Angola, for example—it is not at present deeply involved in politics. There are very few military officers or armed group commanders who have obtained senior positions in government or in state-run companies. Similarly, this military elite has not sought to control the private sector, as for example the Nigerian military attempted to do in the 1970s or as officers in Egypt, Rwanda, or Myanmar do through nationalized industries.[20] Instead, it has largely extracted resources through illegal taxation—extortion—as well as smuggling, protection rackets, and embezzlement.

This inchoate class has carved out a space within Congolese society that is relatively free of accountability. There has never been a parliamentary audit of the military, nor by the army auditor (Inspection de l'armée). Procurement for the army is opaque and not subject to any of the official public procedures. While there have been an increasing number of prosecutions of military abuses, few senior officers are punished, and crimes are rampant. According to the United Nations, the number of convictions of members of the army and police as a percentage of the number of violations they committed ranged between 4 percent and 6 percent in the 2017–2019 period.[21] The proportion of convictions for armed groups is even lower.

What has the impact of this military bourgeoisie been on conflict? It has reshaped local societies, militarizing the economy and linking customary chiefs and businesspeople to armed groups. One can see the importance of this military bourgeoisie in the geography of cities and rural areas in eastern Congo. The military and armed groups are omnipresent—as mentioned above, researchers have documented 798 roadblocks in the Kivus, most of which are manned by armed actors. Over half of the 1,615 mining sites the NGO visited were also militarized.[22]

In urban areas, the military presence is less intrusive—the most frequent harassment is from traffic police—but a visit to Goma, the largest commercial hub in the region, reveals a large presence of military actors in business. A senior UN logistics officer told me that they had a hard time renting trucks and houses, as many of them belonged to actors that were linked to armed groups.[23] Walking through town, well-informed friends would point out large houses, hotels, and construction sites belonging to FARDC officers. In rural areas outside of Goma, I found military officers and armed groups leaders heavily invested in purchasing dredges for gold mining in rivers as well as *concasseurs*, rock crushers for use in mining pits. In Masisi territory, home to large cattle ranches, many landowners had links to armed groups or the army, while in the area around Beni and Butembo, many military officers were involved in smuggling across the Ugandan border.

Perhaps most importantly, this new class of armed men—and, to a much smaller extent, armed women—has changed the social and moral worlds of people living in the Kivus and Ituri. According to polling conducted by the Harvard Humanitarian Initiative, 57 percent of people in those regions thought they were going to die of the conflicts at some point between 2002 and 2014, 19 percent had experienced a physical assault due to the conflict, and 32 percent had a member of their household killed.[24] A primary school teacher in central Masisi told me, "AK-47s are as much part of the drawings that children make as toys or cooking pots."

All of this suggests that the persistence of conflict in the Congo is partly baked into the structure of society. The conflict has reached a critical momentum, reproducing itself without requiring additional fuel from other conflicts. In this, it resembles Christian Geffray's description of Mozambican National Resistance (Renamo): "Its bellicose machinery is not at the disposition of a state or of interests that go beyond it or its command. It is not the armed branch of a nation, nor does it serve a particular class. Renamo is a social body: an institution without another goal other than its own reproduction."[25]

The emergence of this small but influential military bourgeoisie has created a significant obstacle for the resolution of the conflict. Either this elite must be reduced in size, or its interests must be reoriented in order to regain stability.

Fragmentation

The second structural trend that has contributed to the persistence of conflict is the fragmentation of the Congolese state and society. In chapter 3, I described this proliferation of political parties, patronage

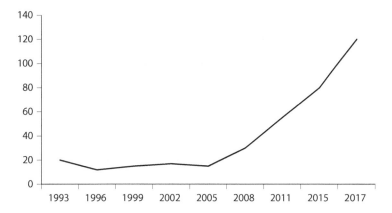

FIGURE 5.1. The proliferation of armed groups in eastern Congo, 1993–2014 (Records in possession of the author; Kivu Security Tracker, https://kivusecurity.org/)

networks, civil society actors, and poles of power. Pluralism, in its be-nevolent and nefarious manifestations, is one of the dominant charac-teristics of the Congolese state and society.

This extends to the conflict as well. During the recent history of the Congo, armed groups have proliferated dramatically (figure 3.2). This fragmentation manifests itself both in the number of belligerents as well as the number of factions and networks within their ranks. As the conflict studies literature suggests, this kind of fragmentation can prolong the conflict by complicating the negotiation process as the number of actors who can block a deal increases.[26] Parallel chains of command in the security services and within the government make it hard for armed groups to trust their interlocutors and for the government to focus on stabilizing the conflict. Analysis of all of the armed groups examined here shows how this fragmentation of the state can undermine negotiations as disparate actors get involved, compete with each other for the patron-age that deals can provide, and complicate both military operations and peace talks by providing conflicting information about the interests, size, and threat of the armed group.

For example, the FARDC's offensives against the CNDP and the M23 were repeatedly hampered by parallel chains of command. Army com-manders mistrusted each other and gave contradictory orders, as each sought to reap the greatest personal benefit from the conflict. The lack of a coherent command structure hampered negotiations, for the rebels had no clear idea with whom they were talking and little faith in the promises of the government.

However, the main challenge fragmentation has posed in the Congo has not been in negotiations—rather, it has reduced the threat of armed violence to the central government. Since 2006, the government has invested relatively little genuine effort, outside of the CNDP and the M23, in negotiating with armed groups. Ten groups of three hundred combatants fighting among each other is much less of a challenge—and more of a headache to organize negotiations—to the government than a single group of three thousand. This, along with the peripheral nature of the conflict, has reduced the government's incentive to bring an end of the fighting. At the same time, the fragmentation has rendered the conflict more brutal to local communities as front lines and the violence associated with them multiply.

There are several reasons for this fragmentation. As the conflict has simmered on, local politicians and businesspeople have leveraged armed groups to promote their own interests, which some researchers have called "the democratization of militarized politics."[27] These elites have used armed groups to intervene in conflicts over land and local power, to intimidate opponents and bolster their standing ahead of elections, and to further their hold over economic rackets. This centrifugal dynamic has led to the splintering of groups. With little impetus from the national government to negotiate an end to conflict, armed groups that lack internal cohesion end up breaking up, furthering this dynamic.

But fragmentation itself has also been a tactic, used by both armed groups and the government to prevent challenges to their control. During negotiations with the Mai-Mai of General Padiri Bulenda in 2002, for example, the government and the UN peacekeeping mission had to contend with at least four different representatives each claiming to speak in the group's name. "Padiri sent us one emissary, who was co-opted by the government and lost clout, that was Anselme Enerunga. Then the next one met the same fate. At the same time, at the local level, we were dealing with around three other representatives," a UN official remembered.[28] When Padiri's group integrated into the government, several factions broke away and formed their own insurgencies.

A similar tactic prevailed in the run-up to the Goma Peace Conference of January 2008, which aimed to bring an end to the CNDP rebellion. According to one senior Congolese intelligence officer, "The government's logic during the Goma Conference was to create new groups in order to dilute the CNDP's power."[29] Examples of these kinds of groups—either created wholesale by the government, or through local initiatives that were endorsed by national officials—included the Mai-Mai Shikito, the Mai-Mai Mahoro, Mudundu 40, the Mai-Mai Ruwenzori, and the Union des jeunes patriotes sacrifiés (UJPS).

How Interests Matter: Involution and Symbiosis

The structural transformation of Congolese society is only part of the explanation for the persistence of violence. To fully understand how conflict becomes entrenched, we must grapple with belligerents' interests.

Between 2001 and 2005, I spent many weeks in the guest house of a church in Burhinyi, a small village lodged in the rocky hills of South Kivu province. The church was run by a group of hardy Polish nuns who had forged a small haven on the front lines of conflict. They had large gardens full of vegetables and fruit; a small herd of goats, cows, and chicken; several small fish farms; and a dispensary with essential medicine. For several years, they were stuck in a midst of a deadly confrontation between local militia, the Congolese army, and the Rwandan FDLR rebels.

One evening, the nuns—*basoeurs*, as the locals called them—organized an informal meeting of the various rival local commanders. All sides attended, albeit somewhat reluctantly, represented by relatively junior commanders. I attended, notebook in hand. As the tense evening progressed, encouraged by their lukewarm beers and a growing familiarity with each other, the commanders began to air similar grievances, albeit in diplomatic terms: they were hungry; their soldiers didn't obey them; their commanders didn't care; they felt responsible for the locals but also angry that they were seen as abusive and mean-spirited. At one point, the FDLR commander said: *"Basi, nani anafaidika hapa?"* (Who benefits from this?).

Not us, was the answer around the table. Low-level commanders, peasants, and most other members of society may squeeze some profits out at the margins, but they are largely confined to hustling for survival. As Stephen Jackson, an anthropologist who has served in senior UN positions in the Congo, argues: "As war—which itself stagnated and turned violently inward—constrains the space for agency more and more, so desperate inventiveness also turns in on itself. All forms of capital, material or cultural/symbolic, are pressed into the service of elite profit or peasant survival."[30]

Jackson is drawing here on the concept of *involution*, most famously developed by Clifford Geertz, who used it to describe how village society in Indonesia responded to population growth, Dutch colonization, and the introduction of sugar as an export crop. Geertz argued that the social and economic structures of rice production did not fundamentally change but merely adapted to these temporary pressures. As a result, the paddies were cultivated more intensively, increasing output per area but not per head. It was a cultural practice, he wrote, that "having reached its definitive form, continued to develop by becoming internally more complicated. . . . it maintained the overall outlines of that pattern while driving the elements of which it was composed to ever-higher degrees of ornate elaboration and Gothic intricacy."[31]

A similar logic has obtained in the Congolese conflict. Over time, the main stakeholders' approach to the conflict turned inwards, becoming invested in their own reproduction, and then became stuck, seeing conflict as an end in itself. There is, however, no grand conspiracy but rather a multitude of actors stuck in a negative equilibrium. Army officers see the conflict as a way of maintaining inflated budgets, embezzling funds, and obtaining opportunities for racketeering at the local level. The national government treats the conflict as a means of coup-proofing by keeping senior commanders content, while the bulk of their troops are deployed far from the capital.

Much like the Javanese rice farmers, the belligerents in the Kivus are not in a position to question the system in which they operate. "If I stick my head out, they will chop it off," said one FARDC battalion commander whom I had known for years. He had been complaining to me about the embezzlement of funds and the lack of resources for operations. I asked him why he didn't do anything about it. He said: "Listen, we are all part of this system, and we have been for a long time. Our salary is almost nothing; our families are not provided for. But we are bosses—that's our power. So we take a little here, a little there. It's not theft; we deserve it. And everyone is doing it, so me protesting against it will not matter." He was visibly upset by my question. The subtext, I guessed from the way he looked away to the hills in the distance when he spoke, was that he felt judged by someone who was privileged not to have to make these kinds of compromises. He continued:

> Look, I am not proud of this. Two kilometers in that direction there is a Mai-Mai position. But I can't go and arrest them because we are low in ammunition, probably because my soldiers sold some to those same Mai-Mai. And even if we arrest them, there will be ten more Mai-Mai to replace them tomorrow. *Njala, ndugu yangu. Njala. Tuko riche lakini tunakufa njala.* [Hunger, my brother. Hunger. We are rich, but we are dying of hunger.][32]

He had a point. Seen from the perspective of any one commander, attempts at reform seemed futile at best, suicidal at worst. This was the case even among elites ostensibly in charge of security, although it was challenging to conduct research about such a sensitive topic. The picture that emerged from my interviews was a decision-making process from which civilians were largely excluded, including parliament and most officials at the Ministry of Defence. Power over deployments, promotions, and funding was largely concentrated among the top military brass, who themselves were internally divided and worried more about maintaining their patronage networks than producing results in the field.

The result has been a curious symbiosis of armed actors, where belligerents on all sides of the battlefield have an interest in continuing the conflict. Many armed groups, even those fighting against the national army, retain close ties with army officers, who are intent on bolstering their own power base and on benefiting from protection rackets.

My argument here has two parts. First, the conflict has been prolonged by the material interests of the various armed groups and the governments involved. Second, the conflict has been prolonged by the perceptions and worldviews of the belligerents, who have come to see violence as acceptable or desirable. The conflict is thus doubly involuted, both in terms of its logic and with regard to its actors.

THE MATERIAL DETERMINANTS OF INVOLUTION

The material side of the equation is perhaps the easiest to document. Simply put, conflicts tend to persist if their protagonists, on balance, benefit more from their continuation than their termination. Unfortunately, for many entrepreneurs of violence and their backers in the eastern Congo, the end of violence would imply an end to the way they have made a living over the past decades. For the political elites and military commanders in Kinshasa, bringing an end to conflict would above all require cracking down on entrenched patronage networks in the security services, which would constitute a dangerous realignment of interests.

These material interests can take different shapes. Countries can develop private industries that are invested in large military deployments—Eisenhower's notorious military industrial complex—although this does not necessarily need to mean an investment in conflict: Germany and Japan, who are constitutionally limited in their deployment of forces, have two of the largest military budgets in the world but few active deployments outside of their countries.

Perhaps the best-known examples of conflict actors whose interests are tied to violence lies in the domain of natural resources. Examples of both government and rebel forces extracting significant revenues can be found in the Niger Delta, the eastern Congo, and the forest regions of Liberia and Sierra Leone. These material interests can lead belligerents to use violence in a bid to maintain control over these rents. In Sudan, for example, Alex de Waal argues that rebellions have become means of rent-seeking: "A commander or a provincial leader can lay claim to a stake of state resources (rents) through a mutiny or rebellion. The government then attacks the leader and his constituency to press him to accept a lower price. After a number of people have been killed, raped, and displaced, and their property looted or destroyed, as an exercise in ascertaining the relative bargaining strengths of the two parties, a deal will be reached."[33]

Belligerents' objectives cannot always be measured in clear financial terms. For many, armed violence is a means of maintaining power and influence and can become intrinsically linked to the continuation of fighting. This use of violence as a form of bargaining—and not to gain territory or overthrow a regime—is not new, nor is it always over natural resources. In the Ottoman Empire, armed dissidence was often used by elements on the periphery to negotiate with rulers at the center.[34] And, as I describe above in the case of both Rwanda and the Congo—for very different reasons—it is not just rebellions but also states that can develop a vested interest in maintaining conflict. Other examples would be the military in Myanmar deliberately instigating violence during the democratic transition to keep a hold on rents from the jade trade or the Mexican ruling party allowing drug cartels and criminality to gain in influence during the democratic transition in states ruled by the opposition.[35]

There is, however, no automatic link between the extraction of resources and the use of armed violence. In all of these cases, belligerents' interests are shaped by social institutions, norms, and historical contingencies.[36] I now turn to these.

THE IDEATIONAL CONTOURS OF INVOLUTION

Interests are not shaped by material factors only. Even core concepts of realpolitik such as violence, gain, and loss are highly subjective and evolve over time. While belligerents have strategic and material interests, they are filtered through ideational lenses: norms, ideas, habits, and identities.[37]

As I argue in chapter 4, the involution of Congolese institutions dates back to the Mobutu period. But aside from those historical roots, what are the ideational forces shaping this involution? Drawing on ethnographic observations, I propose two mechanisms that result in belligerents becoming invested in the conflict, prolonging the violence. The first, normalization, works to prolong the conflict by engendering apathy and resignation. The second, essentialization, pushes in almost the exact opposite direction, by making belligerents feel that the conflict is tightly linked to their core identity. This peculiar blend of both processes made the conflict especially stubborn.

Normalization is the process through which ideas and behaviors that initially fall outside of what is deemed acceptable come to be regarded as normal, while the historical context in which they arose is effaced.

Evidence for this can be seen in how a high proportion of Congolese combatants understood the meaning of violence. In the previous chapter, I described interviews I conducted with forty-three lower-ranking members of the Congolese security services, in which it was clear that they themselves thought that violence had become part of the everyday. In contrast with depictions of violence in popular films, however, most soldiers argued that the rampant violence they observed and participated in was not desirable, but rather that it was either necessary or the unintended side effect of war.[38] For example, one soldier reported this attitude when he began as a RCD combatant in 1999: civilians often protected combatants who come from their community, and "you have to scare them, to control them [*inabidi kubaogopesha, kubamaitriser*]" in order to get them to give you information about these militias.[39] For him, violence against civilians had initially been entirely instrumental, a necessary evil required by the kinds of brutal counterinsurgency they were fighting. Or, much like Dara Cohen describes armed group socialization in wartime Sierra Leone, another combatant described how soldiers needed to be "made like iron [*bakuwe chuma*]" by making them commit acts of violence.[40]

Over time, however, this end/means rationale began to shift. Expressions such as "What some of us do today would never have been acceptable twenty years ago" in the interviews were common. One Mai-Mai combatant told me: "Killing changes you. I have seen it in my own behavior. The first time it happens, it makes you crazy [*unapata wazimu*].

But then you get used to it. You have to, otherwise you really would go crazy."[41] Many other interviews confirmed this. Another combatant said: "You wouldn't understand, you are a civilian. We fight; that is what we do. Would you ask a fisherman if he thinks twice about cutting the head off a fish?"[42] A different combatant told me: "You learn how not to think too much about hurting other people. That's part of the job."[43]

This process of normalization also took hold, albeit in a much more distanced fashion, among the political elites in Kinshasa as well. As described in chapter 3, politicians there were rarely sanctioned for failing to take action, whereas they had a vested interest in allowing army officials to continue racketeering. This made it convenient to see conflict in the eastern Congo as inscrutable and tragic but also normal. In part this apathy was due to a lack of democratic accountability, but the absence of urgency in popular discourse also contributed. Some of my interviews pointed to this. In 2013, a government minister told me: "This conflict in the East has been going on for decades. We are trying to solve it, but you also have to know that fighting is a way of life for people in the Kivus."

Portrayals of the conflict in popular media have also fed into this normalization of violence. An analysis of fifty articles written in two Kinshasa newspapers—Le Potentiel and La Prospérité—during the first part of the postconflict escalation between 2003 and 2013 shows that the conflict was largely framed as a Rwandan invasion, as a battle over minerals by multinational companies, or as a quagmire of dozens of armed groups fighting for no clear reason. This framing placed an emphasis on the actions of rebels, usually without explaining the complex histories behind their motivations, instead of highlighting the inaction of the government. Articles were relatively infrequent—for example, in 2010 the popular daily Le Potentiel wrote an article on violence in the East roughly once a week, and only rarely on the front page.[44]

Some of this framing had to do with economic constraints. Like most newspapers in Kinshasa, Le Potentiel relied on irregular stringers based in Bukavu and Goma who were paid less than $50 for an article and had no allowance for research expenses.[45]

The flip side of this mechanism was *essentialization*. Instead of operating by rendering violence normal and almost invisible, it makes it fundamental, highlighting its importance. While normalization suggests that violence is "the way things are done" someplace else—in the Kivus, in the Middle East—essentialization operates by tying violence to a core part of the belligerent's identity, rendering it an exercise in the expression and affirmation of its legitimacy. This argument has also been made with regard to the War on Terror, which was closely linked to a hegemonic discourse about American identity and values. Terrorists were framed as driven by hatred of the "American way of life," characterized by freedom, democracy, and secularism.[46] The campaigns fought in Iraq, Afghanistan, Somalia, Chad, Syria, and elsewhere were framed in a rhetoric of American exceptionalism, which claimed a providential role for American power in the world. To deviate from this frame meant to implicitly challenge these tropes, which are deeply anchored in the cultural grammar of US foreign policy.

The Rwandan government is a good example of this process, as I detail in chapter 4. Intervention in the Congo became an exercise in upholding its legitimacy as the protector of the nation—and in particular of the Tutsi people—against the forces of genocide and divisionism. The conflict there was framed in these existential terms, justifying authoritarian measures domestically and military aggression in its neighbor. This narrative also draws on notions of Rwandan greatness, often linked with its history of military expansion into the eastern Congo in the nineteenth century.

Similarly, for many Congolese combatants, violence was justified in essentialist terms. As I detail in chapters 6 to 8, almost every armed group in the eastern Congo articulates its raison d'être in terms of identity. In particular, the immigration of hundreds of thousands of Hutu and Tutsi to the Kivus during the pre-colonial and colonial periods, together with the manipulation of ethnicity by the central and provincial governments, were deeply influential in the initial phases of the AFDL and RCD wars. A discourse of autochthony—the binary division of society into indigenous and foreign—furthered a bellicose worldview that facilitated armed mobilization.

The importance of national myths and narratives in fostering military policy has been highlighted by other scholars. Examining the civil war in Sri Lanka, Bruce Kapferer argues that Sinhalese narratives of the state, drawing on Buddhist mythologies, required a hierarchical ordering of society that Tamil nationalism threatened.[47] Violence became necessary and justified to reaffirm core notions of identity. In a similar fashion, Zulaika argues that Basque separatist violence drew on narratives of manhood, exclusion, and victimization that had been cultivated in northern Spain and furthered by local priests, Franquist repression, and the collapse of agricultural society.[48] Even after Spain's democratic transition, this ritualistic use of violence persisted, as it was tied to an expression of identity.

International media often dealt in this kind of essentialization by placing the emphasis on ethnic conflict—Nkunda's ethnicity, for example, was often mentioned in articles, implying an inherent connection between it and the insurrection—and on minerals.[49] While the media often spoke of violence, by attributing it to abstractions such as ethnic conflict or the international mineral trade, responsibility was difficult to locate. Little mention was made of foreign complicity in the decline of the Congolese state, nor in the propping up of the current Congolese and Rwandan states through donor aid and private investments.

This was the systemic nature of violence that prevailed during this period in the Congo. Violence was at once brutal, even grotesque, and also invisible and normal. It was banal and quotidian—especially for decision-makers in the remote capital—but also deeply embedded in the core identities of the main belligerents fighting in the bush.

The notion that violence is shaped by belligerents' worldview and is steeped in local tradition and culture is not new in the study of African conflicts. Stephen Ellis's work on Liberia and Paul Richards's ethnography of combatants in Sierra Leone are examples of this, and there are numerous examples of scholars who study the Congo.[50]

However, the emphasis in this book is different. The main impetus for mobilization in the eastern Congo did not come from rank-and-file combatants but rather from political and military elites in Kinshasa and the eastern Congo who drove mobilization. As one PARECO commander told me, when I asked him whether he would be able to get enough recruits to face down the CNDP: "*Bale ni manpower tu, ni ba-kurutu* [They are just manpower, simple recruits]."[51] The main challenge for his group was not mobilizing enough recruits—he pointed to an abundance of unemployed, disgruntled young men in his community—but keeping his officers together, getting access to funding and weapons, and courting political elites. Appeals to ethnicity helped with this.

For the CNDP, ethnicity was so important that it was built into its name: Congrès national pour la défense du people (National Congress for the Defense of the People). Leaders drew on enduring fears of discrimination within the rwandophone (Hutu and Tutsi) community of North Kivu. In 1998, hundreds of Congolese Tutsi officers had been killed in army camps around the country. Many ex-RCD officers justifiably feared for their lives, and most of their families had fled to neighboring countries. But here, as well, the use of ethnicity was often contradicted by lived reality of combatants. Indeed, that the CNDP abused Tutsi and forcefully recruited Tutsi youth contradicted their image as a protector of the community.[52]

In general, as chapters 6 to 8 bear out, even when recruits joined voluntarily, over time their networks became progressively decoupled from the local dynamics out of which they were born. Commanders obtained sources of financing of their own, developed contacts among political and business elites, and moved away from their areas of origin, in some cases even joining the Congolese army.[53] "The relationship has been turned on its head," one local chief in Shabunda said. "We used to control the youths. Now they control us. All we can do is obey what they ask us to do for them."[54]

Polling data bears this out. In one survey in 2016, 64 percent of respondents in North and South Kivu agreed to this premise: "Armed groups always end up abusing the population and should never be supported." Only 8 percent in North Kivu and 13 percent in South Kivu took this position: "Sometimes it is necessary to create an armed group to protect the local population."[55] In addition, there is almost no record of any of the armed groups pushing hard for the rights of their communities during negotiations with the government. For those who did strike deals with the government, such as PARECO in 2009, rewards for local elites were crucial in brokering the terms, which consisted almost solely of ranks and positions in the national army.

Does the Theory Travel? Application to Other African Conflicts

To what degree can this approach be generalized? There are ways in which these features—the emergence of a military bourgeoisie, fragmentation, and the involution of interests—of the Congolese conflict are mirrored across the African continent.

In his well-known typology of African conflicts, Christopher Clapham presents four categories of rebellion: liberation insurgencies, prominently featured in battles for independence; separatist insurgencies, such as those in Eritrea and Cabinda; reform insurgencies, such as Yoweri Museveni's National Resistance Army in Uganda, which aimed at capturing the state in order to transform it; and warlord insurgencies, such as those that made headlines during the civil wars of Sierra Leone and Liberia.[56] More recently, scholars have added to this list a new kind of internationalized Islamist insurgency that has emerged during the War on Terror, epitomized by Al-Shabaab in Somalia and Boko Haram in Nigeria.[57]

Most armed groups on the continent, however, defy these categories.[58] There are few rebellions today that aim to capture state power or to secede, which constitute the objectives of Clapham's first three categories. Most of the insurgencies that aimed to topple the government have petered out—the Democratic Forces for the Liberation of Rwanda (FDLR) have not mounted a serious attack on Rwanda since 2001, and the various Burundian rebel groups based in the eastern Congo have splintered to the point of near extinction. The complex insurgencies in Somalia, which feature a host of different belligerents, largely coalescing around clan identities or Al-Shabaab, resemble violent bargaining much more than attempts to overthrow the federal government of Somalia.[59]

The recent exception to this has been the conflict in South Sudan, but by 2020 it appeared that the conflict that erupted in 2013 as result of a power struggle between President Salva Kiir and Vice President Riek Machar has settled into a state in which violence is also largely deployed as a means of bargaining at the center and extracting resources at the periphery.

A similar situation prevails with separatist insurgencies, although there are exceptions here as well. Groups like the Front for the Liberation of the Enclave of Cabinda (FLEC) and the Movement of Democratic Forces of Casamance (MFDC) are inactive, and political changes in Sudan since 2018 and 2019 have ushered in the prospect of demobilizing long-standing insurgencies there. Even the Tuareg insurgency in Mali, which began with separatist ambitions in the 1990s, has been transformed, engaging in racketeering and bargaining with the central government. As Morten Bøås and Liv Elin Torheim have argued, "The heart of the matter was who should be the main focal point for the connection between the Malian state and the northern periphery and who should thereby also control the flow of state resources from Bamako."[60]

Meanwhile, most of the insurgencies on the continent are "repeat civil wars."[61] Almost every single civil conflict on the continent takes place on top of the ruins—and, more importantly, on top of social networks, worldviews, and grievances—of previous episodes of violence. As in the Congolese case, this has created entire social classes and networks invested in conflict, and armed mobilization has become an available and acceptable means of conducting politics. As one can see in the case of the Central African Republic and Chad, armed conflict has become a *métier*, an occupation, as Marielle Debos calls it.[62]

Many of the armed groups in the Democratic Republic of the Congo, the Central African Republic, Nigeria, South Sudan, Sudan, and much of the Sahel do not aim at overthrowing the government or seceding. Rather, violence has become an end in itself, a language of bargaining, a lifestyle, and a form of governance. In addition, and despite the battlefield rivalries, these incidents reveal an increasing symbiosis between the government and its armed opponents. In all of these cases, rebellion involves insurgents at the periphery interacting with political elites at the center of the state apparatus in a form of violent equilibrium. The description here of armed violence in the Congo is therefore not an anomaly on the continent. It is no surprise, as William Reno and Christopher Day argue, that counterinsurgency in many African states often looks more like patronage, aiming at co-opting regime strategies for exercising authority outside of warfare.[63]

This does not imply a grand conspiracy to perpetuate conflict. It is more likely, as in the Congo, that the wars have reshaped societies, promoting actors with a vested interest in the conflict economy and whose goal is no longer to seize power but to carve out fiefdoms on the margins of the state. A confirmation of this can be seen in the dramatic growth in the number of conflicts in Africa between non-state actors; these now outnumber those between the state and insurgencies.[64] By 2019, there were twenty-four state-based conflicts and forty-two conflicts between non-state actors.

This trend is compounded by a combination of apathy, opportunism, and pragmatism that has resulted in a government approach that shies away from cracking down on patronage networks or reforming the structure of the state and economy. Imposing stability and dismantling insurgents are perceived by key decision-makers as too risky or not important enough. Violence thus becomes a means of governing as much as a means of protest or obtaining power.

These ambiguities can be found throughout the conflicts in contemporary Africa. In Chad, outright aggression can alternate with camaraderie. As Debos has written, "Soldiers and rebels feel that they are divided by circumstances and divergent tactical choices rather than by irreconcilable identities or political stances."[65] Henrik Vigh explores a similarly broad spectrum in relationships in the conflict in Guinea-Bissau, oscillating between friendship and enmity.[66] Here, as in the close relations between opposition parties and the regime, is evidence for what Achille Mbembe called the "intimacy of tyranny" in postcolonial Africa, demonstrating that "the postcolonial mode of domination is a regime that involves not just control but conviviality."[67]

Political and Economic Liberalization and Conflict

What has caused this new trend in African conflicts that produces violent bargains and involuted conflicts? While further qualitative and quantitative research is required, some trends stick out. The wave of democracy sweeping across the continent after the end of the Cold War, along with the liberalization of African economies, have produced hybrid political systems that have been able to accommodate low-level insurgencies. At the same time, economies were liberalized, making it easier for armed groups and criminal gangs to capture rents, and while average incomes grew, so did the number of poor people. Sub-Saharan Africa is now home to over half the people in extreme poverty, with the extreme poor increasing from 276 million in 1990 to 413 million in 2015.[68]

The introduction of multiparty democracy across most of Africa in the 1990s drew would-be insurgents away from the battlefield and into electoral contention.[69] Meanwhile, the support for armed rebellion that had flowed during the Cold War—from apartheid South Africa, the United States, Cuba, and the Soviet Union—dried up, while large amounts of resources became available for political parties and elections. Norms changed as well. In its Constitutive Act of 2002, the African Union included an obligation to reject the unconstitutional change of government.

There are several mechanisms that connect democratization with these kinds of conflicts. Political elites can resort to backing armed groups in order to bolster their status, to intimidate rivals, or to extract resources. The Congo has been a showcase for this, as have militias in the Niger Delta, which began as enforcers for local politicians.[70] The opening up of a closed political system to electoral competition can also create instability as decisions are made around how public patronage is shared. Scholars have argued that democratization in Mali in the 1990s—much hailed by Western observers—was hijacked by national elites and regional "big men," feeding into the cycles of insurgency there since then.[71] Finally, strongmen who are forced to democratize can use conflict and ethnicized governance in order to divide their opponents and stay in power. This was certainly the case during the final years of Mobutu, as it was in the various spates of ethnically tinged violence in Kenya's Rift Valley; Paul Biya's manipulation of the discourse of autochthony in Cameroon, which has recently produced armed violence, is another example of this.[72]

Economic liberalization, which had begun with structural reforms in the early 1980s, also played a role in this shift in conflict dynamics, creating new sources of profit for armed groups and militia. The civil wars of Sierra Leone and Liberia were examples of this: the state apparatus was weakened, creating security and regulatory vacuums that criminal networks could exploit, all the while social safety nets were eroded.[73] The example of cigarette and human smuggling through the Sahara, a key source of revenue for armed groups based in the Sahel, showcases how these new informal flows of goods can contribute to conflict. The dramatic increase of artisanal mining in the eastern Congo, in mining areas that had been controlled by the state into the 1990s, is another example.

At the same time, structural adjustment programs hit rural peasants hard, leading to the concentration of agricultural capital and land in the hands of a small elite and creating increasing disparities between urban and rural areas.[74] More than ever, cities beckoned, promising consumerism and opportunity, resulting in sprawling slums and large numbers of subsistence farmers with shrinking farms.[75] However, whereas in previous generations urban intellectuals recruited among rural peasants, bridging the two spheres, many recent rebellions—those in Kordofan, Darfur, the Democratic Republic of the Congo, and increasingly in the Central African Republic and South Sudan, for example—feature armed groups hunkering down in rural areas with little intention of taking control of large towns. Armed rebellion has thus become at the same time increasingly peripheral and integrated into the logic of state governance.

International actors became complicit in this production of violence, through a process of extraversion in which local elites draw on outside actors—in particular donors, diplomats, and aid workers—in order to extract resources and bolster their status.[76] There have been different forms of this complicity. Tobias Hagmann, for example, has documented how Somali elites have "regularly turned their participation in transitional governments into a resource appropriation tactic" from outside actors.[77] Similarly, anti-Islamist military backing from the United States has become increasingly important as a source of financing for national armies. In Niger, US support to the army totaled 15 percent of their military budget between 2012 and 2019, while in Uganda it provided an amount equivalent to a third of its military budget in 2016.[78] The United States is not the only source of such funding— the Burundian government was able to obtain $13 million dollars a year by sending peacekeepers to the Central African Republic to serve in a United Nations force there, amounting to around 20 percent of its total military budget.

Similarly, the predilection for power-sharing agreements by international organizations has institutionalized and legitimated the kinds of violent bargaining processes that I describe above.[79] This kind of unwitting complicity is aptly described by Alex de Waal, who shows how diplomats unfamiliar with the terrain and with much less invested in the conflict can be outmaneuvered by belligerents.[80] A different form of complicity takes place when local elites in conflict situations, such as those in the Niger Delta or mining areas of the eastern Congo, draw on international markets to extract resources.[81]

I return to these different forms of international complicity in chapter 9.

Conclusion

This chapter extrapolates from my analysis of the Congolese conflict to offer broader theoretical conclusions about conflict in general. I highlight three trends that have contributed to the intractable, entrenched nature of the Congolese conflict. First, as conflict grinds on over decades, a military bourgeoisie has emerged, spanning state security services and armed groups and with a vested interest in the continuation of conflict. Second, there has been a dramatic fragmentation of armed groups, as local elites seek armed muscle to defend to their interests and as the government uses divide-and-rule tactics to further its survival.

And finally, the interests of the actors have turned inward, focused on their own narrow survival and reproduction within a system that has been detrimental to a large majority of Congolese.

The trends can be seen replicating across Africa. Despite the rhetoric of governments, many conflicts have increasingly become part of a strategy of governance. In Nigeria, for example—the country with the most fatalities in Africa due to conflict in 2020[82]—only 9 percent of the electorate said that violence should be the priority for the government.[83] And yet, in a country that has seen nine military coups since independence and where militias are often instrumentalized by politicians to bolster their status and influence, the existence of violence by militias, gangs, and armed groups—*pace* Max Weber's famous definition of the modern state—has become a feature of the state. In many African countries, violent conflict is peripheral and devastating for the affected population, but it remains a key consideration for government survival.

There are two theoretical contributions being proposed here. First, I argue that we should not treat belligerents' interests as epiphenomenal to material factors—they are not entirely determined by considerations of material gain and loss, or even physical survival. Concepts such as violence, gain, and loss are highly subjective. Interests should therefore by studied as a subject in their own right.[84]

This goes to the heart of constructivist thinking, which holds that ideational factors and inter-subjective beliefs can be just as important as material forces in determining human action.[85] This approach has been applied to international conflict—for example, to Soviet foreign policy or the approach of the United States to the Cuban Missile Crisis. Curiously, however, there are few articles on civil wars explicitly referencing this literature.[86]

The second shift in emphasis is sociological and relational, arguing for a greater appreciation for the internal structure and the social foundations of armed groups. In particular, the rise of a military bourgeoisie that is invested in the conflict, along with the dramatic proliferation of conflict actors—both the sheer number of belligerents as well as their internal fragmentation—has made a peaceful settlement of conflict difficult.

After laying down this theoretical groundwork, I now turn to the microdynamics of conflict in the Congo between 2003 and 2020, charting the path the Congolese conflict took—the critical junctures and the dynamics that transformed and prolonged it. This will flesh out and provide more evidence for many of the arguments I have made in this and the past two chapters. I begin with the creation of the CNDP.

6

The CNDP and the M23

THIS IS THE FIRST OF THREE CHAPTERS profiling armed groups in the eastern Congo.[1] It fleshes out and provides evidence for the theories of the past three chapters while giving a detailed account of the events that undermined the peace process and led to continued violence.

The Congrès national pour la défense du peuple (CNDP) and its successor, the Mouvement du 23 Mars (M23), have been at the center of the conflict in the eastern Congo since 2004. Both groups were led by members of the Congolese Tutsi community and received backing from Rwanda. Both groups triggered a vigorous, if often incoherent, military response from Kinshasa and led to the proliferation of other armed groups.

Conflict in the eastern Congo would have persisted without the CNDP, but it would have looked very different. Conflict, like all major political processes, is deeply contextual and path-dependent; events at a specific point in time can narrow or broaden the possible outcomes at a later point in time through feedback loops, indelible consequences, and increasing returns.[2]

This was the case with the CNDP, which became the linchpin of violence in the eastern Congo. By the time it officially emerged in 2006, internal displacement had dropped by two thirds from its peak in 2003 to 1.2 million people. Armed groups had broadly committed to disbanding and joining the new national army; barely a handful of substantial groups persisted in the eastern Congo in 2005. The CNDP rebellion undermined timid reforms within the new security forces, prompting army leadership to fall back on parallel networks inside and outside of the army to mobilize against this threat, thereby expanding and entrenching the conflict. Finally, the emergence of the CNDP—and its ally in South Kivu, the Forces républicaines fédéralistes (FRF)—also became the main justification for disgruntled army officers to defect and forge new armed groups, pointing to the "Rwandan aggression."

This chapter discusses the emergence of the CNDP and its transformation into the M23. Four factors linked to shifting social structures and their interests supported its creation: (1) the emergence since 1990 of a Congolese military Tutsi elite with tight links to the Rwandan government; (2) the crystallization of a belief within the Rwandan government and this Congolese Tutsi elite that their interests in the eastern Congo could be defended only through armed rebellion; (3) the dramatic marginalization of the RCD political party during the transition, which pushed some of its leaders back into rebellion; and (4) increased competition between Nande and Banyarwanda elites in North Kivu.

The history of the CNDP provides concrete examples that detail the theory outlined in the last chapter. It documents the emergence of a military bourgeoisie in the eastern Congo, a clique of military officers who—despite their professed ideology of communal protection—were relatively dislocated from their community and formed a class in themselves, with their own interests. It also showcases the dynamics that drove the fragmentation of armed groups across the eastern Congo: the centrifugal force the CNDP introduced into the fledgling army, as commanders defected and both the central government and local politicians mobilized armed groups to promote their interests.

Finally, the CNDP and the M23 reveal the ambivalence of the central government toward conflict in its eastern periphery. They were the only Congolese armed groups that became the targets of large, sustained military campaigns between 2006 and 2014.[3] Nonetheless, even these offensives were compromised by the complicity of army officers with the enemy at critical moments, while other officers treated the operations as a source of patronage, sapping the army of critical focus and resources.

The chapter begins with a detailed historical tracing of the CNDP and the M23 and then analyzes the factors that shaped their trajectories.

The CNDP: A History

The Forerunner of the CNDP: Synergie

June 30, 2003, was a day of celebrations across the Congo, especially in the East, where I watched from Bukavu, in a part of the country that had been occupied by the Rwandan army for the previous five years. But not everyone was joyous. The transitional government created anxiety among the former RCD rebels who had been backed by Rwanda and were now joining the national government and army. As explained in chapter 3, the logic of the peace process was a sort of "bait and switch," as one US diplomat argued in retrospect: "You entice former belligerents into a bloated transitional government, sweetened by lucrative government jobs and generous donors, and then three years later kick out a large part of those former belligerents through elections."[4] The key challenge of the transition would be to convince the RCD, the least popular but militarily most powerful group, to join.

The thorny nature of this challenge became clear almost immediately. In September 2003, while the transitional government was still being set up, General Laurent Nkunda and two fellow RCD senior officers based in Goma refused to join the newly integrated national army, citing security concerns for themselves and their community. The Rwandan government, afraid of losing influence, backed them.

Nkunda, a charismatic and imposing figure who would become the leader of the CNDP, is a Congolese Tutsi born into the family of a customary chief close to the border with Rwanda and Uganda.[5] Having relocated to Lubero territory when he was a child, he grew up surrounded by people from diverse backgrounds but remained keenly aware of the vulnerable position of his own Tutsi community. After spending several years as a local schoolteacher, he joined the Rwandan RPF rebellion before it overthrew the regime of Juvénal Habyarimana in 1994. He then participated in the Rwandan-backed AFDL, which toppled Mobutu in 1997, and then in the RCD rebellion between 1998 and 2003. Just before the transition began, and with backing by the Rwandan government, he was named commander of North Kivu province.

While in public he highlighted his concerns for his Tutsi community when justifying his refusal to join the new army, in private he also said he was afraid he could be arrested for crimes he had committed and mentioned a general mistrust of Kinshasa.[6] His fears were justified: as a brigade commander for the RCD, in May 2002 Nkunda had helped lead the suppression of a mutiny in Kisangani, where he was complicit in the killing of at least 160 civilians.[7]

Even before the transitional government was inaugurated, Nkunda and his supporters in the RCD and Rwanda had started to prepare a new armed movement. He set up an organization called the Synergie pour la paix et la concorde to rally like-minded RCD leaders.

As Nkunda mobilized in the Kivus, developments in Kinshasa bolstered his movement. By early 2004, tensions within the transitional government were mounting: army integration was stagnating; little progress was being made toward unifying the country and holding elections; and the RCD felt that Kabila was monopolizing power. A confidential code cable sent from the US embassy in Kinshasa to Washington, D.C., summed up the situation:

> After an initial burst of activity—swearing-in of the new government in July, inauguration of parliament in August, creation of an integrated military command structure in September, and appointment of military region commanders in October—the DRC's transitional government has settled into a lazy pattern of drift and neglect. The country is still divided in fact, with each of the former warring factions still effectively in control of "its" territory. There has been virtually no organized progress on demobilization of former combatants or unification of the various armies. The police, intelligence, immigration, territorial administration, diplomatic services and state-owned enterprises all remain unintegrated.[8]

The governmental inertia in Kinshasa compounded the burgeoning crisis in the East. In early 2004, Azarias Ruberwa, the RCD leader and a vice president in the transitional government, met with Nkunda and the other defectors, asking them to write to Kabila for forgiveness for not having joined the army. Ruberwa told me that the officers did as he suggested, but Kabila never answered the letter.[9] President Kabila and his associates did not take the dissidents seriously until it was too late. It is not clear whether they underestimated the danger, did not care, or thought that renewed conflict might be in their interest.

Nkunda's goal from the beginning was to mount a new insurgency.[10] Planning for this likely began months before the inauguration of the new government in June 2003. "Do you think it was an accident that Nkunda was named commander of North Kivu just before the transition? The plan was always to start something new," one of the officers involved in the rebellion remembered.[11] After defecting from the army, Nkunda began contacting Banyarwanda RCD army officers, laying the groundwork for the CNDP. When Rwandan troops withdrew from the Congo in mid-2002, the RCD had called many of its Banyarwanda commanders back to North Kivu to strengthen its rear base in the run-up to army integration and to provide a buffer for Rwanda against the FDLR rebels.

At this time, the FDLR were the most important armed group in the eastern Congo, numbering between 8,000 and 10,000, although they had not been able to mount an effective attack against Rwanda since 2001. Rwanda's ambitions, however, went beyond defeating the FDLR, as I argue in chapter 4, to maintaining a sphere of influence and maintaining cohesion within its own army. In order to do this, as several former CNDP commanders told me, Rwanda needed either to maintain disorder in the eastern Congo or to establish outright control.[12] It was not initially clear which of these was the initial intent: disorder or control. "At the time, we thought they wanted to set up something like the RCD. Looking back, it looks like it was a strategy of chaos," one interviewee told me.[13]

In the run-up to the transition, the Rwandan government had backed the formation of the 81st, 82nd, and 83rd brigades, which would eventually became the backbone of Nkunda's army.[14] These troops, while officially part of the national army after June 30, 2003—and, bizarrely, receiving salaries from the national government well into the transition—also resisted integration into the new Forces armées de la République démocratique du Congo (FARDC) by refusing orders to redeploy elsewhere in the country.

The Bukavu Mutiny and a Return to Arms

It was not in the RCD heartland of Goma that tensions bubbled over but in Bukavu, a border city and the capital of South Kivu, where locals had long resented the RCD due to its abuses and the perception that it was a Rwandan proxy. Significantly, just before the beginning of the transition in 2003, the Rwandan government played a key role in appointing to local government several senior officials whose presence obstructed the peace process. This included Xavier Chiribanya, who was appointed as governor and Colonel Déo Mirindi, the new provincial military commander. Both had been sentenced in absentia by the Kinshasa government for assassinating Joseph Kabila's father in 2001. It was clear that the current president would never accept an amnesty for their alleged crimes; the Rwandans appeared to be setting up the transition for failure.[15] According to the head of the RCD at time, the party had no say in the appointment; I also spoke with a local eyewitness who said he had seen Chiribanya being brought across the border under a Rwandan military escort.[16]

The scene was thus set for confrontation. Under the terms of the transitional agreement, a former member of Kabila's Forces armées congolaises (FAC), General Prosper Nabyolwa, was appointed military commander in South Kivu, with an ex-RCD deputy. Nabyolwa accused the RCD of stockpiling weapons to launch another rebellion, while the RCD thought Kabila was trying to encroach on their power base and dismantle their military networks.

The crisis erupted in February 2004 when General Nabyolwa arrested Major Joseph Kasongo, another RCD officer who had been sentenced to death in the Laurent Kabila trial. In response, former RCD officers led by Colonel Jules Mutebutsi mutinied, splitting Bukavu into two parts.

The fighting took an ugly ethnic turn when army officers rounded up about fifteen Tutsi, including children, and killed them.[17] While the UN leadership wavered, a small group of UN employees in Bukavu, including myself, began evacuating hundreds of Tutsi, or people who looked even vaguely Rwandan, across the border—a Malian expatriate was targeted, for example, due to his appearance, and I witnessed the tearful separation of a young Tutsi from his adopted family.

This violence prompted accusations of genocide by both the Rwandan government and Nkunda, who began to mobilize the networks he had maintained among the ex-RCD officers in North Kivu for a march on Bukavu. Critically, this expedition was backed by the Hutu governor of North Kivu, Eugène Serufuli, who sent trucks and former RCD officers who had remained associated with him. Nkunda's troops arrived on the outskirts of Bukavu on May 26 and began looting and carrying out targeted killings. Once again, my colleagues at the UN and I began evacuating people, this time to a camp surrounding the UN headquarters in Bukavu.

According to reliable sources, the Rwandan government provided modest military support for this operation and conducted a media and diplomatic campaign.[18] In a meeting with foreign diplomats in Kigali, President Kagame declared that it was not a matter of fifteen Tutsi having been killed but a million and fifteen, linking the killings in Bukavu to the genocide in Rwanda in 1994.[19]

The battle of Bukavu, which lasted about ten days, pushed the transition to the brink of collapse, with the transitional government declaring war on Nkunda's dissidence and the RCD almost reneging on the peace deal. It crystallized a new rebellion around Nkunda; although he was forced to retreat from Bukavu under international pressure, the nucleus of his future insurgency had formed around him. Even after his retreat, much of the "Petit Nord"—the southern part of North Kivu comprising the territories of Walikale, Masisi, Rutshuru, and Nyiragongo, along with the town of Goma—fell under the control of ex-RCD units hostile to the transition. Over the next year, Kinshasa would reinforce the East with twenty thousand troops to carry out by force the military integration that diplomacy could not achieve.[20]

Growing Splits within the RCD, Nkunda's Radicalization

The RCD, always a fractious group, began to collapse under the strains of the transition, which further radicalized the new rebellion. The Bukavu mutiny was the first inflection point, but the breaking point came several months later, in August 2004, when 152 Banyamulenge refugees were killed in the Gatumba refugee camp in neighboring Burundi. The head of the RCD—Azarias Ruberwa, himself a Munyamulenge[21]— accused Congolese security forces of being involved in the massacre and withdrew his party from the transition.[22] Many RCD leaders refused to obey, splitting the party.

However, tensions and consequences went beyond this massacre, Nkunda's defection, and the Bukavu mutiny. The transition was exacerbating preexisting centrifugal forces within the RCD. Since its inception, the party had lacked cohesion, largely because Rwanda constantly interfered in its internal affairs and its initial leaders had been motivated largely by their own personal ambitions and not a shared ideology. Deep fissures persisted throughout its existence: while part of the RCD was, in the words of its own former President Ernest Wamba dia Wamba, a "syndicate controlled by former Mobutists opposed to financial accountability and professionalism,"[23] another faction clustered around the Congolese Tutsi communities and was very close to Kigali.

As outlined earlier, provisions in the peace process deepened these divisions. The transitional government was supposed to culminate in a series of parliamentary, provincial, and presidential elections in which the deeply unpopular RCD was projected to fare poorly. In addition, the transitional arrangement required political parties to represent the whole country. This forced the RCD to name politicians from different ethnic communities across the country to the transitional national assembly and other institutions. Many of these politicians had little sympathy with Banyarwanda concerns and little commitment to the party.

These factors combined to increase defections among RCD members and radicalize some within the rump of the party. "With over half of our members in the transition flirting with Kabila, many of us began to realize that Nkunda had a point," one former RCD parliamentarian said. "What use was it to participate in a transition whose fate was already sealed?"[24]

These disaffected officials had a well-organized constituency to fall back on, both among ex-RCD military officers and within the local political elite. Since the early days of the RCD rebellion in 1998, the Rwandan government had encouraged the creation of a Hutu-Tutsi alliance as the backbone of its new strategy for the eastern Congo. A Rwandan security official said: "We learned from history. As long as there are problems between the Hutu and Tutsi in North Kivu, there will be problems for Rwanda."[25] Eugène Serufuli, the Hutu governor of North Kivu since 2000, was emblematic of this strategy. In an attempt to cultivate a new, pro-Rwandan leadership within the Hutu community, Serufuli appointed new local chiefs, set up several large businesses, and recruited thousands of youths into a local militia, all backed by the Rwandan government.[26] To prop up this alliance, local leaders, with the blessing and encouragement of Rwandan security services, created a pressure group called *la rwandophonie* in January 2004, formalizing a consortium of political and business leaders that had existed for several years.[27]

This *rwandophonie* initially provided support to Nkunda, backing his attack of Bukavu in May 2004. Soon after Nkunda returned from Bukavu, however, this coalition fell apart. The Congolese Hutu community had always been a reluctant partner of the Rwandan RPF government. Some of its leaders had been close to Rwandan president Juvénal Habyarimana's government prior to the genocide, and when the perpetrators of the Rwandan genocide—the Forces armées rwandaises (FAR) and its affiliated militia—fled to the Congo in 1994, they forged alliances with local Hutu militia in Masisi and Rutshuru territories.[28] When the RPF then invaded the Congo under the guise of the AFDL in 1996, they targeted both Rwandan Hutu refugees and Congolese Hutu civilians, whom they saw collectively as complicit with the *genocidaires.*[29] According to United Nations investigations, they likely massacred thousands of Congolese Hutu civilians during this period.

This historical distrust made it difficult for Serufuli to sustain his alliance with Kigali during the transition.[30] "I was under a lot of pressure from my own local community to distance myself from Rwanda and from Nkunda," Serufuli told one of my research colleagues.[31] Realpolitik played a role as well: Hutu leaders noted that obtaining good positions in provincial and national institutions would require an alliance with Kabila, who was favored to win the upcoming elections.[32] At the same time, Serufuli's leadership in the community was being challenged by a pro-Kinshasa Hutu elite. In December 2004, a group of Hutu military officers and local leaders from the RCD wrote letters denouncing the manipulation of Banyarwanda identity and expressing sympathy with the central government.[33] Many of the signatories had been at odds with Kigali in the past and had fought against Rwandan troops between 1996 and 1998.

Soon afterward, Serufuli himself began to switch sides—"He felt that his authority was being challenged by Nkunda, that he didn't control him," Robert Seninga, one of Serufuli's close collaborators, told me.[34] In 2004, he met with security agents from Kinshasa and was courted by Kabila. As Serufuli told one of my researchers, "I had felt since [the peace deal of] Sun City that the RCD didn't have a future. That's why I took my decision to get closer to Kinshasa."

These splits, both within the RCD and between Hutu and Tutsi elites, worried Nkunda and his backers in Rwanda. Nkunda decided to radicalize his language and provoke an open confrontation.[35] Nkunda hoped that by stoking violence he could play on their fears of being marginalized in Kinshasa and victimized in North Kivu. "Violence makes you think about today and tomorrow, not about the long term," one of Serufuli's advisors said. "Nkunda thought a crisis would bring us back toward him, that he could protect us."[36] On August 25, 2005—his first official appearance since the Bukavu crisis—he issued a statement threatening to take military action to get rid of the "Kabila regime." His language was caustic, accusing "the Kabila clan" of divisionism, tribalism, political immorality, and bad governance.[37]

His timing was strategic. In 2005, the Congolese army was in the middle of *brassage* (brewing), the process of integrating the various former belligerents into a new national army. Nkunda's declaration aimed to dissuade ex-RCD commanders who were still uncertain from integrating into the army. If they joined the FARDC, they could expect to be deployed elsewhere in their country, and that would dismantle the military networks upon which Nkunda relied. By the end of the year, around half of the 82nd Brigade, about a thousand soldiers, had defected to join Nkunda, along with many troops of the 81st and 83rd brigades. Alarmed by these developments and Nkunda's belligerent statements, the government issued an arrest warrant for the dissident general on September 7, 2005.[38]

The Outbreak of Hostilities

The next major bout of fighting was triggered in late 2005 by the deployment of the 5th Integrated Brigade of the Congolese army to Rutshuru territory, an area that had been occupied by RCD troops for the previous seven years. The brigade commander, Lieutenant-Colonel Shé Kasikila, a former Mai-Mai officer from the Nyanga community in Walikale territory, had spent the past decade fighting against Rwandan-backed rebellions and made no secret of his antipathy toward the RCD establishment in Goma. He began with cordon-and-search operations to retrieve some of the weapons distributed to civilians in Rutshuru by ex-RCD officials. According to a Congolese intelligence officer in the area at the time, he openly disparaged Tutsi and Rwandan involvement in the Congo.[39] Perhaps most offensive to Rwandan officials, he helped to expose mass graves that, according to locals, resulted from massacres carried out by the Rwandan army and its Congolese allies against Hutu civilians in 1996 and 1997.[40]

Nkunda accused Kasikila of systematically abusing Banyarwanda, an allegation that was likely an exaggeration and that even some ex-CNDP commanders later told me was a pretext.[41] Troops loyal to Nkunda tried to assassinate Kasikila and then launched an attack against Rutshuru and many of the villages surrounding Rutshuru town, pushing Kasikila out.

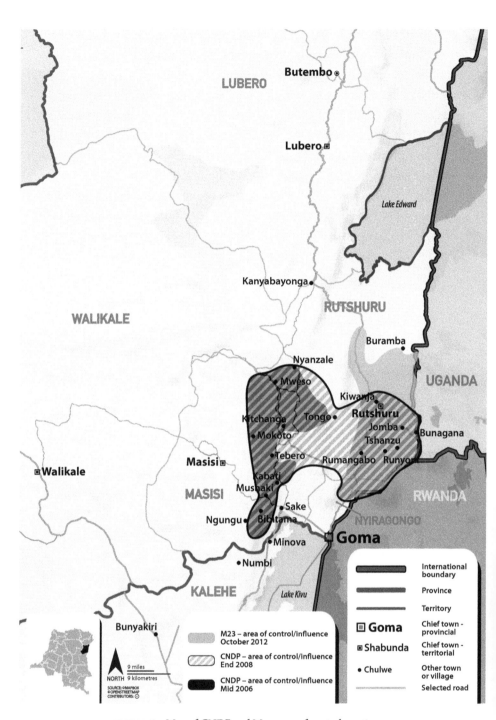

FIGURE 6.1. Map of CNDP and M23 areas of control, 2006–2013

If Nkunda had intended to strengthen Hutu-Tutsi solidarity, his actions had the opposite effect. Within days of the attack on Rutshuru, Governor Serufuli issued a communiqué condemning Nkunda's actions. Shortly afterward, Colonel David Rugayi, the Hutu commander of the 83rd Brigade who had recently been designated the president of Nkunda's military organization, the Conseil militaire pour la défense du peuple (CMDP), defected from Nkunda with around 1,400 soldiers to join the national army. He was followed several months later by Colonel Smith Gihanga, the Hutu commander of the 81st Brigade. The Hutu-Tutsi alliance that had underpinned the RCD's strength in the province was broken.

Elections and the Creation of the CNDP

This was the scene as the political transition was heading to its end, with nationwide elections to take place in July 2006: Nkunda had rallied several thousand soldiers to his side and controlled much of the Masisi highlands. Kinshasa still felt that it could strike a deal with the rebels, especially as it had won over important Hutu leaders in Goma and persuaded a fair share of Nkunda's troops to defect.

According to several high-ranking CNDP officers, however, Nkunda was in it for the long haul and had no intention of striking any quick deals. "Nkunda did not start off with a big head," a member of his high command told me. "But the more interviews he got in foreign media, the more he was vilified, the more he also realized that his future was conflict. Without conflict, he was cooked."[42] This tension persisted throughout Nkunda's insurrection—he argued that all he wanted was a peaceful resolution of his officers' demands and those of the Tutsi community, but at the same time he realized that if there ever was a peace deal, his days would be numbered. "Nkunda never really wanted peace," another senior CNDP officer, who had fallen out with his former boss, told me. "He told us he would never be able to trust Kinshasa. Nkunda wanted war."[43]

During this period, Nkunda also began developing a sophisticated political-military organization, with training camps, a public relations apparatus, and an elaborate network of supporters. For the day-to-day management, he set up an *état major* (general staff office) and began to structure his troops into brigades and battalions. In early 2006, General Bosco Ntaganda, a Tutsi from North Kivu and the former chief of staff of the Union des patriotes congolais (UPC) in Ituri, joined him after the UPC was defeated, his transfer facilitated by the Rwandan government. Within several months, with Rwandan backing, Ntaganda would be promoted to the CNDP chief of staff.

Nkunda also started preparations to set up a political wing and to craft his public image. For this purpose, he merged the political leaders of Synergie with the CMDP's military wing to create the Congrès national pour la défense du peuple (CNDP) on July 26, 2006, with himself as chairman and supreme commander.

In these early days, as its name suggests, the movement's main demands were mostly linked to the Tutsi community. As conditions for integrating into the Congolese army, it insisted on the eradication of the FDLR rebels and the return of the forty-five thousand Congolese Tutsi living in refugee camps in Rwanda. To put this in context, the FDLR, while still a serious threat to the local population, had not mounted serious attacks against Rwanda since 2001 and by 2006 had lost around half the strength it had possessed in 2002 through battlefield deaths and desertions. It was, however, true, that many of the Congolese Tutsi refugees in Rwanda could not return to the Congo because of insecurity in their home villages.

The 2006 elections produced brief hopes that Nkunda would be able to strike a deal with Kinshasa. Kigali told Kabila that they would support him during the elections if he included the RCD in the postelectoral government, and Nkunda allowed Kabila's party to campaign in his territory.[44] The lull in fighting, however, was brief. Kinshasa had little genuine interest in striking a peace deal with a group considered by many Congolese to be Rwandan proxies. That many Congolese accused Kabila of being Rwandan, a sort of Manchurian candidate representing Kigali, also made it hard for the president to strike a deal. On the other hand, elections underscored the challenges for a minority in this new democracy: only one Tutsi was elected to the national assembly, and none to provincial assemblies.[45]

The Sake Crisis and Mixage

As in Bukavu in May 2004, and in Rutshuru in January 2006, it was news of an attack against Tutsi that triggered the next round of violence. On November 24, 2006, police at a checkpoint in Sake—a town 25 kilometers west of Goma on Lake Kivu—got into an argument with a Tutsi businessman who had been bringing fuel into CNDP territory and shot him dead.

The CNDP reacted disproportionately to this incident, launching an offensive against the lakeside town of Sake and then advancing on Goma. It is likely that the CNDP had been preparing an offensive before the incident. This decision to renew hostilities was linked to internal tensions within the CNDP. Just weeks before, the commander of the 81st Brigade, Colonel Smith Gihanga, had deserted from the CNDP, triggering a stream of defections. According to officers in his high command at the time, Nkunda attacked Goma because he needed to maintain momentum and instill order within his own ranks.[46]

The Congolese army scattered as the CNDP advanced and the United Nations peacekeeping mission, called MONUC, was forced to defend Goma. In probably of the bloodiest day of fighting for a Congolese armed group since 2003, between 150 and 400 CNDP soldiers were killed by UN helicopters and armored vehicles in the open terrain that separates Sake from Goma.[47] The attack, in which MONUC may have killed more armed combatants than in any other United Nations operation in decades, had a deep impact on Nkunda, who had perceived the UN as risk-averse and pliable.[48]

This defeat, along with international pressure, forced both sides to negotiate. As with every subsequent round of negotiations, Rwanda would play a crucial role as a mediator. Nkunda flew by helicopter to Kigali alongside the chief negotiator for the Congolese government, General John Numbi.[49] A peace deal was hashed out that would provide the blueprint for subsequent deals as well: it required the integration of CNDP units into the Congolese army, but the integrated brigades would remain in the Kivus. These units would then be tasked with an offensive against the FDLR, a key demand from the Rwandan government. This deal, dubbed *mixage*, led to the creation of six mixed brigades deployed in Masisi and Rutshuru.[50]

Operating with much better troop control than his Congolese government counterparts, Nkunda was able to manipulate *mixage* to his favor. He made sure that his troops remained intact at the battalion level and that his general staff was not affected by the integration exercise. "*Mixage*—that's how we built the CDNP," one of the senior officers told me.[51] According to Congolese government documents, Nkunda's troops received around $190,000 a month in salaries, based on purposely inflated troop numbers.[52] At this point, the CNDP was claiming to have 7,221 soldiers. According to a former senior administrative CNDP officer, that was around 40 percent more than they actually had.[53] The CNDP also received a modest amount of ammunition for operations against the FDLR. As Nkunda explained to me himself: "The government was our logistician."[54]

Mixage also marked a watershed in the CNDP's area of control. Previously, the group had been largely confined to the highlands of Masisi and the northwestern corner of Rutshuru, stretching from Ngungu in the south to Nyanzale in the north. Around the time of the Sake war, Nkunda's high command decided to send a battalion to Runyoni, a series of hills close to the Rwandan border. "This was for two reasons," according to a former senior CNDP commander. "We wanted to open up a second front to disperse the government forces. And we needed to get new recruits and equipment in through Rwanda as fighting heated up."[55] This expansion effectively doubled their territory and allowed them to control the lucrative Bunagana border crossing, where dozens of large trucks crossed every day into Uganda, and with easy access to Rwandan territory.

Mixage was supposed to be an interim measure, but the peace deal turned out to just be a placeholder mechanism, as there was no agreement on any sort of comprehensive, long-term solution. Each side had ulterior motives: Kinshasa wanted to use the arrangement to siphon off soldiers, especially Hutu, from the CNDP—a strategy that was partly successful, as around five hundred soldiers deserted during this period.[56] Nkunda, who in private was unable to articulate a long-term strategy to his officers, pursued his tactic of using negotiations as a means to stall and accumulate more resources.[57]

The military operations against the FDLR provided the trigger for the collapse of *mixage*. Many of the operations took place in areas where the FDLR had been living side by side with the Congolese Hutu population for years. Unsurprisingly, the offensive led to widespread abuses against civilians, especially by CNDP officers.[58] In the meantime, as the cohabitation between FARDC and CNDP officers frayed, skirmishes broke out between the two sides.

Another critical factor in the collapse of *mixage*, and in conflict dynamics more broadly, was the proliferation of militias in the province, often backed by Kinshasa. Worried about the CNDP expansion, army officers and politicians began backing the creation of various armed groups as counterweights in early 2007. The most important one was a coalition of militia called PARECO. One of its backers, FARDC general Mayanga wa Gishuba, told me openly: "We couldn't trust the army, it was often complicit with the enemy—so we had to create our own militia."[59] One of Serufuli's associates justified his support for the group, saying "*Mixage* was an existential threat to us. We needed to act."[60] As argued in chapters 3 and 4, this fragmentation was also driven by national dynamics: the faulty integration process had produced a pool of discontented officers eager for new opportunities, and the run-up to elections also prompted some politicians to back armed groups to bolster their standing and to intimidate opponents.

Finally, in December 2007, Kinshasa declared *mixage* over and launched a broad offensive against the CNDP in collaboration with the FDLR and various local militia. This, too, ended in failure for the FARDC. After the army had massed troops and weapons in the hillside town of Mushaki, the CNDP executed a sneak attack at night that took the army by surprise and killed dozens, including several high-ranking officers.[61]

The Goma Peace Conference

Following this embarrassing Mushaki defeat, Kinshasa decided to return to the negotiation table. Once again, it involved peace talks that ended up serving as a way of siphoning off government funds and preparing troops in the field for the next round of operations. One of the government officers quoted to me Mao Zedong's aphorism, pointing at the strategic value of negotiations: "Talk, talk, fight, fight."

For several months, leading Kinshasa politicians had been discussing the idea of a peace conference that would involve local communities as well as armed groups.[62] The idea was noble—the transitional government had never dealt with many of the root causes of conflict in the Kivus, including community reconciliation, local power struggles, and the presence of the FDLR. A new peace process was needed, its proponents argued, to address these deep challenges. This also came on the heels of an agreement between the Rwandan and Congolese governments on November 7, 2007, in which Rwanda and the Congo committed themselves to cracking down on the CNDP and the FDLR, respectively. It was now time to forge a comprehensive peace deal with all armed groups.

The Goma Peace Conference, held between January 6 and 26, 2008, was, in many aspects, a positive and cathartic experience. Community leaders got up and expressed their anger and grief over decades of war, voicing emotions they had never had a chance to put into words in front of their rivals. The Goma Peace Conference also transformed the CNDP. Its political wing, which had been largely in Nkunda's shadow, became more prominent, featuring political spokesperson René Abandi, military spokesperson Séraphin Mirindi, and the head of their delegation, Kambasu Ngeve. At the same time, the negotiations and the subsequent escalation in fighting shone the media spotlight on Nkunda. Film crews from around the world vied to get in touch with the media-savvy general. "It went to his head," one ex-CNDP officer said. "And the Rwandans didn't like that."[63] Many other ex-CNDP officers agreed, saying they became increasingly disenchanted with their leader around this time.[64]

The Escalation of Violence and the Demise of the CNDP

The new peace initiative was only another lull in fighting. Both sides began rearming almost immediately, this time with various elites and government officials backing new and old armed groups in an effort to marginalize the CNDP. Large-scale fighting began on August 28, 2008, and the CNDP gained the upper hand, seizing the Rumangabo military camp on October 26 with the support of Rwandan military units.[65]

This period saw a sharp increase in Rwandan interference inside the CNDP. "The Rwandans were not that important until 2008," one ex-CNDP officer remembered when I interviewed him in 2012, echoing the sentiments of many others. "That's when their influence became serious and we became less independent."[66] Rwandan troops also participated in the shelling of Congolese army positions when the CNDP pushed toward Goma, reaching its doorstep on October 28, 2008, and sending the Congolese army fleeing. The siege of Goma became a major international incident, triggering meetings at the UN Security Council and bringing dozens of foreign correspondents to Goma.

The attack on Goma led Kabila's government, after four years of fighting and at least six major offensives, to decide to negotiate with Rwanda directly. In October 2008, delegations began visiting Kigali from Kinshasa to try to hammer out a peace deal. Rwanda was coming under increasing pressure from the international community; the report of the United Nations Group of Experts, of which I was the coordinator, revealed extensive Rwandan support to the CNDP, and major newspapers like the *New York Times* conducted their own investigations.[67]

The terms of the deal between Kigali and Kinshasa seeped out slowly, but its impact was felt almost immediately. On January 4, 2009, Bosco Ntaganda announced the removal of Nkunda as the head of the CNDP due to mismanagement. On January 22, 2009, Nkunda was arrested after having been invited across the border by Rwandan officers. All CNDP officers were called across the border to the Rwandan town of Gisenyi and given orders to integrate into the Congolese army; they had little choice but to fall in line.[68]

While the Congo-Rwanda deal was secret—and possibly only an unwritten agreement—it is clear that, much like the 2007 *mixage* deal, it was built around operations against the FDLR. In the days following Nkunda's arrest, the Rwandan army launched joint operations with its Congolese counterpart against the FDLR, sending up to four thousand troops across the border for a month, an operation called Umoja Wetu (Our Unity).[69] In addition, the CNDP were promised top positions within the Congolese army and told they would not be moved out of North and South Kivu.

While the main agreement was concluded in secret, the Congolese government did sign two formal, public agreements on March 23, 2009—one with the CNDP, another with other armed groups.

The Flawed Integration of the CNDP into the Congolese Army

As during the *mixage* deal, the CNDP relied on the complicity and disorganization of Congolese officers, who looked the other way as the CNDP manipulated the process in its favor. While the CNDP consisted of 5,276 soldiers, it again submitted an inflated list, this time containing more than twice that many.[70] However, only about half as many light weapons were handed over as there were soldiers, and almost no heavy weapons; most of these were hidden in arms caches that were discovered several years later.[71] The CNDP even integrated a small number of Rwandans into the Congolese army who had never been part of the CNDP.[72]

Ntaganda became deputy commander of the Kimia II operations, the code name for the military offensive against the FDLR and Congolese armed groups that followed on the heels of Umoja Wetu. As such, he wielded extensive influence over the appointment of ex-CNDP commanders to lucrative areas in the Kivus: the mining areas around Nyabibwe, Bisie, and Bibatama all fell under the control of ex-CNDP in 2009, and they later extended their control to other mining areas.[73] When the commander of military operations in the eastern Congo, General Dieudonné Amuli, was injured in a plane crash in July 2011,

Ntaganda became even more influential, signing off on all major operations and nominations in the Kivus.

Why did the Congolese government allow this? A senior Congolese intelligence officer told me in 2012: "It was part appeasement, part disorganization, part greed. Kinshasa didn't want to offend the CNDP, that was sure. But we were also disorganized, we didn't follow up [. . .]. And then I have to say that some [Congolese officers] made a fortune with the CNDP in some of these areas. Why complain if you are all making money?"[74]

But the peace deal also came at a cost for the ex-CNDP. Many of their officers were unhappy with Rwandan meddling, especially after the arrest of Nkunda, who had commanded the respect and loyalty of many in senior positions. When he was arrested in January 2009, fissures within the group broke open, largely along the fault line that had emerged between Ntaganda and Nkunda but also along clan and ethnic divides.

The strongest opponent to Ntaganda's leadership was Colonel Sultani Makenga, who had been the commander of the key Rutshuru sector—where supplies from Rwanda were organized and the Bunagana border was taxed—for the CNDP before integration. Immediately after Nkunda's arrest, Makenga returned to Rutshuru, where he talked to his officers about fighting against the Rwandans. One officer described the scene in Rumangabo military camp: "Makenga told us we would fight the Rwandans, but we looked up into the hills around us and saw Rwandans deployed everywhere. We told him we couldn't."[75]

Makenga eventually accepted army integration and was appointed deputy commander of South Kivu operations, the second-highest position for an ex-CNDP officer. Many of the other pro-Nkunda officers moved with him; they benefited from his patronage by being appointed to important positions in the province. Tensions, however, remained between Makenga and Ntaganda, and they were often expressed along ethnic lines. While both of them are Tutsi, Ntaganda was accused by many ex-CNDP of favoring officers from his Gogwe sub-ethnic group, as well as officers who had been with him in Ituri when he led the UPC.

All the ex-CNDP officers interviewed for this study agreed that ethnic divides sharpened notably under Ntaganda's leadership.

The M23 Mutiny

For Kinshasa, the integration of the CNDP had always been a temporary solution. "We were going to integrate them, slowly wear down their chain of command, then deploy their officers elsewhere in the country," said a high-ranking Congolese army officer in Goma.[76] Instead, the integration process had the opposite effect: it strengthened the CNDP, making many of them rich and allowing them to co-opt officers from other armed groups. Ntaganda made millions of dollars from mineral smuggling, embezzlement of military funds, and taxation rackets. Some of his actions were brazen—in December 2011 and March 2012, Ntaganda's soldiers stole over a million dollars from a bank in downtown Goma; in February 2011, he and other senior officers were involved in a gold heist worth over $6 million.[77]

Starting in September 2010, the Congolese government tried several times to deploy ex-CNDP commanders outside of the Kivus—to Kisangani, Ituri, and further afield.[78] The CNDP always refused, citing security risks, anti-Tutsi discrimination, and the continuing existence of the FDLR. In response to this pressure, Ntaganda began strengthening his alliance with ex-PARECO officers (once the CNDP's worst foes), which still had links to the FDLR, and other armed groups.[79] The government also tried to weaken Ntaganda's grip through the "regimentation" process, which began in February 2011.[80] The goal was to merge army units into regiments of 1,200 soldiers, getting rid of parallel chains of command—including those managed by the ex-CNDP—and purging the army of fictitious soldiers. The operation backfired, as had so many similar initiatives before it. Instead of weakening Ntaganda's web of patronage, it reinforced it as he named his associates to new command positions.

Eventually, it was the November 2011 elections that provided the trigger for a new rebellion. Kinshasa wanted to wait until after elections before cracking down on ex-CNDP networks, while Ntaganda believed he would be able to sway failed candidates to his cause.

Tensions within the ex-CNDP also contributed to the mutiny. Despite reconciliation efforts (allegedly sweetened with the sharing of spoils), relations between Makenga and Ntaganda were still chilly. However, both knew that they could not succeed if they were divided. They also knew that Kinshasa was grooming Colonel Innocent Gahizi, the ex-CNDP deputy commander of North Kivu, as an alternative to Ntaganda. Both Makenga and Ntaganda were vulnerable and grew uneasy.[81] Rebellion seemed a safer option than doing nothing.

The November 2011 elections, marred by large-scale rigging and irregularities, prompted a push toward rebellion from another quarter. Donors decided that a re-run would not be feasible, but they nonetheless wanted to take advantage of Kabila's perceived illegitimacy to push for other reforms.[82] One of these was the arrest and transfer of Ntaganda to the International Criminal Court, which had issued a warrant for his arrest for crimes he committed in Ituri. Pressure increased when media around the world broadcast news of the conviction on March 14, 2012, of Thomas Lubanga for child recruitment, the court's first ever conviction. Ntaganda, as Lubanga's chief of staff in Ituri during the peak of violence there, was clearly afraid of an impending arrest.[83]

At the end of March 2012, Ntaganda ordered some of his associates to defect from the army. However, the mutineers overestimated their strength and ability, and the mutiny almost collapsed as the Congolese government rounded up the first wave of defectors in South Kivu. "The soldiers were tired of seeing their commanders get rich and not give them anything," one ex-CNDP officer who refused to join the mutiny said. "Why risk your lives for commanders you don't believe in?"[84] Another lamented, "Officers told Ntaganda: 'We can do this, we are prepared.' But they weren't."[85] One of the problems was that Ntaganda, who had antagonized many of the Tutsi officers, for this new insurrection had to rely on weak alliances with less loyal officers.

On April 9, 2012, in an effort to staunch the flow of defections, a delegation of Congolese officials met with their Rwandan counterparts in

Gisenyi. According to both sides, the meeting concluded that Ntaganda should be allowed to stay in his ranch in Masisi while a commission of integration would be set up to decide the fate of other mutineers.[86] When Kabila arrived in Goma the next day, however, frustrated with the ongoing defections, he said the deserters would have to face military justice instead of being reintegrated. He also decided to begin sending ex-CNDP troops elsewhere in the country, a move that they had long resisted.[87]

This was a crucial turning point. "Up until mid-April," one foreign diplomat said, "the Rwandan government appears to have played a positive role, dissuading deserters and talking to the Congolese."[88] It is possible that Kigali, as so often, was playing at brinksmanship, encouraging Ntaganda to defect but also preserving the possibility of reconciling with Kinshasa. However, when they saw that Kabila wanted to definitively dismantle the ex-CNDP networks, the Rwandan government began throwing its weight behind the rebellion. In particular, Rwandan officials began courting Sultani Makenga. Their efforts included pressuring Laurent Nkunda, to whom Makenga continued to look up, to defect. "At one point, they even promised that Nkunda would be released," one Makenga loyalist remembered.[89]

On May 4, 2012, the mutineers, under heavy military pressure from the Congolese government, moved out of Masisi to a narrow stretch of hills close to the Rwandan border. On the same day, Makenga and his officers defected from Bukavu across the border into Rwanda, where they met with Rwandan officers before joining Ntaganda. Two days later, the group issued a statement announcing the creation of the M23 rebellion, with the goal of implementing the stalled March 23, 2009, agreement. It announced a political leadership composed mostly of former members of the CNDP's political wing, although there were also some new names, allegedly appointed after pressure from Rwanda.[90]

The M23 set up a training camp in Tshanzu, close to the Rwandan border, and trained between 800 and 1,500 new troops between May and August 2012. It also tried to strengthen its ties with other armed groups in the region. These alliances were crucial, for they tied down Congolese troops and potentially broadened the M23's support base.[91] The alliances were also intended to highlight that the rebellion was just one of many the Congolese government was facing. For example, opinion pieces in the Rwandan government-owned newspaper, *The New Times*, argued that the real problem in the Congo was not the M23 but the lack of a strong, efficient state.[92] A pundit close to Kigali published a similar piece in the *New York Times*.[93]

The irony of these alliances is that, after sixteen years of Rwandan intervention in the eastern Congo, many of Kigali's natural allies from the Hutu and Tutsi communities were no longer willing to participate in a Rwandan-backed rebellion. This forced the M23 to reach out to other local militias that were much less reliable and were often steeped in anti-Tutsi and anti-Rwandan rhetoric. They included the Raia Mutomboki, as well as militia in Ituri and the southern half of South Kivu.[94]

The Fall of Goma and the Decline of the M23

The fall of the M23 can be traced to their capture of the regional trade hub of Goma, a city of half a million people, on November 20, 2012. Taking Goma represented the apex of the group's power, but—as when the CNDP fought its way to the outskirts of Goma in October 2008—the city's fall crystallized tensions within the group, mobilized the international community, and brought about increased scrutiny of Rwanda's role.

In the immediate aftermath, a regional body, the International Conference for the Great Lakes Region (ICGLR), stepped in to host negotiations between the Congolese government and the M23, leading to the group's withdrawal from the city after ten days. Meanwhile, pressure was increasing on Rwanda to cut support to the M23. In June 2012, UN investigators released a report linking Rwanda to the M23, and in subsequent months donors suspended over $200 million in funds to that aid-dependent country.[95] The fall of Goma several months later only increased the pressure on Kigali.

The Goma crisis also exacerbated the internal feuding within the M23 between Ntaganda and Makenga. After their retreat from Goma, their two factions fell out over the sharing of spoils and even set up competing checkpoints and local taxes. In April 2013, open conflict broke out, which eventually led the Ntaganda faction, consisting of 682 troops and officials, to flee to Rwanda.[96] Ntaganda handed himself over the US embassy, apparently afraid that his fate would be worse in Rwandan hands, and was extradited to the International Criminal Court.

Finally, the fall of Goma led to calls for international military intervention in the conflict. An intervention force, first proposed by the ICGLR and then by the Southern African Development Community (SADC), was integrated into the United Nations peacekeeping mission. The Force Intervention Brigade, consisting of troops from South Africa, Malawi, and Tanzania, was given a more robust mandate than the other UN troops in the Congo, and came equipped with snipers, attack helicopters, and special forces. Meanwhile, the Congolese army also underwent an internal reorganization, firing its commander of the land forces and removing dozens of the senior military officers in North Kivu who had been embezzling funds and creating parallel command structures.

In late October 2013, the Congolese government, backed by this UN brigade, launched a renewed offensive against the M23. This time the Rwandan government did not step in to prop up its faltering ally. With little help from the Rwandan government, the M23 were defeated within a week, and their remaining troops fled mostly into Uganda, ending the CNDP/M23 insurgency.

Analysis: The Constituency and Interests of the CNDP Insurgency

It would be easy to get lost in this complex history. Let's return to the theoretical level and recall the questions that guide this study: Why did the CNDP and the M23 emerge as the two most important armed groups in the eastern Congo, and what were the factors that led to their dismantling? What can the groups tell us more broadly about the conflict dynamics schematized in chapters 3 to 5?

The answers lie in the dynamics generated by the peace process, which led part of the RCD, along with the Rwandan government, to believe that their interests could not be guaranteed by the transitional government. On the other hand, the path charted by the CNDP and the M23 also reveals how the Congolese government has engaged with the most formidable rebellions it has faced since the 2002 peace deal, pouring in military resources while also seeing conflict as an opportunity to provide patronage. This analysis will focus on understanding these key players and how they perceived their interests.

Who Backed the CNDP?

The question of the constituency of the rebellion is not just an academic matter. The CNDP stood at the center of an escalation of violence that almost derailed the peace process and displaced millions of people between 2006 and 2013. Any understanding of the dynamics of conflict requires scrutiny of the main actors involved, their relations to each other, and their interests.

CONGOLESE OFFICERS AND POLITICIANS

The main protagonists of the CNDP/M23 were the officers and politicians who staffed the rebellion, beginning with Laurent Nkunda himself. While this core group was initially composed of both former RCD politicians and military officers, the military came to dominate the movement.

Who were these people? When Nkunda initially refused to join the national army in August 2003, he was surrounded mostly by civilians from a wide array of ethnic groups. Synergie, the brain trust he set up that year, was led by Dieudonné Kabika, a former political advisor to the secretary-general of the RCD, Azarias Ruberwa, and included politicians from different backgrounds and ethnicities. Other leading members of Synergie included:

- Denis Ntare Semadwinga, Tutsi, former chief of staff of Governor Serufuli and advisor to Mobutu;
- Déogratias Nzabirinda, Hutu, a *chef de poste* (local administrator) from Masisi and a former schoolteacher;
- Emmanuel Kamanzi, Tutsi, a former minister of finance for the RCD;

- Xavier Chiribanya, Shi, governor of South Kivu and former chief of staff to AFDL leader Anselme Masasu;
- Kambasu Ngeve, Nande, former governor of Beni under the RCD/Kisangani–Mouvement de libération (RCD/K-ML), a breakaway faction of the RCD rebellion;
- Stanislas Kananura, Tutsi, former administrator of Masisi territory for the RCD;
- Dr. Guillaume Gasana, Tutsi, former RCD minister of health;
- Moses Kambale, Nande, former officer in the Ugandan army;
- Patient Mwendanga, Shi, former governor of South Kivu.

These leaders shared a deep distrust of Kinshasa. Some, like Nzabirinda, Kabika, and Chiribanya, had obtained their positions thanks to the RCD and the Rwandan government and were worried that the transitional government would marginalize them. Others, like Kamanzi, Gasana, Ntare, and Nkunda, had been given positions in the transitional government only to reject them, privately citing ethnic discrimination.[97]

While their stated ambition was to promote ethnic reconciliation, it was clear that they were also trying to lay the groundwork for an alternative to the transitional government. When it became obvious, however, that the government would not collapse, they realized that this political grouping alone was not strong enough to contest the expansion of Kinshasa's authority into the East. Dieudonné Kabika, head of Synergie, told me: "We had initially come together as a means of reconciling local communities. The goal was to show people in the East that we didn't need Kinshasa. But just sitting together in reconciliation meetings wasn't going to make that happen."[98] The disintegration and unpopularity of the RCD during the transition left these leaders with few peaceful options.

Once Nkunda began reaching out to the military leaders of the 81st, 82nd, and 83rd brigades, the influence of these civilian cadres faded. "At the beginning we relied on civilians," one former CNDP colonel remembered. "They helped us mobilize support among Tutsi exiles in

Rwanda and local businessmen. All of our funding in these early days came from individual contributions. But once the fighting began, we got our own sources of funding, and when Rwanda became more involved, that all changed."[99]

By 2006, when the CNDP was formalized, most of the main decision-makers came from a core network of Congolese Tutsi officers. Their intimate ties had been forged over fifteen years of intermittent warfare in the region. They exemplified a broader trend, highlighted in chapter 5—the emergence, after two decades of war, of a military bourgeoisie with the resources to fuel an insurgency and a vested interest in doing so. Once the impetus behind the CNDP was transferred from politicians to this military class, the chances for peace dwindled.

The importance of this military elite was particularly pronounced among the Tutsi of North Kivu. This community is relatively small, probably numbering between 120,000 and 300,000 in the whole province; however, a large number of young Tutsi men joined the RPF between 1987 and 1994 to overthrow the regime of Juvénal Habyarimana in Rwanda.[100] Almost all of the Tutsi officers who joined the CNDP received their initial military training in the RPF and then joined the AFDL and the RCD together. This shared history, along with their similar ethnic and personal backgrounds, forged close ties among these commanders.

THE RWANDAN GOVERNMENT

The second important constituency of the CNDP was the Rwandan government, particularly members of the Rwandan security establishment. However, Rwandan support was not steady; its nature and magnitude changed significantly across the various phases of the insurgency. At first, the Rwandan government provided impetus, encouragement, and guarantees of help, although this support was mostly symbolic. As the insurgency developed, Rwanda increasingly provided material support. Rwandan involvement peaked under the M23, which was much weaker in terms of internal cohesion and military strength than the CNDP.

TABLE 6.1. Members of the CNDP high command, 2008

Name	Ethnicity	Clan	Socioeconomic class	Position in CNDP	Military history
Laurent Nkunda	Tutsi	Jomba	Upper[a]	Commander/ Chairman	RPF, AFDL RCD
Bosco Ntaganda	Tutsi	Gogwe	Lower[b]	Chief of Staff	RPF, AFDL, RCD, RCD-K-ML, UPC
Sultani Makenga	Tutsi	Jomba	Lower	G3—Operations	RPF, AFDL, RCD
Innocent Gahizi	Tutsi	Jomba	Upper[c]	G4—Logistics	RPF, AFDL, RCD
Christophe Hakizimana	Hutu		Upper[d]	G1—Administration	AFDL, RCD
Claude Micho	Tutsi	Gogwe	Lower[e]	G2—Intelligence	RPF, AFDL, RCD
Innocent Kabundi	Tutsi	Mwega	Lower[f]	Brigade commander	RPF, AFDL, RCD
Faustin Muhindo	Tutsi	Gogwe	Unknown	Brigade commander	RPF, AFDL, RCD
Christian Pay-Pay	Tutsi	Mwega	Upper[g]	Police commander	RPF, AFDL, RCD
Baudouin Ngaruye	Tutsi	Gogwe	Lower	Brigade commander	RPF, AFDL, RCD
Sebarera Bahati	Hutu		Unknown	Brigade commander	AFDL, RCD
Moses Kambale	Nande		Upper	Commander, training wing	UPDF, RCD
Eric Ruohimbere	Munyamulenge		Lower	G3—Operations	RPF, AFDL, RCD
Séraphin Mirindi	Shi		Unknown	Military spokesperson	AFDL, Mudundu 40
Fred Ngenzi	Tutsi		Upper	Personal assistant to Nkunda	
Antoine Manzi	Tutsi		Upper	G2—Intelligence	RPF, AFDL, RCD

[a] According to Nkunda himself, his uncle had been a customary chief in Jomba, Rutshuru territory. His family had been forced to move to a different part of Rutshuru when the colonial administration appointed a new administrator hostile to his family, but his family was still well-off, with 1,200 hectares and over 100 cows. Scott, *Laurent Nkunda et la rébellion du Kivu*, 48.

[b] Ntaganda is widely considered to have been born in Rwanda and to have moved to Ngungu, in Masisi territory, when he was an adolescent. His family was wealthy enough to have sent him to secondary school, but he was still considered to come from the lower class.

[c] Gahizi comes from a landed Tutsi family from Rubaya, in Masisi territory. His family had enough money to send him to study in Goma. He has spent most of his military career in administrative positions, dealing largely with logistics and supplies.

[d] Hakizimana is from a well-off Hutu family from Mokoto, Masisi territory. He spent several years in the Catholic school run by monks in Mokoto and is considered to be educated. He worked in the civilian intelligence service before joining the rebellion.

[e] Micho is from a cattle-herding family in Nyamitaba, Masisi territory.

[f] Kabundi's parents were cowherds for Trappist monks in Mokoto, Masisi territory.

[g] Pay-Pay's mother is from the family of the customary chief of Nyiragongo territory. His father was a wealthy Tutsi. Pay-Pay studied at a respected school in Goma before joining the RPF in 1993.

Rwandan support was evident from the beginning of the CNDP. When interviewed years later, several of Nkunda's former RCD colleagues testified that the Rwandan government heavily influenced his decision to refuse an appointment as commander of the Congolese army in North Kivu. "Rwanda told Nkunda and others to refuse," said a senior former CNDP commander. "The order came from Kigali; they needed a plan B in case the transition didn't work out."[101] Four other senior ex-CNDP officers close to Nkunda told me or researchers working with me that Rwanda played a key role in their decision to defect, although some insisted that Nkunda was his own man and charted his own path within the parameters provided by Rwanda.[102] This corresponds with comments made to me by the former head of Rwandan external intelligence, Patrick Karegeya, after his defection from the government.[103]

This support of Nkunda accompanied other signs that the Rwandan government was trying to undermine the transition. As described above, just before the beginning of the transitional government in July 2003, Rwanda had named several bitter enemies of Kabila to the RCD leadership in South Kivu, including a governor and a provincial military commander who were accused of having helped assassinate Joseph Kabila's father.[104] On the eve of the creation of the transitional government, the Rwandan government helped set up military units that would be difficult to dismantle in North Kivu: three ethnically homogeneous brigades—the 81st, 82nd, and 83rd—composed almost exclusively of Hutu and Tutsi. According to officers who served in these brigades, they were encouraged by Kigali not to join the transitional government.[105]

The first material Rwandan support to Nkunda came during his siege of Bukavu in May 2004, when he reportedly received some weapons and ammunition from Rwanda. After that offensive, Nkunda spent some time in Rwanda planning his next steps. In mid-2005, the Rwandan chief of defense staff, General James Kabarebe, called several high-ranking ex-RCD officers and told them that Nkunda was going to return to the Congo and that they should take care of him.[106] Soon afterward, Nkunda crossed the border and made his way to

Kitchanga, the headquarters of the 83rd Brigade. Rwandan officers then arranged for Bosco Ntaganda, who had never been close to Nkunda, to join the insurgency in early 2006—reportedly against Nkunda's wishes—along with several other Congolese Tutsi officers who had been backed by Rwanda during the conflict in Ituri.[107]

As military pressure from the Congolese army and its militia allies increased between 2006 and 2008, Rwandan support also increased. In particular, once Nkunda lost the support of his main Hutu allies—Governor Eugène Serufuli and his allies fell out with Nkunda during 2005—the Rwandan government stepped in to help with recruitment and reorganization. Their support would include, at various times, the provision of uniforms, ammunition, and free passage to recruit soldiers in Rwanda.[108] The links between Rwanda and the CNDP were so close that, according to three ex-CNDP officers, General Kabarebe spoke with Nkunda almost every week to discuss military and political strategy.[109] Kabarebe has a long history of involvement in the Congo stretching back to the AFDL rebellion, when he led the Rwandan army operations against Mobutu.

The high point of Rwandan military support, according to both UN investigators and former members of the CNDP, came in October 2008, when the CNDP overran the army barracks at Rumangabo with help from the Rwandan army. The CNDP then advanced on Goma, assisted by artillery fire from Rwandan units across the border.[110] Rwandan influence over the CNDP was once again evident in January 2009, when senior officers invited Nkunda across the border, arrested him, and then ordered his troops to integrate into the Congolese army. Nkunda has been under some degree of detention or supervision in Rwanda ever since.

Nonetheless, it would be wrong to depict the CNDP as puppets of Rwanda or created solely by Rwandan officials for Rwandan purposes. Much of the material—mostly uniforms and ammunition—that the CNDP got across the border it had to pay for, and even when Rwanda sent troops across the border in 2008, the force numbered only several hundred. "Relations between us and Rwanda were always tense," one commander remembered. "We had different objectives. And the

Rwandans wanted to control us, we didn't want to be controlled. They tried to divide us internally, threaten us, and eventually even killed some of us. They were allies, not friends, we knew that even then."[111]

By comparison, the involvement of Rwanda was much more obvious between 2012 and 2013 during the M23 crisis. Rwandan interference and the co-optation of ex-CNDP cadres by Kinshasa had deeply divided the core group of ex-CNDP officers. The arrest of Nkunda had eroded its internal cohesion, leaving it factionalized and unable to galvanize widespread support when Bosco Ntaganda launched his mutiny in April 2012. The collapse of the new rebellion forced Rwanda's hand, obliging Rwandan security officials to become much more involved than they had expected or hoped to be.

By mid-2012, this support had provoked substantial international criticism. In contrast to the CNDP period, the main Western backers of Rwanda—in particular the United Kingdom and the United States—no longer believed the government's remonstrations that it was not supporting the M23.[112] In addition, the Southern African Development Community (SADC) strongly condemned Rwandan support of the M23. Malawi, Tanzania, and South Africa increased their contribution to the UN peacekeeping mission by dispatching three thousand troops as part of a new Force Intervention Brigade. When in late October 2013 the Congolese army and the UN launched a new offensive, they quickly overran the M23 positions. According to interviews with UN officials, diplomats, and non-profits, when the Rwandan government decided to withdraw support from the M23, the group crumbled.[113]

Other Potential Explanations

Were there other potential constituencies? While there is substantial evidence that the Rwandan government and networks of Congolese Tutsi military officers combined to form the key constituency of the insurgency, others also could have been involved. The literature on conflict in the eastern Congo suggests two possibilities: political and business elites, and the broader Tutsi community.

POLITICAL AND BUSINESS ELITES

The notion that minerals underwrite the conflicts in the eastern Congo is common in journalism and activism related to the Congo. Writing in *Foreign Affairs*, the US activist John Prendergast wrote that the demise of the M23 was, among other reasons, because organizations—including his own Enough Project—had been successful in cutting off their profits from mining:

> Numerous corporations, including Apple, Hewlett-Packard, Intel, and Motorola Solutions worked to reform international supply chains that had allowed illegally extracted minerals to trade on global markets and end up in cell phones and computers everywhere. Congressional legislation and corporate initiatives have dramatically reduced the money available to armed groups such as the M23, which previously financed themselves by smuggling minerals and other natural resources.[114]

However, there is little evidence that either the CNDP or the M23 made much money directly from mining. After it was pushed out of the mining areas of Walikale in 2004, the CNDP did not directly control any mining areas, nor did the M23 during its brief existence. While both armed groups derived substantial profits from the transport of minerals through their territory, there is no evidence that mining companies were major contributors or that mining profits alone were the main motivation for the rebellions.

This is not to say that economic and political elites did not play a role. As mentioned earlier, at the start of the CNDP, Tutsi leaders played an important role in fund-raising and recruitment. Raphael Soriano (a.k.a. Katebe Katoto), a former vice president of the RCD who had seen his political fortunes fade, reportedly gave money and equipment to the CNDP to gain a foothold in local politics.[115] Ethnic solidarity prompted others, such as businessman Victor Ngezayo and the Anglican bishop Emmanuel Kolini, to act.[116] Others contributed under duress.

However, as the CNDP grew more financially independent and hostilities with Kinshasa flared up, the risks for such contributions grew while the need diminished. Politicians such as Guillaume Gasana, Xavier Chiribanya, and Emmanuel Kamanzi, who were influential in Synergie, also saw their importance diminish. "It was only natural," Kamanzi said, "that as the group engaged in a full-blown war with the government, it would be harder for us to raise our voices and still live in Goma."[117]

THE BROADER TUTSI COMMUNITY

Some scholars have emphasized the importance of the peasantry and grassroots mobilization networks in fueling armed mobilization, arguing that the M23 insurrection was tightly linked to communal resentments that date to the colonial period. Both Mahmood Mamdani and Séverine Autesserre argue that such local conflicts over identity are core drivers of the violence in the eastern Congo.[118]

There is no doubt that ethnicity helped to shape the insurrection; most senior M23 officers were Tutsi, and they consistently mentioned discrimination as one of the main reasons for insurrection. But this tells us little about the social networks and structures involved in mobilization and reduces the complex nature of ethnicity to a simple causal story. In the case of the M23, the Tutsi community had been scattered across the region, lacked any strong communal organizations, and had been kept in the shadow of the Rwandan government, which, according to many Tutsi interviewed, did not want an autonomous Tutsi movement to emerge across the border and become a potential threat to its own security.[119]

It is difficult to find much written evidence on strong Tutsi peasant organizations. This may have been because the community, which was always very small and vulnerable, had strong organizations based in the elite, such as the Association coopérative des groupements d'éleveurs du Nord Kivu (ACOGENOKI), a livestock cooperative dominated by large landowners, as well as strong links to the Catholic and Adventist churches in North Kivu.[120] In addition, during the Mobutu era, powerful Tutsi businessmen and politicians like Barthélémy Bisengimana, who was Mobutu's chief of staff, and Cyprien Rwakabuba, a member of

Mobutu's powerful *bureau politique* and business magnate, represented the community.

During the Rwandan civil war of 1990 to 1994, local mobilization cells for fundraising and recruitment called *umuryango* were put in place by the Rwandan Patriotic Front throughout the region, but those structures had a military aim and were quickly subsumed into the AFDL and RCD when the Rwandan government occupied the eastern Congo. Only during the transition from 2003 to 2006 did the Tutsi community, feeling threatened by demographics, develop some more rooted community structures. Their development was bolstered by the RCD's attempt to foster ethnic reconciliation through the *baraza intercommunautaire*, a structure in which each ethnic community in the province was represented. Once the CNDP emerged, however, Rwandan influence again became dominant, and the importance of the leaders of the Tutsi community diminished. As one member of Nkunda's high command lamented: "We were too important for Rwandan ambitions to allow us to have any independence. They wanted to control us."[121]

This is not to say that the CNDP did not try to cultivate a grassroots following—it was clear from the beginning that Nkunda hoped to create a social movement, and CNDP radio programs, youth groups, and propaganda were aimed at mobilizing popular support. These tools worked with far greater sophistication than those of any other armed group in the country, with regular press statements, two websites (www.cndp-congo .org and www.kivupeace.org, both now defunct), and a radio station.

The CNDP also set up a series of *syndicats*, support cells that held regular meetings, gathered funds, and spread the word about the CNDP's goals and deeds. At least in the first several years of the organization, Nkunda also put on a well-publicized campaign of public reconciliation rallies, called *umusabane*, during which he would criticize the government and urge the population to live together peacefully. Finally, the group carried out training seminars for civilians and military alike, during which they provided some basic military training, articulated the CNDP philosophy, and taught Congolese history.

During the early stages of the rebellion the CNDP sought funds from volunteer grassroots donations. However, as the CNDP grew, the funds mobilized through this network—which according to one former CNDP leader might reach $40,000 in a good month—became less important than revenues coming in through local taxation rackets. Perhaps more important, the CNDP struggled to reconcile the abuses it committed with its calls for popular support. This was perhaps most apparent in the widespread forced recruitment of civilians, including children, which was documented by Human Rights Watch and UN investigators in both the Congo and camps in Rwanda.[122] Forced recruitment revealed how shallow the popular appeal of the CNDP and the M23 was. As one civil society leader said: "If the CNDP was really representing Tutsi, would it be abusing them?"[123]

While there is no doubt that some Congolese Tutsi, especially those living in exile in Rwanda, supported Nkunda, there is little evidence of a broader influence of this community. If there had been strong involvement by the broader Tutsi community, we should have observed their physical presence in the decision-making process, and we should have been able to observe situations where they compelled the CNDP/M23 to take action against its will and in the interest of that community, for example during peace talks. Instead, there is only circumstantial evidence of their influence on the group, and substantial evidence that contradicts such hypotheses.

The Interests behind the CNDP/M23 Rebellion

The peace process provided the backdrop that framed the interests of both the Rwandan government and the Congolese Tutsi military networks that formed the CNDP/M23. As described in chapter 3, the RCD was afraid of being marginalized during the transitional government, that instead of sharing power with the other belligerents, President Joseph Kabila would absorb the other parties into his fold.

Early in the transition, there were already signs that the president was trying to outmaneuver the other parties to the agreement. Two of the four vice presidents were his allies,[124] and Kabila was able to maintain control over many of the informal networks where power resided. Moreover, the transition was set to culminate in national elections, when their party would go from controlling a third of the country to representing just a few percent in national institutions.

At the same time, the RCD was facing challenges at the local level, compounding its marginalization. When provincial elections in North Kivu took place in October 2006, Kabila's coalition won 25 seats, with the RCD only claiming 7 out of a total of 42 seats.[125] Just as critical was the ethnic breakdown: 25 Nande were elected, 10 Hutu, and not a single Tutsi. The provincial assembly then elected a governor from the Nande community.[126]

All of these shifts in power affected the control of economic resources in the area around Goma, which was crucial for the CNDP/M23 and its backers. As elsewhere in the country, access to lucrative business opportunities depended on patronage provided by government officials. The Nande community, in particular, which had built strong international trade networks through their home territories of Lubero and Beni in North Kivu, stood to gain from the new political dispensation. Numerous Banyarwanda businessmen interviewed by my team lamented this competition, as did several CNDP members.[127]

With this backdrop in mind, what were the interests behind these successive rebellions? In chapter 4, I examined the Rwandan government's interests at length; here I focus on those of the Tutsi officers at the core of the CNDP and the M23.

CONGOLESE TUTSI OFFICERS

There is no doubt that narrow personal interests motivated Congolese Tutsi officers when they began the CNDP rebellion. Nkunda was afraid of being arrested for crimes he had been accused of committing in Kisangani in May 2002, a fact that he mentioned in conversations with his colleagues in 2003. Many other CNDP officers had similar concerns about joining the transitional government—they were afraid of being arrested or losing rank and status.

Almost all of the senior operational officers—the brigade and battalion commanders and many of the staff officers—had been members of the Local Defense Forces (LDF), a paramilitary force that Governor

Eugène Serufuli had created at the beginning of the transition in 2003. The LDF enabled many officers to obtain promotions, giving them more access to resources than ordinary commanders. But these promotions were not recognized by the official RCD military hierarchy, leaving the officers uncertain about their fate once they were integrated into the national army. The social environment cultivated by life in ethnically homogeneous units, in close contact with Rwandan officials, also bred mistrust and fueled rumors. "We didn't trust Kinshasa. That was the main problem," one ex-CNDP officer said. "We thought we would be killed, or at the very least marginalized."[128] Another said: "By 2005, we could see that those RCD officers who had joined the army were just looking out for themselves. If we joined, who would make sure we got our salaries, that our families were looked after?"[129]

This uncertainty was informed by the deep history of tensions and violence between Congolese Tutsi and other communities. In addition to broader communal tensions, CNDP officers cited the killing of Tutsi officers in army camps in 1998, when the RCD rebellion first broke out. Troops loyal to President Laurent Kabila had rounded up hundreds of Tutsi civilians and soldiers in cities around the country and summarily executed them.[130] As Nkunda put it to me, "The last time we had been part of an integration exercise, we had been butchered. And now they wanted us to go right back into the lion's den?"[131]

Almost every CNDP officer interviewed for this research cited persecution or discrimination as the main reason they joined the CNDP. There is little doubt that this sentiment was genuine—even prominent Tutsi civilian leaders critical of the CNDP agreed that discrimination fueled the movement.[132] While many other Congolese communities have suffered from discrimination and abuse—including at the hands of attacks led by Tutsi soldiers—the Tutsi community felt particularly vulnerable given its small size, the genocide in neighboring Rwanda, and the spread of virulent anti-Tutsi stereotypes in the region. When I told Nkunda that his rebellion was only exacerbating anti-Tutsi sentiment and that feelings toward his community had actually improved since the beginning of the transition, he said: "What do you want me to do? Stand around while my people are killed?"[133]

Nonetheless, it should be pointed out that many other Congolese Tutsi—in particular from the Banyamulenge community of South Kivu—who had faced similar persecution and violence mostly joined the transitional government, which suggests that vulnerability itself was not enough to fuel action.[134] A small number of Tutsi officers, from North and South Kivu, held leading positions in the new national army: General Malik Kijege was the head of logistics, Colonel Bonané Habarugira became brigade commander, General Jean Bivegete was a senior military judge, and General Obed Rwibasira and General Pacifique Masunzu were both commanders of military regions.

There are other signs that suggest that ethnic discrimination alone was not sufficient, and at times even contradicted the CNDP's actions. An oft-mentioned grievance was the presence of up to fifty thousand Congolese Tutsi in refugee camps in Rwanda. This may have been up to 30 percent of the North Kivu Tutsi population; many of the refugees had been there since 1994. In every interview I had with Nkunda, he mentioned these refugees. For instance, on one occasion he said, "We are fighting so our brothers and sisters in the refugee camps in Rwanda can return. They are suffering there! The graveyards next to the camps are larger than the camps themselves!"[135] Many CNDP/M23 officers felt strongly about these camps; some had relatives living there. One non-Tutsi senior ex-CNDP official said, after having defected from the CNDP: "If you take care of the refugee camps, you will get rid of most of the problem."[136] An indication that others shared this belief were the riots that erupted in the camps when news of Nkunda's arrest was announced on January 25, 2009.

However, the CNDP also manipulated this refugee population, suggesting that for them there was little to distinguish motive from pretext. The CNDP and the M23 carried out forced recruitment of soldiers, including child soldiers, in these camps, and descriptions of the camps suggest a high degree of militarization and intimidation by Rwandan officials and refugee leaders.[137]

On several occasions when refugee returns took place, they were poorly managed, in particular in 2011 when ex-CNDP soldiers helped organize the operation. According to UN investigators, many of the so-called refugees that were resettled were not from the area and some were not even Congolese. Rather, the CNDP was using the refugees—or, as some evidence suggests, Rwandan civilians posing as refugees—as a means to resettle and control strategically important areas.[138] In addition, according to two separate sources within the CNDP, none of the senior CNDP officers had close family left in the refugee camps at the time they started the rebellion.[139] One said, "The senior officers all had money, enough money to make sure their families didn't have to live in those camps."[140]

The importance of ethnic grievances also shifted over time. During the later M23 mobilization, the importance of ethnic discrimination shifted. Many Tutsi ex-CNDP officers did not join the new insurrection. Why? In interviews, many pointed to their disaffection with Rwanda. One former CNDP brigade commander told one of my fellow researchers:

> Why should I rebel again? I didn't see the purpose. Tutsi are still persecuted here, that's true. But I don't see how joining Bosco would have helped. There was no strategy behind this rebellion. All I could see was Rwanda, Rwanda, Rwanda.[141]

By 2012, many Tutsi officers within the Congolese army had begun to prosper. By then there were at least eight Tutsi generals in the police and army, many with lucrative and powerful positions. For them and other Tutsi officers, the notion that a rebellion would somehow better the status of the Tutsi community, or tackle the long-standing discrimination they faced, rang hollow.

In interviews with Tutsi officers, both those who had joined the rebellions and those who did not, it became clear that ethnicity was a nuanced, textured marker of their identity. It was interpreted through their relationships—in the case of those who remained with the government or defected from the CNDP/M23, it was often due to appeals from close Tutsi colleagues or family members, which allowed them to shift their perception of threat and to trust the offers made by the central government. As scholars of the Congo have proposed, building on sociological understandings of war, ethnicity is a form of social capital, which is neither merely an instrument of power nor an essential, immutable characteristic. It is constitutive of the identity of armed groups, even as their leaders seek to manipulate it to recruit followers, forge alliances, and legitimate their existence.[142]

In sum, the complex interests of the core Congolese Tutsi military networks included both self-interest and grievances regarding the persecution of Tutsi and the suffering of Tutsi refugees. When those grievances clashed with strategic objectives—for example, the need for recruits—the community usually lost out. And when first Banyamulenge and then North Kivu Tutsi officers fell out with Rwanda, they abandoned the rebellion, regardless of communal grievances, suggesting that they realized that an alliance with Rwanda no longer helped their personal or collective goals.

Conclusion

This chapter provides detail and nuance to the arguments made in chapters 3 through 5. The peace deal created a backlash, which then forged both the CNDP and M23 rebellions, from two constituencies— Congolese Tutsi military networks and portions of the security establishment in Rwanda. Both groups were motivated by the threats posed by a peace process in the Congo that jeopardized their interests.

It is clear that while communal self-defense provided an important frame for mobilization and solidified their internal military networks— and it is indeed difficult to separate individual from group interests— the rebellions were informed and triggered by narrower forms of self-interest. As I argued in chapter 4, the Rwandan government seemed less interested in protecting its ethnic kin and more intent on protecting its security and economic interests across the border while preserving its internal cohesion and discipline; Nkunda and his fellow commanders were worried about being arrested and losing influence. These distinctions between self-interest and communal protection are, however, difficult to make, given how deeply tied perceptions of self-worth are to ethnic identity.

This story is also a good illustration of how the Congolese government—as well as the international community—has managed conflict in the eastern Congo. A clear tension can be discerned in this regard. On the one hand, the government mobilized against the CNDP and the M23 as with no other group, sending thousands of troops to fight and seeking to galvanize domestic and foreign opinion. On the other hand, some government officials appear to have been complicit with the CNDP, providing them with intelligence and dragging their feet on offensive operations. One several occasions, the government provided funding to the CNDP and, when it was integrated into the national army in 2009, allowed it to take control of large parts of the command structure in the Kivus.

This ambiguity can be explained in part by the general neglect and opportunism the Kinshasa government has displayed regarding conflict in the eastern Congo. It looked the other way when commanders like General Gabriel Amisi were complicit with the CNDP and the M23, afraid that punishing Amisi could offend other senior officers. And the government was too internally fragmented to control the integration of the CNDP, giving Bosco Ntaganda and fellow commanders a large margin to maneuver. But it is also clear that when the government felt that its survival was at stake, it was able to act decisively—to remove dozens of commanders who were clogging up the chain of command in Goma in 2013 and to send troops and money when needed. This shows that the weakness of the government is not merely a matter of capacity but also of will. It shows how the internal fragmentation within the government has furthered the involution of the security services, which in turn has made fragmentation one of the main strategic approaches of the government toward the conflict.

We now turn to a very different armed group, the Raia Mutomboki, in which fragmentation and the involution of political and military elites also manifests itself, albeit in very different ways.

7

The Raia Mutomboki

IN 2011, a new kind of armed group emerged in rural areas of eastern Democratic Republic of the Congo.[1] The Raia Mutomboki ("Outraged Citizens") were a grassroots response to rampant insecurity, in particular to the abuses perpetrated by the Forces démocratiques de libération du Rwanda (FDLR, Democratic Forces for the Liberation of Rwanda), a largely Rwandan Hutu rebel group.

In contrast to the other groups examined here, this one was decentralized, lacked cohesion, and was closely tied to local communities and their interests. Supported by customary chiefs, former militia members, and army deserters, young people rallied around the idea of *dawa*, a magical medicine in the form of an amulet or salve they believed made them invincible, and quickly drove the FDLR out of many of their former strongholds. United by a common ideology and belief in *dawa*, this conglomeration of fractious groups spread their influence to an area that was almost the size of Belgium between 2011 and 2013.

Despite its parochial character, the appearance of the Raia Mutomboki, like that of the CNDP, was prompted in part by the peace process. However, whereas the CNDP was propelled by military and political elites who felt marginalized by the transitional government, the Raia Mutomboki drew on frustrations at the grassroots level.

Three developments stand out as key steps in the emergence of the Raia Mutomboki, first briefly in 2005 and then in earnest in 2011:

1. the failures of the demobilization program, which reinserted thousands of former combatants into the Kivus without follow-up;

2. the launch of massive military operations (Umoja Wetu and Kimia II) against the FDLR between 2009 and 2011 that resulted in widespread abuse against the local population; and

3. the renewed security vacuum produced by the restructuring of the army in 2011.

The story of the Raia Mutomboki fleshes out many aspects of the theory that was laid out in chapters 3 to 5. It shows how a generation of combatants was recycled into a new armed group. The rural military elite they formed was not nearly as affluent or well connected as the national military bourgeoisie but has proven extremely difficult to dislodge. It also elucidates some of the local dynamics behind the extreme fragmentation of armed groups—at this writing in early 2021, there were between twenty and thirty Raia Mutomboki groups in the two Kivu provinces.[2]

Finally, the Raia Mutomboki also showcase the importance of interests. The Congolese government only rarely paid much attention to them, confirming that the army placed little emphasis on groups that did not threaten core state interests. Conversely, most Raia Mutomboki factions displayed little interest in using insurgency as a means to obtain ranks or money from the government, although they have been abusive and predatory.

Although the Raia Mutomboki are marginal groups, they have persisted much longer than the UPC and CNDP. Today, the Raia Mutomboki groups active across the Kivus appear more similar to other armed groups active in the eastern Congo in 2020 than to the CNDP or UPC: lacking cohesion, posing little threat to the Congolese government, but harassing the population and preventing durable development. These features could make them a thornier problem to solve than the more imposing CNDP or M23.

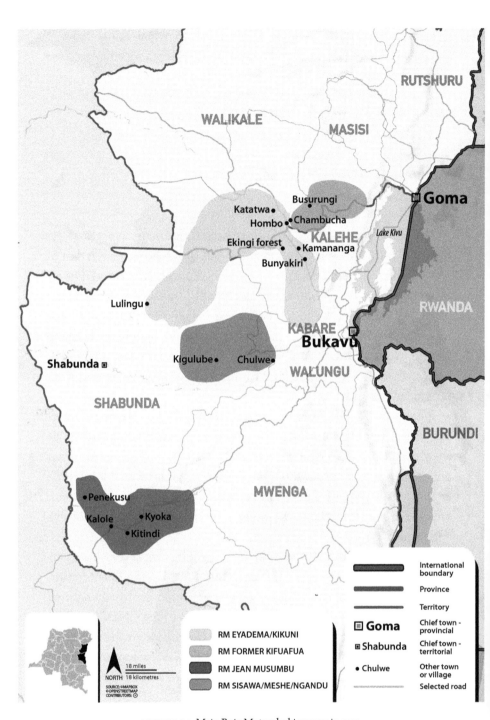

FIGURE 7.1. Main Raia Mutomboki groups in 2013

The Historical Backdrop to the Raia Mutomboki

The events that led to the first use of the name *Raia Mutomboki* now form part of the militia's folklore. On March 29, 2005, a group of local traders was on its way to sell food to gold miners in Kyoka, a jungle village in the far south of Shabunda territory. The group was ambushed by combatants of the Rwandan FDLR rebellion; four traders escaped and alerted a nearby Congolese army patrol. When they finally found their kidnapped colleagues, it emerged that all twelve of them, including two women and four children, had been brutally butchered with machetes.[3] Outraged, they formed a local militia to fight against the FDLR.

The Rwandan rebels had been based in this area since 1998. While similar abuses had been occurring for years, it was the shifts in local power and social relations brought about by the peace process in 2003 that prompted a new mobilization. These shifts included the increased isolation of the FDLR and the infusion of thousands of demobilized, underemployed combatants into local communities.

Until 2001, the Congolese government maintained thousands of FDLR as units inside its army and provided modest material support to other FDLR units in the eastern Congo.[4] Alongside the various Mai-Mai factions, with whom the FDLR often collaborated, these troops formed part of Kinshasa's strategy of pinning down Rwandan and RCD troops by fueling an insurgency behind the frontlines.

In 2003, however, this anti-Rwanda coalition, which had held solidly across rural districts of the Kivus for five years, broke apart. The national peace deal required the integration of the main belligerents, including most Mai-Mai groups and the RCD, into the new national army. In places like Shabunda, most Mai-Mai fighters slowly started leaving for integration camps in early 2004, producing a security vacuum, which in some places was filled by Mai-Mai defectors who had refused to join the national army and in other places by the FDLR.

The FDLR were the clear losers in the peace process. The departure of the Mai-Mai deprived them of allies, and their supply chains to Kinshasa and Lubumbashi were cut off. In addition, the political logic of the peace process meant that the FDLR would face a military offensive that included its previous allies. "Making peace meant that we had to foster a deal between Kigali and Kinshasa," Cindy Courville, then senior director for African affairs at the National Security Council, told me. "Part of that would lead to a withdrawal of Rwandan troops. In return, the Congolese would then get rid of the FDLR."[5] This has been a constant throughout the peace process: diplomats seeking a grand bargain to reconcile the Democratic Republic of the Congo and Rwanda by eliminating the FDLR, often at great cost to local populations.

Beginning in April 2004, the newly formed FARDC launched initial attacks against the FDLR; they then began joint operations against the rebels in 2005 with the UN peacekeeping mission.[6] While these operations were limited and sporadic collaboration between Congolese army commanders and the FDLR continued until 2009—especially against the CNDP—the FDLR felt increasingly worried about their security. Betrayed, in their view, by the Congolese government, they no longer had local allies in Shabunda or a strong central command to rein them in. This prompted a vicious backlash from a group that had already become notorious for its brutal violence, in the apparent belief that violence against civilians could give them political clout. Nor were their abuses confined to Shabunda: on July 9, 2005, they attacked Ntulu-mamba in Kalehe territory, massacring thirty-nine civilians. Other, similar abuses intensified around this time.[7]

It was in Shabunda, in response to the Kyoka massacre, that these parallel developments produced a countermobilization. It is not clear why this area—an extremely remote part of South Kivu that had not seen much fighting during the war—produced the first Raia Mutomboki group. At the center of this uprising was the local *muganga* (natural healer) and Kimbanguist Church minister Jean Musumbu.[8] He rallied local youths and set up a self-defense force. While Musumbu did not have military experience, many of the youths who joined were former Mai-Mai.[9]

Key to the popularity of the Raia Mutomboki was a magical amulet devised by Musumbu, the *dawa* that its wearers believed rendered them impervious to bullets, as long as they followed a strict set of conditions. Initially a thin armband called *bijou* ("jewel") made by local *bachawi* ("witches"), the *dawa* drew on initiation ceremonies of the local Rega ethnic community as well as on a tradition of Mai-Mai militia activism that dates back to the pre-colonial period in this part of the Congo.

The mobilization was initially confined to southern Shabunda and was surprisingly successful.[10] Armed only with spears, machetes, and bows, the Raia Mutomboki were able to drive most FDLR out of the area. The idea of a popular militia with magical powers, fortified by astounding success, proved contagious: the Raia Mutomboki spread to neighboring areas of Maniema and Katanga provinces, where young people organized, copied the name, and sent emissaries to obtain the ritual amulets from Musumbu. These groups were not linked through any joint command structure.[11]

The first wave of Raia Mutomboki mobilization, albeit small in scale, lasted into 2007, but it was barely noticed on the national or provincial levels.[12] Musumbu's group only appeared in the fairly comprehensive United Nations monitoring reports a few times, in the context of battles with the Congolese army and the FDLR in late 2005. This confirms statements made by a former member of this group: "We had little interest in national politics or even in becoming soldiers in the national army. We just wanted to defend our local villages."[13]

The Raia Mutomboki groups of these early days were similar to those that would appear in 2011 throughout Shabunda.[14] They were loosely organized, and Musumbu did not have had direct control. This diffuse nature of the organization was not surprising: Musumbu had little experience as a commander, and the large area he controlled had few roads and no cell phone coverage. One former Raia Mutomboki member from the area recalled his limited leadership role:

> Musumbu went from village to village in those early days, talking to local chiefs and spreading the word. He named a commander in each village, after speaking with local chiefs, but he didn't really control them. He was powerful because of the magic that he spread.[15]

The traditional structure of Rega society was also crucial in shaping the internal structure of the Raia Mutomboki. The Rega are the dominant ethnic group in Shabunda and parts of southern Walikale, Mwenga, and eastern Maniema. They traditionally live as a decentralized society—anthropologists often use the terms *segmented* or *acephalous*— in which chiefs rarely have influence outside of a cluster of several villages. In pre-colonial society, authority resided largely with clan chiefs whose position was not hereditary and who shared power with other local moral and political authorities.[16]

During colonial rule, the Belgians created hereditary positions of customary rule, including the *chef de village, chef de localité, chef de groupement,* and *chef de collectivité.* Today, however, it is still the lineage chiefs and, in some cases, the *chefs de village* who retain customary power and are the most influential in rural areas. When Musumbu began recruiting soldiers, it was these leaders who threw their weight behind him in the southern part of Shabunda, encouraging youths to join and authorizing food collections. But the segmented nature of Rega society also contributed to keeping the groups decentralized and difficult to control. By 2007, Musumbu's group had largely disappeared. One local leader who knew Musumbu told me: "There were still youths clustered around Musumbu, but they were mostly reservists—they only had a few old Kalashnikovs. The rest were local hunters or farmers."[17]

Over the next four years, the scattered, sporadic re-emergence of the Raia Mutomboki was linked to opportunistic military and political entrepreneurs who sought to use the Raia Mutomboki brand for their individual benefit. While these leaders tried to harness local discontent, they contrasted with other Raia Mutomboki in that they were less rooted in local communities and tried to impose more hierarchical forms of organization.

As argued in previous chapters, this rise of a military bourgeoisie was linked to political and social developments at the national level. The 2002 peace deal had created a new class of disgruntled officers. Participation in insurgencies had become a bargaining device for frustrated officers who wanted better ranks and positions; some of them supported or created Raia Mutomboki groups.

Another impetus came from the national government, which was eager to forge alliances against the CNDP. The trend became most clearly visible during the Goma Peace Conference in early 2008, when Kinshasa encouraged the participation of many friendly armed groups—some of which had been created from scratch for the occasion—to dilute the CNDP's influence.

Among the representatives at the Goma Peace Conference were two alleged members of the Raia Mutomboki, Sadiki Kangalaba Devos and Salumu Kaseke, who signed the Actes d'engagement, the peace deal that resulted from the Goma Peace Conference. According to customary chiefs and civil society leaders, however, these representatives did not have Musumbu's blessing or that of other Raia Mutomboki commanders. "They signed the agreement, took their per diems, and then disappeared," said one Congolese intelligence officer involved in the conference.[18]

The opportunism did not stop there. In Shabunda it became fashionable to name armed groups Raia Mutomboki because that label implied popular support and legitimacy. A telling example was a militia that was mobilized by former Mai-Mai fighters and allied politicians between 2006 and 2010. The group was launched by Misaba Bwansolo, better known as Mwami Alexandre, who had been a Mai-Mai commander during the war against the RCD. Alexandre launched a new armed group in southern Shabunda in 2006, only to be arrested a year later by the Congolese army and sentenced to prison for recruiting child soldiers.[19]

Alexandre's insurgency was followed by that of Kyatend Dittman, a Rega musician who had been living in Germany since the 1980s. In 2003, he returned to the Congo to try his hand at local politics.[20] He launched a music group, the Armée rouge ("Red Army"), and became involved on the board of Bukavu's OC Muungano soccer team, which is popular within the Rega community.[21] In November 2006, Kyatend was ousted from the presidency of the OC Muungano club and, increasingly marginalized within the community, tried reviving the militia set up by Alexandre in Shabunda, starting in early 2007. He achieved only modest success, although from 2009 onwards he benefited from the active support of Alexandre, who had escaped from prison in Bukavu.

Kyatend's group often went by the name of Raia Mutomboki, although its legitimacy was contested by Musumbu.[22] It was based in a mineral-rich area around Kitindi in southeastern Shabunda, undoubtedly attracted by the profits to be made from taxing and trading gold and tin in the region. The local customary chief, Mwami Muligi V, supported this group, as he would later support other Raia Mutomboki factions. While some said this was due to a succession struggle, Muligi V himself insists it was out of concern for the local population.[23]

Kyatend's militia fell apart when the Congolese army arrested Muligi V in 2010. When the latter called on young people in his *chefferie* (chiefdom) to turn in their weapons, only twelve were handed over to the FARDC, probably an indication of how small the group was. The local population then captured Kyatend and handed him over to the government. Both Kyatend and Alexandre were imprisoned in June 2010.[24]

The Expansion of the Raia Mutomboki (2009–12)

Before 2011, very few people in the eastern Congo knew of the Raia Mutomboki. Security problems in Shabunda barely registered as a national priority for the government, the United Nations, or donor nations. Their reappearance and rapid expansion were sparked by the side effects of the treatment of the CNDP insurgency by the government and the international community.

After the deal between Kinshasa and Kigali in late 2008, CNDP troops were integrated into the national army, and the FARDC launched a series of offensives against the FDLR, code-named Umoja Wetu ("Our Unity," 2009), Kimia II ("Peace II," 2009–2010), and Amani Leo ("Peace Today," 2010–2012).

This deal was widely hailed by foreign diplomats for bringing an end to the CNDP insurgency and mending ties between the Democratic Republic of the Congo and Rwanda. But in solving some problems, it created others. The 2008 deal was skewed in favor of the CNDP and its main rival, the Coalition des patriotes résistants congolais (PARECO, Alliance of Resistant Congolese Patriots), which created resentment among officers in rival militias. The joint operations against the FDLR—one of the conditions of the peace deal— also sparked considerable insecurity in rural areas. The growing insecurity, coupled with anti-rwandophone resentment, sparked the revival of the Raia Mutomboki.

In 2009 alone, when the FARDC carried out a poorly planned counterinsurgency offensive, operations against the FDLR displaced over eight hundred thousand people. In many areas, the government employed local militiamen and hunters as guides and trackers who provided crucial information about FDLR positions. These included some former FDLR allies who would later join the Raia Mutomboki, such as the Mai-Mai Kifuafua in southern Masisi. Their support for FARDC operations would later lead to brutal retaliation by the FDLR. "The army rattled the hornet's nest and then left us to face the consequences," a local chief from northern Shabunda lamented.[25]

Beginning around May 2011, all Congolese army units based in Shabunda territory left to join the regimentation process, which was supposed to streamline the Congolese army's organization by getting rid of fictitious soldiers, undercutting patronage networks, and breaking up the parallel chains of command maintained by ex-CNDP troops.[26] This left Shabunda territory—with its lucrative trade routes and mining areas—unprotected. The FDLR took advantage of this security vacuum, moving into mining areas and carrying out raids in villages previously controlled by the Congolese army. This triggered the scattered remobilization of the Raia Mutomboki throughout Shabunda, in the three main following areas.

Musumbu remained the focal point of the first group, based between Kalole and Penekusu in the Wakabango chiefdom of southern Shabunda. Ironically, his earlier success in getting rid of FDLR in the area kept mobilization to a minimum. "The Mutomboki were always meant as a response to a security problem," said one local chief who knows Musumbu. "In Wakabango I, the security problem had largely disappeared, so not many youths took up arms."[27]

The second Raia Mutomboki group—which would become the most significant military force—was based in Nduma, along the edge of the Kahuzi-Biéga National Park in northern Shabunda. This area had a scattering of mining areas and an FDLR military base that included a training camp, schools, and health centers for their dependents.[28] Albert Mutima Muba, the group's chief of staff, told me about a pivotal incident that took place in Nduma in January 2010: "The FDLR killed thirty-six people in Nduma, they buried people alive, they made them eat cassiterite [tin ore], or tied them to the trees or beat them to death. Three of these miners survived and came to tell us about the massacre. But when we went to tell the Congolese army, they arrested us! They made us pay a fine of $100 to set us free.[29]

The massacre and the FARDC's response catalyzed local outrage and led to the mobilization of a self-defense group. To make matters worse, the population's security concerns were mocked during a visit by the South Kivu governor, Marcellin Cisambo, to Shabunda in July 2011. Replying to a question in a town hall meeting about the withdrawal of Congolese troops, he reportedly replied dismissively: "Liberate yourselves!"[30]

The local population took up his call, although not in the way the governor probably intended. According to one version of events, Eyadema Mugugu, a young mineral trader from Nduma who had been one of Musumbu's followers, traveled to southern Shabunda to get advice and the magical *dawa* from his former leader.[31] Eyadema proceeded to mobilize networks of demobilized combatants and artisanal miners claiming, initially at least, that the main motivation was self-defense. Mutima, an elderly man who was previously the principal of the high school in nearby Nyambembe, described his own experience:

> Major Cimanuka [an FDLR commander] came to Nyambembe and demanded [from the population of Nyambembe, Tchonka, and Lulingu] $10,000 and thirty goats from the local population in July 2011 for "reconciliation." The population gave him this, but then he went and pillaged the village anyway. He said the government had given the east to the Rwandans, that this was theirs now. I was there! I was a teacher at the local school. I contributed six thousand Congolese francs, all teachers got together $30. But this was not enough! They came back to pillage the village and burn it down.[32]

The Raia Mutomboki under Eyadema were able to accomplish what the Congolese army had been unable to achieve: by early 2012 they had chased out almost all of the remaining FDLR from northern Shabunda.

The third group that appeared in Shabunda was the most opportunistic and internally fragmented. It was launched initially by Rega Congolese army officers who were upset by their treatment. The defectors
mostly came from the 11th Integrated Brigade, which included an entire
battalion of officers without jobs, the so-called *battalion cadre,* created
by the Congolese army as a place for officers who did not have the connections, education, or physical fitness needed to obtain more lucrative
deployments. "It was ridiculous," one of the officers in the battalion
remembered. "Lieutenants and captains were foot soldiers, majors were
platoon commanders. It was humiliating."[33] Among them were several
Rega Mai-Mai officers who believed that they had been marginalized
because of their ethnicity by the former Mai-Mai leader General Padiri,
who came from Bunyakiri and was a Tembo. "Just look at the army. We
fought for Padiri, but he rejected us as soon as he went to Kinshasa. Are
there any high-ranking Rega in the army who could help us? No!"[34]

Those who sympathized with these officers argue that their mistreatment prompted their defection. Several sources suggest that the
Lega-Lusu *mutuelle,* an ethnic community organization based in Bukavu,
encouraged these officers to return to Shabunda to protect the population from the FDLR during regimentation.[35] According to the Congolese army, however, there was another factor: many of the deserters
were fleeing arrest warrants issued by military tribunals.[36]

The first to defect was Lieutenant Musolwa Kangela, who went to
Mulungu in early 2011. He was followed by several other officers, the
most prominent being Major Donat Kengwa Omari and Major Ngandu
Lundimu. While these officers did not defect together, by late 2012 most
of them had gathered in northeastern Shabunda, close to their villages
of origin.

That many of the FARDC commanders operating in this area were
Congolese Hutu or Tutsi—largely a result of the integrated of the CNDP
and PARECO—further inflamed relations. Almost all of the FARDC
regiment commanders deployed to Shabunda in 2011 and 2012 were
from these communities, as was the deputy commander of operations
for South Kivu, Colonel Innocent Kabundi, and the military region

commander, General Pacifique Masunzu. Shabunda had witnessed a brutal occupation by RCD soldiers, many of whose leaders were Tutsi, between 1998 and 2003. It had also been the site of massacres by Rwandan troops in 1997.[37] In October 2011, Major Donat, addressing the population in Tshonka, said that he would only welcome non-rwandophone FARDC troops in Shabunda territory.[38]

Two other local combatants joined the diffuse cluster of ex-FARDC commanders: Wangozi Pascal, otherwise known as Sisawa, and Daniel Meshe. By most accounts, Sisawa was a former miner and young rank-and-file soldier working with Eyadema who struck out on his own.[39] He had two main assets: his mother was a well-known *muganga* with powerful *dawa*, and he was a valiant fighter, "always to be found on the front lines during military operations," as one civil society leader put it.[40] Meshe, on the other hand, had stumbled into militia politics almost by accident. A former member of President Laurent Kabila's entourage, he had left for Germany after Kabila's assassination in 2001. He returned in 2011 to mine gold in his home village, Mulanga, in northeastern Shabunda. Failing in that endeavor, in part due to the insecurity caused by the FDLR, he decided to launch his own armed group. Lacking military experience but prone to boasting about his elite networks and education, he quickly allied himself to Sisawa.

Expansion into Kalehe and Clashes with the FARDC (2011–12)

Despite its lack of cohesion, there is little doubt about the success of the Raia Mutomboki in Shabunda. By the end of 2011, they had pushed the FDLR out of many of their previous strongholds, confining them to a few positions in the far east of the territory.[41] This success propelled the Raia Mutomboki beyond its initial ethnic and territorial confines.

It was Eyadema's group that proved to be the most zealous and efficient at expanding its reach. By September 2011, there were reports of Raia Mutomboki activity in North Kivu's southern Walikale territory, where early the following year, Eyadema's chief of staff had arrived "in hot pursuit of the FDLR," as a local civil society activist put it.[42] By the end of the year, the Raia Mutomboki were moving southwards into Kalehe territory.[43]

Success and expansion created challenges for the Raia Mutomboki. For the first time it moved into areas inhabited largely by other ethnic communities where armed groups were already active or where a tradition of armed resistance had developed. Yet these barriers did not stop the movement. In FDLR-affected areas, the movement was enthusiastically welcomed by the general population and by demobilized Mai-Mai combatants, for whom the new arrivals presented an opportunity to improve their own position.

As the armed group spread into Kalehe territory, it became enmeshed in local power struggles, further complicating the security situation. Here the movement was transformed from a scattering of loosely connected self-defense groups into a better structured armed movement that became closely connected with, and involved in, local power dynamics.

One key factor in Kalehe was the presence of hundreds of demobilized soldiers. This area, where the movement arrived in January 2012, had been the bastion of the Padiri Mai-Mai, one of the largest and most formidable Mai-Mai groups in the country between 1996 and 2003. When the war officially ended, many combatants had returned to civilian life but had few opportunities. As one of them recalled:

> I was a simple soldier for Padiri. When the war was over, I went home and was demobilized. I got $200 and bought a motorcycle. When that broke down and I didn't have money to fix it, I carried cassiterite across the mountain for a *négociant* for $50 a month, but I had to pay $10 in taxes to the FDLR and the FARDC. CONADER [the demobilization commission] said they would give us jobs, but they never did, they said they ran out of money. So when the Raia Mutomboki came, I volunteered.[44]

Bunyakiri had long been an important transit point for the FDLR, who visited markets on the Bukavu-Walikale road and had a liaison position in Hombo through which they traveled from North Kivu to South Kivu. The strategic importance of the area for them, along with the presence of Rwandan refugees whom they were protecting, made for bloody confrontations with the Raia Mutomboki. In an initial operation in January 2012 in the forest of Mangaa, the Raia Mutomboki destroyed an entire FDLR village and massacred its inhabitants. On their return to Kalonge, the Raia Mutomboki fell into an ambush and their two leaders were killed. This immediately boosted recruitment into their ranks in Bunyakiri, the home of the two leaders. Mobilization was fueled by a vicious—or, as local leaders had it, a virtuous—cycle: Raia Mutomboki attacks inflicted considerable losses on the FDLR, which prompted retaliation, which fueled further mobilization.

In January 2012, for example, the FDLR killing of thirteen civilians in Lumendje led local youths to take up arms;[45] in a revenge attack, more than 20 FDLR members were killed. On May 14, 2012, the FDLR killed more than thirty civilians in Kamananga, a village on the road from Bunyakiri to Hombo.

By the end of July 2012, the Raia Mutomboki were active over a vast area that stretched from southern Shabunda to southern Masisi, a distance that would take two weeks to walk. Once the FDLR was flushed out of Bunyakiri, Raia Mutomboki combatants started to patrol openly in larger villages, first hesitantly and only at night, but then later also during the day.

In early 2013, the Raia Mutomboki movement was confronted with various divisions in Kalehe and Walikale as a result of growing tensions between Rega commanders and Tembo recruits over the movement's strategy, its impact on local society, and competition between former Mai-Mai commanders and new recruits for leadership positions.

ETHNIC VIOLENCE IN MASISI (2012–13)

What was probably the bloodiest chapter in Raia Mutomboki history unfolded in southern Masisi between April and September 2012, as the battle between the Raia Mutomboki and the FDLR moved into areas inhabited by a large Congolese Hutu population. Here, the Raia Mutomboki's tactics, accentuated by long-standing communal tensions, resulted in the massacre of over two hundred people. A report by the

UN's Office for the High Commissioner for Human Rights, the most reliable investigation of the violence in southern Masisi during this time, suggests that this probably underestimates the number of deaths.[46]

Southwestern Masisi had been an FDLR bastion for many years. They had their main headquarters here, and many of their families lived in these remote and fertile hills. It was a strategic area, given its proximity to South Kivu and to the mineral-rich areas of Walikale and Kalehe. Most important, there was a very large Congolese Hutu population in these areas, and the FDLR had established alliances with local Hutu elites and militia.

The arrival of the Raia Mutomboki in this area upset a delicate balance that had been established over the previous decade. Southern Masisi—especially the *groupements* of Ufamandu I and II and of Nyamaboko I and II—is more ethnically mixed than the rest of the territory, with large Tembo and Hunde populations often in conflict with the Hutu and Tutsi communities. The latter are perceived as immigrants, with many arriving only in the 1970s from overpopulated parts of Masisi, as well as from Goma after a volcano erupted there in 1977.[47] Customary power in this area lies in the hands of the Hunde and Tembo, who consider themselves to be indigenous, which makes many Hutu anxious over their claims to land.

Militarily, however, the area had been relatively united until the arrival of the Raia Mutomboki. Hutu militia collaborated with the FDLR, as did the Mai-Mai Kifuafua, who are predominantly Tembo and who control much of Ufamandu I and II *groupements*. "We had no choice," Limenzi "Bridge-Cutter" Kanganga, the deputy commander of the Kifuafua, told me. The FDLR were "too strong."[48]

With the arrival of the Raia Mutomboki, the balance of forces shifted, as Rega commanders convinced the Tembo to join them in their battle against the Hutu rebels. This change became visible in Chambucha, a village in southern Walikale territory, when the Raia Mutomboki began preparing for their entry into Tembo territory by crossing the Bukavu-Kisangani road in pursuit of the FDLR. On April 20, 2012, the FDLR invited local Tembo chiefs and Kifuafua commanders to a meeting in Karaba, southern Walikale. According to one participant, the FDLR commander presiding over the meeting said: "We have fought the Raia Mutomboki in Shabunda for a year now. We know them and the troubles they will bring here. Know that if you join them, it will bring you nothing but death and destruction."[49]

This standoff did not last long. On April 28, 2012, the FDLR attacked Chambucha, allegedly in response to the killing of FDLR dependents in Shalio, triggering a massive recruitment of young Tembo into the Raia Mutomboki. "All the kids from our village went to Katatwa, where the Rega had their *dawa*, and were initiated into the movement," one village elder in Chambucha remembered. "We couldn't control them. The Kifuafua couldn't control them. It was like a frenzy."[50]

The Kifuafua quickly followed suit and changed their name to Raia Mutomboki. "The FDLR didn't trust us, they thought we were Raia Mutomboki," said Limenzi, "and the local youths all wanted us to fight against [the FDLR]."[51] Interviews with local elders, however, suggest that the top Kifuafua leadership under Colonel Delphin Mbaenda saw an opportunity in the Raia Mutomboki to enhance their reputation, pad their ranks with new recruits, and increase their military power with a new kind of magical bracelet. "Delphin took the *dawa* because it was a craze here, all the youths wanted to have it to be able to fight," one of them said.[52] Delphin delegated his own son to become one of the witch doctors deployed with the Raia Mutomboki troops in the area. Two commanders who refused to support the group were forced out of the Kifuafua.

After the initial altercation in Chambucha, the Raia Mutomboki spread quickly into Masisi, burning many villages settled by Hutu.[53] The violence was compounded by the Congolese army's decision in April 2012 to withdraw its troops from this area to reinforce their positions against the M23 rebellion in Rutshuru and northern Masisi. Much as it had in Shabunda during the regimentation process, FARDC withdrawal produced a vacuum that other armed groups sought to fill.

The Raia Mutomboki offensive reinforced collaboration between Rwandan and Congolese Hutu armed groups, as the FDLR joined forces with the Nyatura, a mostly Hutu militia based in the highlands of Kalehe and Masisi led by deserters from the Congolese army.[54]

Abuses were committed on both sides; a UN investigation concluded that while the Raia Mutomboki attacked with the specific intent of killing civilians, the FDLR/Nyatura coalition burned villages and killed at least 143 civilians between April and October 2012.[55]

The group's ideology was not always consistent. Many Raia Mutomboki commanders and soldiers told me that they were fighting against Tutsi and Hutu domination of the eastern Congo and that the FDLR and the M23 were all part of the same foreign conspiracy. However, in 2012 the Raia Mutomboki of southern Masisi began to collaborate with Colonel Eric Badege, a Tutsi M23 commander who defected from the FARDC in late July 2012. Badege traveled to southern Masisi, where he contacted local Raia Mutomboki and Kifuafua commanders to convince them that they both had the same Hutu enemies and that he would help them find arms caches that the CNDP had left behind near Ngungu. Several sources report that officers close to Badege had laid the groundwork for his defection and collaboration with Tembo leaders earlier in the year, not least by providing the latter with weapons and ammunition.[56] These leaders were further swayed by cash incentives as well as by Hutu militia who had begun to join forces with the FDLR against the Raia Mutomboki. "For the Tembo, the priority was fighting against the Hutu. If they had to ally briefly with the M23 to do so, that was acceptable," observed a local civil society leader.[57]

Over the ensuing years, the Raia Mutomboki would continue to splinter and spread, skirmishing with the FARDC but only rarely the focus of major military offensives. By late 2017, they had chased the FDLR out of most of Shabunda, Kalehe, and Walikale territories, and the Raia Mutomboki's rhetoric shifted toward opposition against the FARDC and the Congolese government.

By 2020, there were twenty-six Raia Mutomboki groups that were still active, managed largely by many of the same leaders—or, in the case of splinter groups, by other senior commanders—as those who had started them years prior. Their area of influence had declined slightly, as the groups in the southern part of North Kivu fizzled out due to competition with the many other armed groups there. However, much of Bunyakiri, western Walungu and Kabare, and Shabunda territories—an area roughly the size of Massachusetts—were still under their influence.

Analysis

When one arrives in Raia Mutomboki territory, the links between the armed group and surrounding society are striking; in fact, it is often difficult to pinpoint where the armed group ends and civil society begins. "We are all Raia Mutomboki," a group of village elders gathering in a church in Kigulube told me. "They are our children, they are fighting for us."[58] Outside under a palm tree, a primary school teacher recounted: "When they launch on operation, over half of their combatants are peasants who leave the fields, take their machetes, and join the youths."[59]

In Hombo, fifty miles north of Kigulube as the crow flies, the head of the local radio station pulled his sleeve back to show me the telltale amulet around his biceps. "We have all been initiated into Raia Mutomboki," he boasted. He gave me his interpretation of why it was so popular: "It's not some corrupt politician, or some militia commander claiming he is going to help you. It's the people."[60] Later, a local Raia Mutomboki commander confided over a bottle of beer: "Most of my troops are reservists." When I asked him what he meant, he said: "They are civilians. Farmers, teachers, shop owners, motorcycle drivers. When we launch an operation, they all come."[61]

The Social Constituency

The relations between the Raia Mutomboki and local society varied considerably over time and space. During the initial period, which resembled a "craze" (*folie*) or "epidemic," in the words of many locals, the influence of customary chiefs, local *notables* (civic leaders), and religious leaders was apparent. As one Protestant minister in Shabunda told me: "When the Mutomboki first arrived here, everyone joined, and its real force was that our community was united in protecting ourselves against the FDLR, chasing them out."[62]

This populist, acephalous nature of the rebellion was initially shaped by two factors: the spiritual nature of the group and the impending threat of FDLR attacks. In Kigulube and Hombo, the two places where I conducted fieldwork on the group, the importance of *dawa* was obvious. All the soldiers I met had been "vaccinated," as the local parlance had it. More tellingly, even civilians who did not belong to the Raia Mutomboki had sought out amulets, and the nearby FARDC were obviously nervous about testing their efficacy.

The power of the *dawa* had an impact on the structure of the group. It was not only the military commander of the group who held power but the witch doctor who knew how to concoct the *dawa*. Even he, according to two focus groups of combatants that I convened in each place, was limited in his power, for they believed the ultimate power lay in the *dawa* itself, being derived from ancestral spirits. "No one can tell us what to do here. We are all in charge, because the *dawa* is in charge," a young combatant in Hombo told me.[63]

The use of the *dawa* and the invocation of tradition drew heavily on initiation rites in the local community, in particular the *lutende* ceremony, also called *yando*. Traditionally this was a coming-of-age ceremony for men, performed at puberty prior to circumcision and lasting several months in both Tembo and Rega communities. It was revived by the Raia Mutomboki with the help of customary chiefs and was transformed into a ritual, lasting only a few days but essential for entering the group and being protected against the enemy by the *dawa*. One customary chief explained: "In the *yando* ceremony, the youths hear the voice of Kimbilikiti, our spirit, who is the same spirit who makes the *dawa* strong. That's why the Raia Mutomboki are also called Force Ntakulengwe, which means: 'Get out of the way, Kimbilikiti is coming!'"[64]

In contrast to the armed groups that previously operated in the area, the Raia Mutomboki was initially an open movement in which people could stay or leave as they pleased, a relatively egalitarian movement with clear prescriptions of conduct within the group but with little command structure or hierarchy. In several areas around Bunyakiri, the local population gathered to elect their own commanders by popular acclamation when the armed group was first formed.[65] The spoils of conflict were often distributed equally among combatants.

However, this initial egalitarianism soon petered out. Broadly speaking, in areas where customary chiefs had tenuous influence over the local population, in particular in Shabunda, the emergence of the Raia Mutomboki empowered youths and quickly became an autonomous movement. In Bunyakiri, where customary chiefs—especially the *chefs de groupement*—had more control, the Raia Mutomboki were more easily incorporated into existing governing structures. In Walikale, the Mai-Mai Kifuafua was already well established, and it briefly changed its name to Raia Mutomboki. However, because the group had already existed, its relationship with the local population did not change, and there was less spontaneous mobilization for military operations than elsewhere.

Over time, in all three places, the Raia Mutomboki distanced itself from the local population as its internal structures coalesced and abuses increased.

A general crisis of local governance contributed to this. As mentioned above, Rega society in Shabunda is known for its acephalous, segmented nature. The lack of local leaders has been exacerbated throughout the war, as customary chiefs have left many remote areas to move to towns. I traveled to Kigulube with two *chefs de clan*, who had considerable legitimacy there but had been forced by security problems to live in Bukavu. It was clear in their interactions with the local population, and with the Raia Mutomboki in particular, that while respected, they had little sway over the armed group. Their attitude toward the Raia Mutomboki was a mixture of disapproval and fear. On one occasion, a chief tried to intercede to prevent a drunk combatant from stealing from a local trader and was almost himself shot. "They have no respect for their elders," he told me.[66] The other chief explained it thus:

> There has been a breakdown of customary rule here. Back in the old days, the *chef de clan* had real power at the local level. Then, under the Belgian colony, they imposed new chiefs we had never seen before, which messed things up. Those are the *chefs de groupement* and

collectivité. Now, during the war, no one has been able to be active at the local level. Those who are, they are bought off by politicians. So these youths operate without any elders to watch over them.

In Bunyakiri, in contrast, the Rega commanders arriving from Shabunda began by eliciting support from customary chiefs, starting in Kalonge. While Tembo customary authority is also in turmoil—there are many succession disputes, and local chiefs are caught between state administrative officials and armed groups—the *chefs de groupement* in particular retain considerable sway. They played a pivotal role in recruiting youth into the movement, organizing popular rallies to explain the objectives of the movement and to mobilize potential fighters.

Throughout these early days in Bunyakiri, customary chiefs, recognized by the group as the real political authorities, were regularly requested to give advice. In some cases, they became the local representatives of the Raia Mutomboki. They also provided the group with direct logistical support and resources, albeit clandestinely. According to local sources, the Raia Mutomboki in the Buloho *chefferie* were even given the customary right to collect taxes from the local population.[67]

This close relationship between customary chiefs and insurgents, however, also caused problems. In many areas of the Kivus, the RCD had named its own customary chiefs during the Second Congo War (1998–2003), sometimes from within an incumbent's family, creating persistent feuds. Elsewhere, conflicts had arisen due to succession struggles following the death of a chief. The Raia Mutomboki began to take sides in these conflicts, setting the stage for potentially brutal internecine altercations.

One example was the case of Kalima *groupement* in Kalehe, where the former chief, Jacques Musikami Nzibiro II, supported the Raia Mutomboki as a tactic in his struggle to regain power. Although he had been designated as chief in his father's will, he was removed by customary elders, who favored his younger brother, Jean-Claude Musikami Ngalamira. The Raia Mutomboki were divided over the issue. Many demobilized Mai-Mai combatants joined the faction supporting Ngalamira, who during the Congolese war had been loyal to Padiri's

Mai-Mai, while others sided with Nzibiro. Such militarization of customary conflicts over succession became a matter of great concern for the population.

There are many other cases in which the Raia Mutomboki have become embroiled in local conflicts, thereby complicating or eroding their support from local society. As one observer stated, "The Raia Mutomboki have already transformed themselves into judges, administrators, police, and local chiefs and are themselves addressing the problems of the local population."[68] While initially the population contributed voluntarily to the movement, these contributions quickly became obligatory, putting the group in conflict with local administrators and, at times, customary chiefs. In the opinion of one local administrator: "The Raia Mutomboki helped us with the FDLR, that is true. But I am afraid that they solved one problem by creating twenty others."[69]

Besides the customary chiefs, two other broad constituencies of local society were often represented among the Raia Mutomboki, although not in a structured fashion: artisanal miners and demobilized soldiers (see table 8.1). In these instances, representation varied depending on the location. In northeastern Shabunda, for example, there is a lot of artisanal gold mining, especially around the remote town of Mulungu. Several prominent Raia Mutomboki leaders, such as Makombo Walike and Natalis, had been artisanal miners or traders. Natalis said he joined the Raia Mutomboki after the FDLR stole his stash of gold,[70] a similar motive for that of Daniel Meshe's initial involvement in the armed group. According to one local chief: "Meshe came here [a mining site close to Chulwe] and began digging for gold. He didn't find as much as he wanted, and then the FDLR began attacking his diggers, taxing them and stealing gold. Eventually, he took up weapons and called himself Mutomboki."[71]

This may also have been the motivation of the group of Eyadema, based in northern Shabunda. There, the violence that prompted the initial mobilization occurred in a tin mining concession in Nduma, and many of the victims were miners.

There were temporal as well as geographic shifts in the constituencies of Raia Mutomboki groups. As a group coalesced and became a more

TABLE 7.1. Raia Mutomboki leaders, 2011–2014

Name	Place	Rank/Position	Background
Bimpenzi	Eastern Shabunda (Mulungu)	Commander, local RM branch	Unknown
Makombo	Southeastern Shabunda (Lubila)	Deputy commander, Musumbu RM branch	Traditional healer (*muganga*)
Natalis	Southeastern Shabunda (Lubila)	Commander, Musumbu RM branch	Former artisanal miner
Sisawa Kindo	Northeastern Shabunda (Kigulube)	Commander, local RM branch	Former Mai-Mai
Daniel Meshe	Northeastern Shabunda (Kigulube)	Commander, local RM branch	Former mineral trader, spent time in Europe
Ngandu Lundimu	Northeastern Shabunda (Nzovu)	Commander, local RM branch	Former major in FARDC, former Mai-Mai
Donat Kengwa	Northeastern Shabunda (Nzovu)	Commander, local RM branch	Former major in FARDC, former Mai-Mai
Maheshe	Eastern Shabunda (Chulwe)	Deputy commander, local RM branch	Former Mai-Mai
Juriste Kikuni	Northern Shabunda (Nduma)	Commander, RM branch (took over from Eyadema)	University dropout, former mineral trader
Albert Muba	Bunyakiri (Kambale)	Chief of staff, Kikuni RM branch	Former secondary school teacher
Bwaare Hamakombo	Bunyakiri (Bulambika)	Local commander, Kikuni RM branch	Former Mai-Mai
Imani Byataa	Kalonge	Local commander, RM branch	Former Mai-Mai
Malinda Lukisa Limenzi	Bunyakiri (Mubughu)	Local commander, RM branch	Customary chief and former Mai-Mai
Munyarakengwa Enaburondo	Bunyakiri (Buloho)	Local commander, RM branch	Unknown
Batumali Muchumbi	Bunyakiri (Bitale)	Local commander, RM branch	Unknown
Chika Matengete	Bunyakiri (Lubengera)	Local commander, RM branch	Unknown
Jacques Lubula	Bunyakiri (Mulonge)	Local commander, RM branch	Former Mai-Mai, member of family of customary chief
Ngubire Chitemi	Bunyakiri (Musenyi)	Local commander, RM branch	Customary chief

sophisticated military organization, its relations with society changed. "Every village needs a chief; every rebellion needs a command," Eyadema's chief of staff Mutima said on a visit to Bunyakiri, where he was attempting to set up a local hierarchy. "We needed to make sure that discipline was maintained."[72] While at the start of the movement in Kalehe it was difficult to distinguish Raia Mutomboki members from the rest of the population, beginning in the summer of 2012 a series of command posts were set up, with commanders either from Shabunda or recruited locally from former Mai-Mai combatants.

Fragmentation

Articles by scholars and researchers about the Raia Mutomboki use descriptors such as "weakly organized and highly decentralized" and a "fluid and flat organization."[73] While these phrases accurately depict the internal structure of the Raia Mutomboki groups, there was significant variation among them. All of the "new" groups—the ones that did not, like the Kifuafua, exist before and just changed their name—were initially relatively egalitarian, with little internal differentiation and a high degree of decentralization. Musumbu's group, for example, did not initially have ranks, and there were no commanders, just members.[74] Musumbu himself was said to have just provided the *dawa* and retained little control over the other leaders. Even in other groups that had obvious leaders and commanders, such as Kikuni's group, there was initially little internal organization. Kikuni's chief of staff told me: "The Raia Mutomboki is a popular uprising. This meant that there was no boss, no leader at the beginning, it was just the population. This eventually became a problem for us. Every movement needs a leader. So we began naming leaders, but we didn't give them ranks. We didn't want to reproduce the love of names and ranks that the FARDC have."[75]

The attempts to develop hierarchies were limited by persistent infighting within the Raia and their inability to forge strong networks. The Raia Mutomboki in Bunyakiri, for example, which started out as one group in 2012, had split into five largely autonomous factions by 2015. Similarly, the five main groups in Shabunda split into nine groups by 2015 and eighteen groups by 2017.

TABLE 7.2. Raia Mutomboki groups, 2012–2020

Territory	2012 RM Groups	2015 RM Groups	2017 RM Groups	2020 RM Groups
Shabunda/ Walikale	RM Eyadema/Kikuni	RM Takulengwa	RM Takulengwa	RM Kazimoto
		RM Donat/Ngandu	RM Donat/ Ngandu	RM FPP-Donat
	RM Donat/Ngandu	RM Makombo		RM Walike
	RM Natalis/Makombo	RM Sisawa		
	RM Sisawa			
	RM Musumbu			RM Musumbu
		RM Maheshe	RM Maheshe	RM 100kg
		RM Kashungushungu		
		RM Ndarumanga	Rm Ndarumanga	RM Ndarumanga
		RM Akilo	RM Akilo	
		RM Mirage	RM Mirage	
		RM Elenge	RM Elenge	
			RM Kabazimia	RM Kabazimia
			RM Kikwama	
			RM Kimba	RM Kimba
			RM Kisekelwa	
			RM Mabala	RM Mabala
			RM Machite	
			RM Mamba	
			RM Shebitembe	
			RM Shemakingi	
			RM Wemba	
				RM Musolwa
				RM Makindu
				RM Charles Quint
				RM Kabé
				RM Bozi
				RM LeFort
Kalehe	RM Eyadema/Kikuni			
		RM Hamakombo	RM Hamakombo	RM Hamakombo
		RM Musole	RM Musole	
		RM Shukuru	RM Shukuru	
		RM Mweeke	RM Shabani	RM Shabani
		RM Butachibera	RM Butachibera	RM Butachibera
		RM Mweeke		
		RM Imani Bitaa	RM Imani Bitaa	
				RM Soleil
	RM Kirikicho	Mai-Mai Kirikicho	Mai-Mai Kirikicho	
		RM Mungoro	RM Mungoro	RM Mungoro
			RM Bipompa	RM Bipompa

Continued on next page

TABLE 7.2. (*continued*)

Territory	2012 RM Groups	2015 RM Groups	2017 RM Groups	2020 RM Groups
			RM Kabanzi	
			RM Manyiisa	
			RM Safari	
Kabare		RM Blaise	RM Blaise	RM Blaise
		RM Gaston		RM Lance
				Muteya
			RM Lukoba	RM Lukoba
				RM Bralima

Note: Groups on the same row are related to each other, often factions of former groups.

What was behind this fragmentation? There did not seem to be the problem of a surfeit of resources attracting opportunists, at least not as Jeremy Weinstein has argued in his analysis of rebellions elsewhere in Africa.[76] While there were indeed some artisanal miners who joined to gain control of mining concessions, interviews with both the population and Raia Mutomboki leaders indicate that the groups were generally very poor and had little revenue other than taxes from the local population.[77] On the other hand, the *dawa* became a resource that provided an initial boost to the movement, but the initial enthusiasm later became one source of weakness. Almost all the groups—with the exception of the Raia Mutomboki of southeastern Walikale, which was simply a rebranded version of the Mai-Mai Kifuafua—expanded so quickly that they had no time to vet, train, or educate their members, failing to inculcate the sense of trust and reciprocity that is the key to collective action.[78] In other words, the rapid growth was one of the main challenges the groups had to face.

Local leaders pointed out another, related weakness of the movement. "The Rega were not meant to produce big groups," one customary chief in Kigulube said. "We never had kingdoms; our strength is in small, local initiatives. We are not elephants. We are ants. Ants can devour elephants, but they will never be big like elephants."[79] This contrast between segmented and centralized societies is well known in anthropology.[80] While it has not, to my knowledge, been drawn on in the analysis of social movements or armed groups, this analysis suggests that armed groups will reproduce the cleavages of the society out of which they emerge.[81]

The Interests of the Raia Mutomboki

As with many local militia forces in the eastern Congo, the Raia Mutomboki are motivated by a complex mixture of opportunism and genuine outrage, a drive for self-empowerment and communal protection against a rapacious state and outsiders. These emotions are layered onto a long tradition of armed mobilization that has generated behavioral repertoires, providing accessible templates for underemployed youths.

In my several dozen interviews with Raia Mutomboki members, the answer to "Why are you fighting?" was almost always the same. "We are here to protect our population against those who come to oppress us [*benye banatugandamiza*]," the commander of a unit in Bunyakiri told me.[82] Very often, the identity of those oppressors has a distinct ethnic shading. Initially, the Raia Mutomboki saw the FDLR as its main enemy, but for some that quickly became all Kinyarwanda speakers. "For us, Hutu and Tutsi are all the same. They are all foreigners," a combatant at a roadblock told me.[83] A *muganga* in Walikale told me that the power of their medicine comes from the soil, "and because it comes from the soil, it protects us against all foreigners. That means all Rwandans, Hutu and Tutsi."[84] This ambiguity about boundaries, the lack of clarity about who is "us" and who is "them," is common in discussions of indigeneity in the eastern Congo.[85]

Anti-Rwandan sentiments—in which Congolese and Rwandan Kinyarwanda speakers are often lumped together—have a deep history in the eastern Congo that starts with large migrations during the precolonial and colonial periods and continues to be reflected in structures of ethnic governance in the Kivus.[86] That many FARDC units deployed in these areas during this time were led by Congolese Tutsi, who were often abusive, has accentuated ethnic tensions and prejudices. It would be easy to dismiss such sentiments as simple bigotry or a mere façade for power politics. Neither is entirely accurate. While no doubt negative stereotypes about Rwandans abound, these notions draw on personal and communal experiences that reach back into the colonial period, combining rational, well-grounded grievances with more generalized anger and frustration.

The role of *dawa* was also critical to the movement, highlighting the degree to which culture and worldview shaped and helped spread the movement. Throughout the interviews, it was clear that the legitimacy of leaders was closely tied to their ability to "manufacture" the *dawa*, often by having access to a particular recipe or to witch doctors. The movement spread through the *dawa*. For example, the leaders of the Mai-Mai Kifuafua were forced to convert themselves into a Raia Mutomboki faction and seek out the *dawa* or risk losing their control over their troops. These magic amulets and potions thus became an important driver of the various groups and a key resource for its leaders.

Soon after the movement emerged, however, its interests became more ambiguous. As an organizational structure coalesced, the importance of self-defense receded, and opportunism appeared. The widely reported abuse of civilians, for example, and the links between Raia factions and the M23 in southern Masisi are indications that the self-defense militias themselves were becoming a security threat for locals. My interviews with civic leaders in Shabunda, Walikale, and Kalehe confirm this.[87] Nonetheless, some of these same interviewees also suggested that, as abusive as they were, the Raia Mutomboki were at least more accountable to the local population than the FARDC or the FDLR and were thus the lesser of two evils.[88]

Conclusion

The Raia Mutomboki represent perhaps the most intractable kind of armed group: a fragmented, grassroots-based militia fighting for interests that are very difficult for the state to guarantee. Ten years after the movement emerged as a significant factor in 2011, it had fragmented into over twenty different militias. Almost none of them has engaged in successful negotiations with the government, which appears to have little interest in the demobilization of any of the groups.

This chapter adds nuance to the arguments laid out in chapter 3 through 5. Perhaps above all, it elucidates some of the factors behind the proliferation of armed groups in the eastern Congo. By privileging a logic of co-optation, and not of institutional reform and accountability, the transitional government and its successors created incentives for armed mobilization. Furthermore, by focusing primarily on what Kinshasa saw as the main threat—the Rwandan-backed CNDP and M23—the Congolese government angered other armed groups and created power vacuums that produced the mushrooming of Raia Mutomboki described here.

The fragmentation was also furthered by the speed at which the movement grew. The Raia Mutomboki spread extremely quickly and became a victim of their own success. Their rapid growth made it difficult to create internal institutions and hierarchies and predisposed them to splinter and factionalize. Moreover, in areas with segmented communities—such as in Shabunda—the Raia Mutomboki detached themselves more quickly from the societies out of which they emerged and also appear to have become more susceptible to internal splits and dissent.

Fragmentation and involution on both sides of the battlefield produced a dismal, violent equilibrium. Their fragmented, communal nature of the groups and their remote location meant that they posed little threat to the Congolese government, which did not prioritize defeating them. In stark contrast with the UPC and the CNDP, the Raia Mutomboki forged a strange interaction with the Congolese army, in which they skirmished but did not engage in open battles. The conflict developed into one in which neither the rebels nor the state have much interest in striking a bargain or in fighting, making low-grade conflict the sad status quo for the population.

8

Ituri and the UPC

THE MAIN AIM of this book is to understand why conflict in the Congo has persisted for so long.[1] Ituri was, until recently at least, the exception to this trend and therefore provides an interesting case study. This district was once one of the most violent areas of the country, with violence peaking between 2002 and 2007 before declining precipitously. The number of displaced people in the district fell from 500,000 in January 2003 to 130,000 in 2010 even as violence in the neighboring Kivu provinces was on the rise.

Although conflict in Ituri did not endure, it resembles the Kivus in terms of land and resources, variables on which conflict scholars often focus. The region hosts many gold, tantalum, and tin mines and has valuable tropical hardwood forests; it consists of a mixture of highlands suitable for cattle herding and thickly forested lowlands. As in the Kivus, there are long-standing communal disputes over land infused with a similar rhetoric of indigeneity.

Why did Ituri not follow the trend of other Congolese areas in conflict? And why did the UPC, one of the most brutal armed groups in the country, fold after only three years of existence? Perhaps the critical factor was geopolitical. The escalation of conflict in Ituri was in large part due to a proxy war involving the governments of Rwanda, Uganda, and the Congo. However, the region was never seen as a core national interest for any of those countries, in contrast with Kigali's relationship to the Kivus. When violence took on grotesque dimensions and international pressure mounted, Rwanda and Uganda were forced to

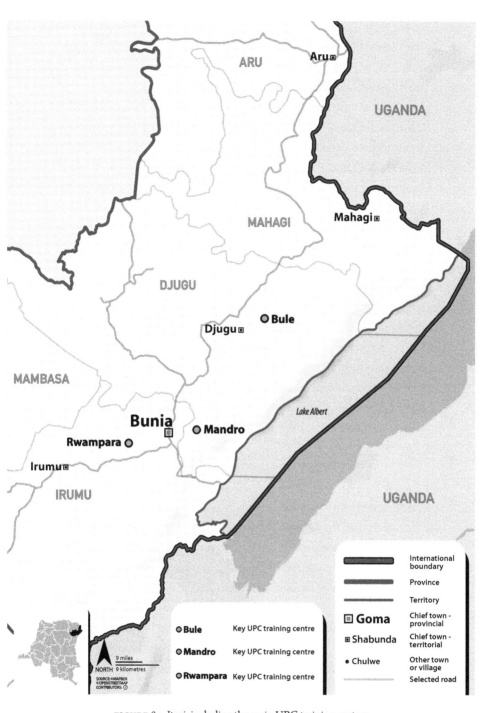

FIGURE 8.1. Ituri, including the main UPC training centers

disengage. The international community and the Congolese government then made Ituri a showcase of what outside intervention could do, pumping in peacekeepers and funding and making Ituri an early focus of the International Criminal Court. This approach eventually led to the dismantling of most of the armed groups.

It bucks the storyline of the Kivus in several ways. The approach was largely coercive. None of the main belligerents in Ituri were invited to join the transitional government, the French army was sent in as part of a European Union military intervention, and the UN peacekeepers used much more aggressive offensive tactics than in the Kivus. This prevented a military bourgeoisie from forming, and Ituri did not become part of the same system of military patronage as the Kivus, and military fragmentation did not take hold.

Local factors were also important. As this chapter will explain, despite its many internal squabbles, the UPC was relatively cohesive, but it was also extremely dependent on outside support, first from Uganda and then from Rwanda. When that support was cut in 2005, the UPC became untethered, for it had few roots in a local society that had been traumatized by the extreme violence of the war. Local business and customary elites who had initially backed the group then backed peacebuilding initiatives, creating critical momentum behind stabilization.

The Historical Backdrop

To understand the violence in Ituri, it is crucial to realize that it lies on the periphery of the Congo, both politically and geographically. Located in the extreme northeastern corner of the country over a thousand miles from the capital Kinshasa, it has closer economic ties to Uganda than much of the Congo.

Ethnicity has been the main prism through which actors in Ituri have expressed their grievances and ambitions in the postcolonial period. There are more than a dozen ethnic groups in Ituri. In late 2002, about 3.5 million people lived in the district, with the Hema and Lendu, the main groups that were involved the tragedy there, accounting for about 40 percent of the population.[2]

Scholars generally agree that the Lendu arrived in Ituri earlier than the Hema—the former around the sixteenth century, the latter in the late seventeenth or early eighteenth century.[3] Both groups settled primarily in Djugu and Irumu territories, those hit hardest by the violence. Northern Hema (from Djugu) are also called Gegere, whereas southern Lendu (from Irumu) are also known as Ngiti. While the extent of inequality prior to colonization is debated, it is clear that Belgian administrators helped the Hema achieve social and political dominance. Nonetheless, Djugu and Irumu differed importantly in both origin and scale of inter-ethnic conflict before 1999.

Irumu had seen several large outbreaks of violence long before 1999, beginning at least as far back as the late 1880s with an expedition by Henry Morton Stanley, who worked with the Hema while encountering fierce resistance from the Lendu. After independence, violence flared up in 1966 and then became what one Lendu community leader called "cyclical," with incidents in 1975, 1979, 1981, and 1992/93.[4] These conflicts originated mostly in disputes about administrative borders: the Hema had incorporated certain Lendu villages into their *chefferies*, depriving the Lendu from access to Lake Albert.

In contrast, Djugu remained relatively peaceful up to the 1990s. Here the conflict was rooted in land disputes related to the General Property Law of 1973, which abolished, at least officially, customary tenure and declared all land to be state property.[5] In a similar way as elites in the Kivus, affluent Hema took advantage of this law and their privileged access to the state bureaucracy, acquiring land that many Lendu considered to belong to their ancestors. Because the law stipulated that land titles would not enter into force until two years after they were bought, buyers simply kept their deeds secret until it was too late to challenge them.

Ernest Wamba dia Wamba, who was the head of the RCD/K-ML rebellion in Ituri—a Ugandan-backed splinter faction of the Rwandan-backed RCD that broke away in 1999—regarded the aggressive appropriation of land as "the real source of the conflict" in Ituri.[6] Likewise, the anthropologist Johan Pottier has suggested that class, not ethnicity as such, triggered the crisis.[7]

Whereas Lendu leaders, when asked about the origins of conflict, typically cited this history of inequality, Hema leaders emphasized the rise in insecurity that accompanied the arrival of the AFDL rebellion in 1996. The district experienced incidents of gang rape and lootings by Mobutu's retreating soldiers between December 1996 and March 1997 but remained relatively peaceful until the arrival of RCD, Rwandan, and Ugandan troops in late 1998. In 1999, Hema leaders claim, the Ugandan army began to exploit ethnic tensions, selling weapons to both sides.[8] It was during this period that local armed groups first emerged in Ituri.

The Formation of Hema Self-Defense Groups

The trigger for the Ituri conflict was a dispute over the Leyna farm in Walendu-Pitsi, a *chefferie* in Djugu territory, that broke out in April 1999. Lendu villagers accused Singa Kodjo, the Hema owner of Leyna, of illegally expanding his concession into Lendu land. The exact chain of events remains contested, but it appears that Kodjo asked the police to evict villagers from his land, triggering a Lendu attack.[9] Similar events occurred in nearby villages, one of which led to the murder of a Hema landowner. At the end of May, Kodjo and other Hema ranchers paid Captain Anthony Kyakabale, the sector commander of the Uganda People's Defense Force (UPDF), to evict Lendu peasants, further militarizing the violence.[10]

As tensions escalated, both sides began to form *autodéfense* (self-defense) groups; most descriptions suggest that the Hema groups were more structured and had more resources than their Lendu rivals. Because the Hema groups were organized at the village level, details of their creation and structure differ across the district. Nonetheless, one can discern shared features.[11] The groups were typically led by Hema farm owners or their sons, while village elders, customary chiefs, and local youth committees all played important roles in mobilization. Material support came from several sources. Wealthy businessmen made large donations, while in market towns such as Fataki, tax collections often went directly to self-defense groups, and door-to-door collections provided both money and food. Meanwhile, in villages close to mines gold was sold in exchange for weapons.

According to one former member, each Hema self-defense group had about three or four assault rifles, often bought from the UPDF, which sold weapons left behind by Mobutu's and Kabila's armies. The UPDF also deployed its own soldiers—usually around a dozen—to each farm in return for payment. When the fighting spread, engulfing all of Djugu in the second half of 1999, the groups intensified their recruitment efforts. Members who had been in Mobutu's army provided hasty military training to new recruits.

The "self-defense" label was misleading, for both Hema and Lendu went on the offensive at times. While the Hema were fewer in number, they had more weapons thanks to their wealth and support from the UPDF. That support was both military and political. Just as heavy fighting broke out in June 1999, the Ugandan commander of operations in the Congo, Brigadier James Kazini, announced the creation of Kibali-Ituri province, combining the districts of Ituri and Haut-Uélé. He appointed the Hema politician Adèle Lotsove as its governor, a move seen as a clear signal that the Ugandans favored the Hema. Although Lotsove organized a pacification commission in August, she was soon criticized for exacerbating the conflict in Djugu.[12]

In September 1999, following fighting between the Rwandan and Ugandan armies in Kisangani, RCD/K-ML president Ernest Wamba dia Wamba moved his headquarters to Bunia. The move, which had little to do with the Ituri conflict, contributed to a sharp intensification and regionalization of the violence there, for the district became the scene of competition among the branches of the RCD/K-ML and eventually between Uganda and Rwanda.

The Armée populaire congolais (APC), the military wing of the RCD/K-ML, initially absorbed the Hema militia, which had close ties to the Ugandan officers backing the APC. Quickly, however, different leaders of the RCD/K-ML and even of the Ugandan army struck up ties with rival Hema and Lendu militias to bolster their local power bases and foster lucrative protection rackets. The creation of the Union des patriotes congolais (UPC) resulted directly from this infighting.

The Creation of the UPC

The RCD/K-ML was never an internally coherent movement. Like many Congolese rebellions, it was riven by factionalism, outside meddling, and disagreements over goals. Soon after arriving in Bunia, Wamba's authority was challenged by his commissioner-general, Antipas Mbusa Nyamwisi, and the latter's deputy, John Tibasima. A native of faraway Kongo Central province, Wamba was considered an outsider in Ituri, making it easier for Mbusa, a Nande from just across the provincial border in North Kivu, and Tibasima, a local Hema, to oust him. These two communities represented the two economically most influential ethnic groups in the area under RCD/K-ML control.

The contrasts between the three protagonists were striking: on the one side, a leftist history professor who had spent much of his life in the United States and Tanzania; on the other, two locally well-connected businessmen. Tibasima, who was in charge of the group's budget, finance, and mining portfolios, had previously been chief executive of the state-owned mining company OKIMO, while Mbusa came from a politically influential family and had been one of the founding members of the RCD in 1998.

From late 1999 onwards, the competition between these leaders began to take a military form. Tibasima began recruiting youth for the Rwampara training camp near Bunia, while Mbusa did the same at the Nyaleke camp close to Beni. Both recruited largely along ethnic lines, although Mbusa's soldiers included both Nande and Lendu.[13] In both camps, UPDF officers trained recruits, illustrating Kampala's opportunistic and fragmented approach to the conflict. Like Lotsove, Mbusa and Tibasima secured Ugandan support by forging business relationships with Brigadier Kazini and General Salim Saleh, President Yoweri Museveni's influential half-brother, offering them access to taxation and protection rackets involving natural resources.[14] Mbusa also managed to buy the support of lower-ranking Ugandan officers stationed in the area.

Outflanked, Wamba tried to curtail his rivals' influence in April 2000, which promptly triggered a coup attempt. President Museveni intervened, bringing Tibasima, Mbusa, and Wamba together in Kampala and forcing them to reconcile. The truce did not last. In July, Hema APC commanders staged a mutiny in protest against what they perceived as a pro-Lendu stance by Wamba, calling themselves the Chui Mobile Force (CMF).[15] Wamba swiftly blamed this revolt on Tibasima.

President Museveni was again forced to step in to stop the violence. He ordered the deployment of UPDF reinforcements, prompting the Hema community to dispatch a delegation to plea with Museveni not to attack its "sons who are demonstrating against injustice."[16] One of the delegates was Thomas Lubanga, a forty-year-old Congolese who had studied psychology at the University of Kisangani. In the 1990s, he had been an active member of Étienne Tshisekedi's Union pour la démocratie et le progrès social (UDPS, Union for Democracy and Social Progress) political party, and he represented Bunia as a member of the provincial parliament during Adèle Lotsove's short-lived governorship.[17]

Accompanied by a high-ranking Ugandan delegation, the committee returned to Bunia to negotiate the CMF's peaceful surrender, in return for which the Ugandans agreed to provide military training to the mutineers. Seizing the opportunity, Hema community leaders in Djugu and Irumu quickly launched a recruitment drive, inflating the number of mutineers from around three hundred to nearly seven hundred.[18] Before being flown from Bunia Airport to Uganda at the end of August, some mutiny leaders stayed in Lubanga's house and chose him as their spokesman, apparently due to his political acumen.[19] After they departed, he assembled a group of educated Iturians, many of whom were Hema. On September 15, 2000, they created the UPC and named Lubanga president.

Some of his co-founders contended that the UPC began as a "purely political movement" with the aim of ending the inter-ethnic violence in Ituri.[20] However, Lubanga's involvement with the CMF immediately prior to the founding of the UPC suggests that the group had military aims from the outset. Lubanga, who spent time in Uganda in 2000 and 2001, maintained links to the former mutineers while the Ugandans trained them in UPDF camps in Kyankwanzi and Jinja.[21]

Meanwhile, the political crisis at the heart of the RCD/K-ML continued. During the CMF mutiny, Wamba tried to suspend Mbusa and

Tibasima, accusing them of treason. Mbusa responded by attacking Wamba's residence. While the roles of Tibasima and Lubanga in this putsch are not clear, UPDF officers were openly divided, with those backing Mbusa seen as Kazini's men.[22] Once again, the Ugandan government ordered all the main protagonists back to Kampala. This would be Wamba's farewell from Bunia—embattled and tired of the endless plotting against him, he left the region and retired from the Congo war.

The Failure of the FLC Merger

In a purported effort to end the constant infighting in Ituri—for which its own army was largely responsible—the Ugandan government invited the three largest Congolese rebel groups it supported to talks in Kampala at the end of 2000: Jean-Pierre Bemba's Mouvement de libération du Congo (MLC), the RCD/K-ML, and Roger Lumbala's RCD-National (RCD-N). The result was the short-lived merger of the three groups into the Front de libération du Congo (FLC, Front for the Liberation of Congo) in January 2001.

Bemba, who was the most successful and charismatic rebel chief and whose troops were in control of Équateur province in northern Congo, was chosen as the FLC leader, to be based in Beni. Mbusa was named executive coordinator, while Tibasima became the national secretary in charge of mining. In other words, the latter two ended up with positions almost identical to those they had when the RCD/K-ML first moved to Bunia. Mbusa, however, having become wary of his Ugandan counterparts, declared that they would no longer accept his "autonomous spirit" and went into exile in South Africa.[23]

While Lubanga gained stature in this new coalition, becoming FLC deputy national secretary of youth, sports, and leisure, the UPC was also marginalized, as the MLC and RCD/K-ML moved to suppress competition. It was not invited to sign the FLC founding statutes; several months after the merger, the UPC office in Bunia was vandalized, its flag burned, and all its documents destroyed. The UPC stopped holding official meetings and went underground.[24]

Eventually, Uganda's attempt to discipline its allies in the eastern Congo clashed with the actions of its own officers deployed there and the ambitions of local leaders. In June 2001, troops loyal to Mbusa, who maintained control over a core of local troops while in South Africa, launched an attack against Bemba in Beni, forcing him to flee. Once again, individual Ugandan officers supported Mbusa, undermining the compromise their government had tried to foster.[25] Riven by internal feuding, the FLC fell apart within months. It was only a brief interlude in what was becoming an increasingly factionalized conflict that was beginning to be much more connected with the ambitions of the military and political elites than with the initial land conflicts.

The broader political context influenced these intrigues. Joseph Kabila, who had become president after his father's assassination in January 2001, reinvigorated the peace process. Beginning in late 2001, talks began in South Africa with the goal of creating a transitional government. At these talks Mbusa sought greater influence and began to court President Kabila. At the same time, he sought an alliance with Lubanga to force Bemba out of Bunia. Meanwhile, Tibasima, the main Hema leader within the RCD/K-ML, left Bunia to focus on the national peace talks, eventually obtaining the ministry of urban planning in the transitional government.[26]

Bemba's troops retreated from Ituri in November 2001. Around that time, Mbusa named Lubanga new RCD/K-ML minister of defense. Nonetheless, Mbusa did not want Lubanga to use the UPC label and refused to allow him to formally register as a political party. When it became clear that he saw Lubanga as merely a figurehead without any real power, their relationship quickly deteriorated.[27] Having benefited from conflicts first within the RCD/K-ML and then within the FLC, Lubanga was now poised to exploit the growing tensions between the RCD/K-ML and the Ugandan government.

From Political Party to Armed Movement

The center stage of the Ituri conflict had thus been occupied by a struggle for power among political elites that used armed violence to settle scores and outmaneuver each other. As the major Congolese belligerents entered peace talks in South Africa and a regional rivalry between

Rwanda and Uganda intensified, Ituri was caught in the crosscurrents, with deadly effect.

In early 2002 Mbusa drew on ethnic divisions in his attempt to consolidate power, demoting Lubanga from his ministerial position and naming Jean-Pierre Molondo Lompondo—another "outsider," from Kasaï province—as new Ituri governor and commander of the APC. He recruited almost only among the Lendu and Nande communities and was openly antagonistic toward Hema. "Mbusa wasn't from Ituri, so the only way he could easily mobilize people was to locate himself on one side of the ethnic divide," recounted a former RCD/K-ML leader.[28] Lompondo was viewed with suspicion by the Hema, who accused him of plotting massacres with Lendu self-defense groups.[29] Then, in early April, Mbusa forced Hema bishop Léonard Dhejju to resign for having supported Hema militias. When a Nande, Janvier Kataka, was sent to replace him, the Hema community rallied protesters against Mbusa.[30]

On April 17, 2002, the situation in Bunia escalated. Lubanga accused Mbusa of selling out Ituri to the Congolese government, planning a Nande takeover of Bunia, and siding with the Lendu in the inter-ethnic conflict. Shortly afterwards, troops loyal to Lubanga staged another mutiny within the APC, managing to cut Bunia into two parts, with one area controlled by Lubanga, the other by Mbusa.[31] This situation lasted from April to August 2002.

The mutiny marked the return to prominence of the commanders who had backed the earlier CMF mutiny. Following their training in the Ugandan camps of Kyankwanzi (for new recruits) and Jinja (for officers), most of them had been sent to Équateur province to join the MLC's armed wing. After some months of fighting for Bemba, the soldiers had grown increasingly frustrated. They knew that fellow Hema were still dying in Ituri's inter-ethnic clashes, and they felt that the MLC were using them "like dogs."[32] When the FLC fell apart in northeastern Congo, these soldiers, led by Floribert Kisembo, rebelled in Équateur, demanding to be sent back to Ituri. Bemba gave in and let them return to Bunia, where they rallied to Lubanga's side.[33]

While Ituri was marginal to the Congolese military—fighting there did not threaten Kinshasa—it increasingly became an arena for regional intrigues within the context of national peace talks. In April and May 2001, Mbusa had gone to Angola's capital, Luanda, twice, the first time to talk to the Angolans, who supported the Congolese government, and then to meet with Congolese President Joseph Kabila and his advisors.[34] By the time Mbusa's troops attacked Bemba in Beni in June 2001, Mbusa had already started to switch sides, hoping to become "Kinshasa's man in the northeast" as the peace process accelerated. Furthermore, in mid-2002, President Museveni tried to mend fences with the Congolese government, not least due to Uganda's increasingly hostile relations with Rwanda. In this context, Mbusa appeared useful as a facilitator between the Ugandan and Congolese governments.

In June 2002, Uganda invited Lubanga to Kampala for negotiations about the impasse in Bunia. Perhaps in an attempt to demonstrate its good will toward the Congolese government, but much to Lubanga's surprise, the Ugandans detained him along with several members of his delegation and put them on a plane to Kinshasa on June 21, 2002. These arrests would have dire consequences. Suspicious of Uganda's intentions, Chief Kahwa, the UPC deputy minister of defense, and Lubanga's security advisor Richard Beiza fled Kampala and went to Kigali, where they asked the Rwandan government for support in their struggle against Mbusa's troops and Lendu militias. The Rwandans agreed, seizing the opportunity to gain influence in Ituri, their Ugandan rival's backyard. Initially without Uganda's knowledge, Rwanda began to supply the mutineers through airdrops to their training center in Mandro.[35]

Continuing to contradict themselves, Ugandan troops helped the pro-Lubanga mutineers chase out Governor Lompondo and take control of Bunia on August 9, 2002; they were reportedly having second thoughts about their rapprochement with Kinshasa.[36] Whether the UPC was behind this operation was later a contested issue in the Lubanga trial at the International Criminal Court. The prosecution argued that Lubanga orchestrated the attack by phone, whereas the defense—emphasizing that he was still under house arrest in Kinshasa at the time—suggested that Lubanga simply "took political advantage of a rebellion which he did not lead."[37] Lubanga was allowed to return to Bunia at the end of August, arriving with Congolese human rights minister Ntumba Luaba, who wanted to convince Ituri's traditional leaders to participate in a peace conference. Chief Kahwa seized the opportunity to take Luaba hostage; he then exchanged him for Lubanga's delegates, who were still detained in Kinshasa following their arrest in June.[38]

That Lubanga had been managing the mutiny from prison, or at least remained its symbolic leader, is suggested by the fact that when he returned to Ituri in August 2002 he appointed Floribert Kisembo and Bosco Ntaganda—the architects of the rebellion against the RCD/K-ML—to lead the armed wing of the UPC, the Force patriotique pour la libération du Congo (FPLC, Patriotic Forces for the Liberation of Congo). This also suggests that the mutineers may have been working for Lubanga all along. Having taken control of Bunia, the UPC now turned its sights on the rest of Ituri.

Six Months in Power

The period from September 2002 to March 2003 was the UPC's heyday; during this period it proved that it was a relatively strong politico-military movement, better organized than the Lendu-dominated armed groups against which it fought. However, that lasted only for the six months that the UPC controlled Bunia.

At the beginning of September 2002, Thomas Lubanga announced the members of UPC executive, which became Ituri's new administration. The UPC's executive was a multiethnic façade with little substantive influence. Some of the non-Hema executive members were threatened into joining the movement, while some traditional chiefs and administrators from other ethnic groups were killed when their loyalty to the UPC came under suspicion.[39]

While the provincial secretaries, also referred to as ministers, represented a broad spectrum of ethnic groups, the inner circle of decision-makers remained mostly Hema, including Lubanga's chief of staff Dieudonné Mbuna, his private secretary Michel Angaika, and economy minister Lonema.[40] These civilian leaders, in turn, were less influential with Lubanga than the military ones, especially Floribert Kisembo (UPC chief of staff), Bosco Ntaganda (UPC deputy chief of staff), and

Aimable Rafiki Saba (chief of security), who had all been involved in the CMF mutiny. While Kisembo was a Hema, Bosco and Rafiki were both Congolese Tutsi. Many Hema think of Tutsi as fellow *nilotiques*—a value-laden and historically problematic term that refers to a common ethnic origin—and thus consider them natural allies.[41]

At its height, it controlled large parts of four of Ituri's five territories. Due to complex relations with Hema self-defense groups, it is difficult to estimate the FPLC's exact numerical strength. Kisembo's former assistant suggested that the troops that seized Bunia in August 2002 numbered 18,000. In an interview from February 2003, Lubanga claimed to preside over 15,000 soldiers. He estimated that the FPLC had 20,000 to 23,000 fighters before it began to fragment in March 2003.[42] In 2004, the various factions that had originally formed part of the UPC were estimated by the national demobilization commission to have around 8,000 combatants.

Escalating Violence and New Alliances

The dramatic intensification of violence that followed was in large part driven by external dynamics: the feuding between Uganda and Rwanda, and Ituri politicians vying for seats in the national government. Between July 2002 and March 2003, the conflict in Ituri left at least five thousand civilians dead and an estimated half a million people had been displaced.[43] Even before Lubanga announced the new government, the troops who had taken control of Bunia launched attacks on Lendu villages. On August 31, Commander Bagonza was allegedly in charge of a large-scale massacre in Songolo in which between 140 and 787 people were killed. In response, on September 5 Lendu militiamen and APC soldiers attacked civilians whom they accused of being combatants for the UPC in Nyankunde. Over a period of ten days, at least 1,200 Hema and Bira civilians were systematically slaughtered.

Regional geopolitics exacerbated this violence. Around that time, Mbusa's RCD/K-ML and the Congolese army together set up the État-major opérationnel intégré (EMOI, Integrated Operational Headquarters) in Beni. The EMOI sent assault rifles and other supplies by air to Lendu militias in Irumu, which until then had often relied on crude weapons. Mbusa thus provided the Kinshasa government with an entry point into northeastern Congo, then still largely under the control of armed groups allied to Rwanda or Uganda.

After taking control of Bunia in August, the UPC began to plan an attack on Mongbwalu, an important gold mining town that was still held by APC and Lendu militias. Human Rights Watch reported that even "before a shot was fired, UPC President Lubanga asked the then general director of OKIMO, Étienne Kiza Ingani, who was himself Hema, to prepare a memo on how mining operations could be managed under UPC control."[44] After a six-day battle from November 18 to 24, Mongbwalu fell into the UPC's hands.

That two separate Human Rights Watch reports differ on whether Rwandan and Ugandan or only Rwandan troops helped the UPC attack Mongbwalu shows how complicated the game of alliances had become.[45] A former UPC member believed that the Ugandans had been aware of the UPC's links to Rwanda in August and had only helped the UPC take power in order to "infiltrate" them and learn more about Rwanda's exact role.[46]

Around this time, Rwandan influence became more noticeable within the UPC. According to several sources close to the UPC, Lubanga helped the Rwandan government provide weapons to the anti-Museveni People's Redemption Army (PRA), which was based in Lendu-controlled Kpandroma, and more than one hundred UPC fighters received training in Rwanda between September and December 2002.[47] On January 6, 2003, the UPC made this alliance official by signing an agreement with the Rwandan-backed RCD, which, unlike the UPC, was party to the national peace negotiations. The RCD pushed for the UPC to be included in the Sun City Agreement that concluded the Congolese peace process.

The Decline of the UPC

Between March and December 2003, amidst escalating violence, the UPC fragmented into five armed groups and twice lost control over Bunia—first temporarily in March, then permanently in June when a French-led multinational intervention force deployed in the city.

Divisions within the UPC had emerged in late 2002. In early December, its deputy minister of defense, Chief Kahwa, defected from the organization and led the first challenge to its control of Bunia. He had become disillusioned by the fact that the Rwandans—while supporting the UPC—were indirectly cooperating with Lendu groups by supporting the PRA in Kpandroma. Former UPC members have also suggested that Kahwa thought he deserved a more important position within the movement, given that he had initially secured Rwandan backing and that the UPC's main power base, Mandro, was in his chieftaincy.[48]

Ugandan president Museveni seized the opportunity to invite Kahwa to Kampala. On September 6, 2002, Museveni and Congolese president Kabila had signed the Luanda Agreement, in which the two governments agreed to put in place the Ituri Pacification Commission (IPC) backed by the UN. Uganda also agreed to withdraw its troops from Bunia within eighty days of the inauguration of the IPC. Behind the scenes, in an attempt to weaken the UPC, Museveni facilitated contacts between Kahwa and Kabila, which led to the creation of a new armed group, the Parti pour l'unité et la sauvegarde de l'intégrité du Congo (PUSIC, Party for Unity and Safeguarding of the Integrity of Congo), led by Kahwa, which initially existed only on paper.

Concerned that Rwanda was encroaching on its territory, Uganda undermined the UPC in other ways as well. When the UPC refused to sign any agreement with Lendu groups, Uganda helped create the Front pour l'integration et paix en Ituri (FIPI, Front for Integration and Peace in Ituri), an alliance that brought together Kahwa's PUSIC, the Lendu-dominated Front des nationalistes et intégrationnistes (FNI) and Force de résistance patriotique d'Ituri (FRPI), as well as the Alur-dominated Forces populaires pour la démocratie au Congo (FPDC). These deals paved the way for more regional conflict, pitting the UPC, supported by Kigali, against various armed groups assisted by both Kampala and Kinshasa.

In January and February 2003, tensions peaked in Bunia. Ugandan army officials openly threatened the UPC, while Lubanga accused the UPDF of reigniting the Hema-Lendu conflict.[49] On March 4, Uganda convinced—or perhaps forced—another UPC commander, Jerome Kakwavu, to break away from the UPC and create his own armed group, the Forces armées du peuple congolais (FAPC, People's Armed Forces of Congo), in Aru and Mahagi. Two days later, the UPDF, supported by Lendu FNI and FRPI militias, attacked the UPC in Bunia, forcing them to retreat to the countryside. Rwandan troops helped evacuate Lubanga and other officers to Kigali.[50] The same alliances that had made the UPC such a formidable force had now become their undoing.

Chief Kahwa helped the Ugandans defeat the UPC during the struggle for Bunia on March 6 by calling troops loyal to him and telling them not to join the fighting. The PUSIC was transformed from a paper tiger into an actual armed group, with Kahwa as president.

On March 18, 2003, the Democratic Republic of the Congo, Uganda, and Ituri's armed groups—with the notable exception of the UPC— signed a cease-fire. The UN peacekeeping mission then helped bring together 177 delegates representing all the main ethnic groups to set up the IPC, which in turn established an interim administration. Shortly afterwards, on April 25, the Ugandan army began to withdraw its troops. To replace them, MONUC sent 720 Uruguayan peacekeepers to secure the airport and protect UN personnel and facilities as well as the IPC meeting sites. The Uruguayans were faced with a chaotic situation, for the UPDF's withdrawal—completed by May 6—left a security vacuum marked by heavy clashes in Bunia among Ituri's armed groups.

In the meantime, the UPC's troops regrouped and, on May 12, retook Bunia together with PUSIC troops. According to former PUSIC members, they realized that they could not contain the massacres perpetrated by Lendu militias in Bunia, so they called on their former brothers-in-arms within the UPC for help. Prior to the attack, Rwanda had supplied the UPC with weapons and brought back Lubanga and Bosco from Kigali. Rwanda reportedly told the UPC that, to improve their bargaining position, they had to retake Bunia before the additional peacekeeping contingents arrived.[51]

During the fighting for Bunia, thousands of civilians sought shelter near MONUC's headquarters, and thousands more fled the city. These events, coupled with reports about other massacres in Djugu and Irumu territories, finally pushed the international community to more forceful action. On June 6, the French-led Interim Emergency Multinational

Force (IEMF) began to deploy in Bunia. It swiftly took control of the city, on a few occasions clashing with both Hema and Lendu groups. The IEMF mandate was limited to Bunia; violence continued in Ituri's countryside.

By the time the IEMF left after three months, MONUC had deployed 2,400 soldiers to Bunia. This number increased steadily in the following months, and MONUC also began to deploy outside of Bunia. It became clear that taking the city was no longer possible for any of Ituri's armed groups.

Two other dynamics slowed the escalation of violence. First, on June 30, 2003, the attention of national politicians turned to the formation of the new national government in Kinshasa, in which Mbusa, Tibasima, and the RCD were represented. Second, the brutality of the Ituri conflict, which in addition to large massacres featured cannibalism and dismemberment, had garnered international media and diplomatic attention that made it much more difficult for Rwanda and Uganda to be overtly involved.

In August 2003, the leaders of Ituri's armed groups arrived in Kinshasa for negotiations. They signed a memorandum of understanding, agreeing to work with the new transitional government, even though none of them was represented there. They also pledged to cease hostilities in Ituri and to bring an end to "uncontrolled" groups that continued to commit massacres.

Back in Ituri, the UPC's fragmentation continued. While the other Ituri leaders had returned after the talks, Lubanga stayed in Kinshasa, hoping to use his contacts with the RCD to establish himself as a national politician. This proved to be a serious mistake: he was placed under house arrest in Kinshasa's Grand Hotel while violence in Ituri escalated. In the meantime, MONUC pressured the UPC's military leadership in Ituri to disarm, with the option of being integrated into the new Congolese army.

In December 2003, the pressure led to the defection of Floribert Kisembo, the chief of staff of the FPLC, from the UPC, splitting the group into two factions: UPC-Lubanga (UPC-L) and UPC-Kisembo (UPC-K). Various reasons have been given for the split. Several interviewees highlighted the role of Dominique MacAdams, head of MONUC's Bunia office, in pushing Kisembo to defect. Some suggested that the Congolese government promised Kisembo that he would not be prosecuted for his involvement in abuses if he were to defect from the UPC. Added to this was a leadership conflict between Lubanga and Kisembo. According to people close to him, Kisembo wanted to disarm the FPLC and integrate it into the army. He was also eager to remove Congolese Tutsi—such as Bosco Ntaganda and Innocent Kaina—from its ranks, which the international community allegedly demanded, likely due to concerns that they were cooperating with Rwanda. Lubanga disagreed on both issues. When Kisembo defected, Lubanga promoted Bosco to the position of chief of staff of the UPC-L's armed wing.[52]

Under military pressure and with its alliances fraying, the UPC tried to portray itself in a friendlier light. Finally, in May 2004, Lubanga as well as representatives from the UPC-K, the FAPC, the PUSIC, the FNI, the FRPI, and the FPDC signed a peace deal—the Acte d'engagement de Kinshasa—with the transitional government in Kinshasa, agreeing to cease hostilities and to support the UN-led Disarmament and Community Reinsertion (DCR) program for Ituri.

Despite the signing of the peace deal, most of Ituri's armed groups kept fighting each other, the Congolese army, and MONUC. However, with the withdrawal of regional actors, the dynamics of violence in Ituri became more tractable, pitting MONUC and the Congolese army against groups resisting disarmament.

At the beginning of 2005, MONUC started to take a more robust approach in Ituri, attacking armed groups and cutting off their supply routes. The killing of nine Bangladeshi peacekeepers in an ambush near Kafé (Djugu territory) on February 25, 2005, reinforced the shift in the conflict. In response to the Kafé ambush, MONUC head William Swing pressed the transitional government to issue arrest warrants for the leaders of the groups responsible. Between March and April, many were arrested, including Lubanga in Kinshasa and Chief Kahwa in Ituri. After Lubanga's arrest, UPC interim president Bede Djokaba Lambi and Secretary-General John Tinanzabo were also temporarily jailed.

This new, aggressive approach spurred the creation of an alliance that brought together many of Ituri's remaining rebel leaders: the Mouvement révolutionnaire congolais (MRC, Congolese Revolutionary Movement). According to Lubanga's former chief of staff Dieudonné Mbuna, the MRC was conceived by former RCD/K-ML commander Frank Kakolele Bwambale, an ethnic Nande.[53] Kakolele, Ngudjolo, Mbuna, and several FNI, FRPI, PUSIC, and UPC commanders met in Jinja, Uganda, in June 2005, to officially create the MRC, signifying the end of the UPC.[54]

Heavy fighting in Ituri continued throughout much of 2005 and 2006. In mid-2006, however, MONUC began to step up its attempts to find a diplomatic solution to the conflict. In November, it facilitated three separate peace deals between the Congolese army and the FNI, the FRPI, and the MRC. Negotiations about the specifics of their integration into the FARDC continued for another year, and in November 2007 their three main leaders—Peter Karim, Cobra Matata, and Matthieu Ngudjolo, all Lendu—finally boarded a plane at Bunia Airport that took them to Kinshasa. While some pockets of armed groups remained, this marked the end of intense violence in Ituri. It would be over a decade before fighting would begin again in earnest, in late 2017.

Analysis

The dizzying switchbacks of the Ituri conflict would make anyone's head spin. Zooming out, what can this story tell us about conflict duration in the Congo more generally? Why did conflict in Ituri scale up and then back down so quickly?

Three factors stand out. A local military bourgeoisie did emerge in Ituri, but it was a short-lived phenomenon with relatively shallow roots in local society. This bourgeoisie was then dominated by outside actors, which—along with Ituri's peripheral status in the Congolese conflict—made it an easier showcase for foreign humanitarian intervention. I will describe these factors here through an analysis of the UPC.

The Short-Lived and Shallow Existence of the UPC

All of our sources, as well as the scholarly literature, agree that the conflict began in April 1999 at the Leyna ranch in Djugu territory. While there had been previous episodes of violence—in 1975, 1979, 1981, and 1992/93—these had all been relatively brief and did not result in standing armed groups with their own interests. In short, there was no military bourgeoisie in Ituri before 1999, when the forerunner of the UPC emerged.

In the early days of the mobilization, the Hema cultural organization ENTE, which emerged alongside many other similar organizations during the democratization period of the early 1990s, emerged as an important actor.[55] One interviewee suggested that ENTE provided the organizational infrastructure for militia mobilization.[56]

While ENTE provided some of the ties and the personal relationships necessary for such high-risk activity, there is little doubt that the initiators were the wealthy landowners themselves, sometimes acting within the business association (Fédération des entreprises du Congo, FEC).[57] According to one source: "The local defense committees were usually led by the landowner or his sons. . . . The committee then called upon the UPDF, which deployed twelve to fifteen soldiers or more to each ranch. When the Lendu attacks became more intense, the Hema defense committee began to recruit former FAZ [Mobutu's army], AFDL, and APC soldiers who were Hema."[58]

The United Nations special report on violence in Ituri, which was compiled in 2003 and 2004 by UN human rights officials, also pointed to these landowners, reporting that the wealthy Savo family, which owned large cattle ranches in the highlands, in particular played a leading role in mobilization:

Witnesses interviewed by MONUC stated that, under the leadership of the Savo family, the *concessionaires* [large landowners] began to organize militias around Fataki. They imposed a fund-raising system on the Hema/Gegere businessmen. Two prominent Hema/Gegere businessmen who were opposing the fund-raising were murdered.

As the collegial leadership of this militia was expecting violence, all of the Hema *concessionnaires* by the end of May 1999 contracted squads of UPDF soldiers to protect their land. On 29 May 1999, important Hema families reportedly paid Captain Kyakabale, the UPDF sector commander, the alleged amount of $12.000 for a punitive action to be undertaken against the populations occupying their concessions.[59]

Throughout this period, the interests of the Hema community were represented by the militias. However, while this "community" was often invoked, ethnicity was an ambiguous shorthand. Some who participated in these militias wanted to safeguard their families, while many of the leaders were strongly influenced by landowners. An individual close to the UPC said: "We were within an ethnic organization, and ethnicity came first. We needed someone who could speak for the ethnic group."[60] What ethnicity meant, however, was contextual and different for its various members.

Their constituency shifted considerably with the arrival of the RCD/ K-ML, which set up its headquarters in Bunia just three months after the initial violence erupted. As one RCD/K-ML leader remembered:

> When we got to Bunia, we met with local militia leaders, many of whom had connections to the UPDF. But these were disorganized groups of militia, there was no central command. When we arrived, as there were internal struggles within the RCD/K-ML, some of our leaders took advantage of local militias to position themselves.[61]

The arrival of the RCD/K-ML elevated the military struggle from one between very localized factions, driven by local agendas, to competition among national and regional leaders. Until the arrival of the RCD/K-ML, few of the local militias had any military training. When dozens of high-profile political and military leaders joined the RCD/ K-ML, dynamics in Bunia changed profoundly. Leaders such as Mbusa Nyamwisi and John Tibasima, the two deputy heads of the rebellion, used their connections with Kampala and their military expertise to rally militias to their side. Tibasima set up a training camp for mostly

Hema militia in Rwampara, close to Bunia, while Mbusa did the same in Nyaleke, close to his hometown of Beni. This distanced the militia from their communities and created a sense of armed group identity.

Evidence of this shift away from the local roots of the UPC was confirmed during the trial of Thomas Lubanga at the International Criminal Court. One of the witnesses, who had been in charge of Hema local defense forces, complained that Hema youth who had been sent for training to the UPC did not return to protect their villages as had been expected.[62] An RCD/K-ML leader also pointed out that it was Tibasima who had recruited Lubanga from relative obscurity as a trader in the Bunia market, and that neither Lubanga nor many of the other senior officials had strong links to the Hema elite. "Lubanga, Tibasima, Bosco, Lotsove—these were all people who owed their political careers more to the Ugandans or Rwandans than to the local Hema community."[63]

The dislocation of the future UPC military officers was physical as well as social: in August 2000, some seven hundred RCD/K-ML mutineers who would form the UPC were transported to Uganda for a month of military training.[64] The leading commanders—including Bagonza, Kasangaki, Kahwa, Ntaganda, and Kisembo—stayed on for a longer military training, lasting over four months, at the Jinja military academy. All of the mutineers, both soldiers and officers, were then sent by the Ugandan army to fight alongside Jean-Pierre Bemba's MLC in Gbadolite for more than a year. They were gone from Ituri for about eighteen months, during which time they established close relations with Ugandan military officers.

These travels distanced the mutineers from their communities, put them in touch with new political networks, and opened their eyes to new opportunities. Even the civilian leadership, including Thomas Lubanga, who stayed in Ituri, became increasingly focused on individual, short-term interests. One source within the RCD/K-ML gave two reasons for this: "First, Lubanga realized that running a military operation, especially this undisciplined bunch of guys, would always put you in conflict with the population. . . . Secondly, he realized that the Hema political elites themselves were deeply divided."[65]

Thus, while Lubanga and other UPC leaders continued to claim to protect the Hema community, rhetoric that was easy to justify given the widespread massacres of the time, they increasingly acted for individual material gain and catered increasingly to their foreign allies. For example, the stubborn attempts by all sides to control Bunia in 2002 and 2003 are difficult to justify exclusively in terms of communal self-protection. They were fueled largely by proxy warfare between Uganda and Rwanda and the desire by armed group leaders to secure representation in the newly announced national transitional government. "You can justify everything with ethnicity," one civil society activist from Bunia said. "No matter whether they wanted to enrich themselves or serve their foreign allies, they always said it was for the community. That may have been true at the outset, but by 2003 it was just words."[66]

Perhaps the starkest contradiction between rhetoric and action was the UPC's treatment of Hema civilians. The UPC forcefully recruited Hema children, including demands that every family send one child to join the UPC or pay a tax. This prompted some families to send their children far away.[67] A witness with intimate knowledge of the UPC, said: "Everybody—everybody, even the Hema, were victims of the other Hema. Actually, everybody was responsible for their own security and safety. You couldn't say anything against the UPC. If you said anything against the UPC, it was finished for you."[68]

A further sign of the disconnect between the UPC and the Hema community was the frequent squabbling among UPC leaders, who were much more concerned with their stature and personal interests than with their communities. The clearest examples of this were the opportunistic alliance of the PUSIC, a splinter faction of the UPC, with Lendu armed groups such as the FNI and the FRPI in late 2002, and then the alliance between remnants of the UPC, the FNI, the FRPI, and PUSIC officers in 2005. This disconnect was confirmed by the attitude of UPC leaders when they went to Kinshasa in 2003 for negotiations. According to a diplomat who followed those talks, "This was all about positions and money for them, they didn't seriously ask for anything for their communities. Concerns such as land tenure, community reconciliation, and ethnic discrimination were mentioned but never insisted upon."[69]

The opportunism of the UPC was also clear in subsequent years, when, under pressure from the Congolese army and MONUC, its remaining officers jettisoned their claims of ethnic self-defense and forged a new alliance, the MRC, with their former Lendu archrivals.

In short, in contrast with the Kivus, armed groups were a relatively recent phenomenon in Ituri, forming a military bourgeoisie that quickly began to be estranged from its local seat of power, becoming beholden to outside interests.

The Dominance of Outside Actors

Meanwhile, foreign governments—first Uganda, then Rwanda— became increasingly influential. Uganda had enough clout to be able to extract the leaders of the entire proto-UPC mutiny in 2000 and then to summon Lubanga and other senior UPC officials to Kampala and arrest them in June 2002. During this time, tensions between Rwanda and Uganda were rising, prompting more aggressive attempts to control militias in Ituri. Lubanga's arrest by Ugandan officials offered an opportunity for Rwanda to become more involved in the UPC, providing weapons, training, and logistical support to the UPC from late 2002 onwards.[70] Some witnesses, both at the International Criminal Court and in Human Rights Watch reports, went so far as to say that Rwanda masterminded the UPC attack on the mining town of Mongbwalu in November 2002, giving orders to the officers in the field.[71] Rwanda was also crucial in evacuating senior UPC leaders, including Lubanga, from Ituri in March 2003 and then bringing them back several months later. When the UPC disintegrated in 2005, Rwanda facilitated Ntaganda's departure from Ituri to join Laurent Nkunda's CNDP.

How much did the UPC depend on these governments? The impression one gets of the UPC during the 2002–2005 period is of a core of cunning military operatives with substantial autonomy negotiating for support between Rwandan and Ugandan governments, invoking the interests of the Hema community when it was convenient, and striking deals with Lendu elites when it was politically expedient or when their foreign allies pressured them to do so. In this relationship, notions of ethnicity, interests, and loyalty were constantly in flux.

To understand the interests of these foreign actors, we need to understand the particular place Ituri occupies in the region. In contrast to the Kivus, neither Uganda or Rwanda has deep-rooted or historical interests in Ituri. No armed group there posed a major threat to the survival of regimes in Kigali, Kampala, or Kinshasa.

It was the superficiality of interests—alongside the neopatrimonialism of the Ugandan government—that first allowed Ituri to become the playground of Ugandan military officers and then allowed the conflict to be shut down relatively quickly once abuses began to mount and international pressure grew. In other words, Ituri was useful to the Ugandan government as a means of providing the UPDF leadership with opportunities of enrichment, at times on both sides of the battlefield. However, Kampala did not have an overriding national interest in the Ituri conflict that could impose a certain amount of order and discipline on its own officers' involvement or that would require their continued intervention once the costs of this deployment began to rise.

Relations between the Ugandan government and the UPC were both close and shallow. The UPDF trained the core UPC officers, provided them with weapons and opportunities for patronage, and was willing to back the alliance with military force. The presence of UPDF officers on the ground in Ituri throughout this period led to close relationships between officers from both sides.

However, the Ugandan army's involvement in Ituri was decentralized and full of contradictions. While the UPDF generally favored Hema self-defense groups, UPDF colonel Peter Karim at times intervened to protect Lendu villages. In at least one incident, UPDF units that supported opposing camps even exchanged fire.[72] When international pressure increased on the Ugandans to disengage from Ituri and with an opportunity to ally with Kinshasa against Rwandan rivals, the Ugandans cut the UPC off, arresting Lubanga and eventually encouraging Kisembo and Kakwavu to turn themselves in to the Congolese authorities.

Similarly, Rwanda's objective in Ituri was always a short-term one of nettling Uganda and accumulating resources. They had no lasting allies or history there—Ituri is some 300 kilometers from Rwanda's closest border. With the humanitarian crisis deepening and the Congo adopting a transitional government, donors leaned heavily on the Rwandan government to end its involvement in Ituri.

By mid-2003, with both Ugandan and Rwandan officials keeping their distance and with local communities cutting support because they were traumatized by the violence, the UPC found itself cut adrift, under military siege, and riven by internal differences.

Foreign support both made and broke the UPC. If it had not been for Ugandan action, the UPC would never have come into existence and taken control of Bunia. However, the UPC's dangerous game of alliances embroiled it in a Rwandan-Ugandan proxy war that proved to be fatal. When the UPC sought support from Rwanda in 2002, betraying the Ugandan army that was still occupying Ituri, it shot itself in the foot. Together with the Congolese government, Uganda responded by dealing the UPC a critical blow. While it might have been able to absorb the loss of Jérôme Kakwavu, the UPC never recovered from the ability of Kinshasa and Kampala to divide its three most powerful Hema leaders—Lubanga, Chief Kahwa, and later Floribert Kisembo.

Intervention by the International Community

Donor intervention in the Kivus was tightly constrained by political considerations. The United Nations and the major international actors in the conflict were always wary that their actions in the Kivus would upset the fragile peace talks underway at the time. When the RCD massacred 160 people, mostly civilians, in Kisangani in the middle of the negotiations in May 2002, there was only temporary condemnation. A similar lack of opprobrium followed the RCD attack against its former ally, the Mudundu 40, in South Kivu in April 2003, during which it killed dozens and raped twenty-seven women.[73]

I personally witnessed this privileging of the political process during Laurent Nkunda's advance on Bukavu in May 2004. When the UN mission's deputy force commander wanted to order troops to use deadly force to prevent Nkunda from arriving in Bukavu, the political leadership of the mission told him to stand down. UN spokesman Fred Eckhard said: "It's for the [Congolese] parties to sort out. When war breaks out, the role of peacekeepers ends."[74] The reason for this, as explained to me by the head of the mission at the time, was that they were afraid the RCD would withdraw from the peace process if the UN engaged military force.

International intervention in Ituri was the opposite of this. The international community wanted to make an example of this region, which was both extremely violent but also geopolitically marginal—two factors that made it a prime candidate for interventions by the International Criminal Court, the European Union, and the United Nations. Here outsiders could invest considerable resources without offending regional powers while claiming to have contributed significantly to a decrease in violence. A researcher who advised the International Criminal Court at the time remembered: "I told them that Ituri would be a perfect place to begin their work on the Congo. The human rights violations there were extreme, and yet the protagonists were minor thugs. An example could be made without getting embroiled in political controversy."[75]

This approach also steered clear of controversy by avoiding close scrutiny of the involvement of the governments in Kigali, Kampala, and Kinshasa. Despite the clear complicity—and even arguably direct responsibility—of government officials in the massacres, the three major International Criminal Court trials focused on Ituri never seriously probed their involvement.

Similar considerations informed international military intervention. The European Union, led by France, was motivated by the brutality of the violence, the embarrassment suffered by UN troops in Bunia, and its own internal considerations to deploy Operation Artemis in 2003. It was clear from the nature of the intervention—it was limited to the town of Bunia and lasted only for three months—that it saw Ituri as a place where the application of overwhelming military force could produce a radical shift in local dynamics, an analysis that proved to be correct. General Patrick Cammaert, the UN commander who continued robust operations against armed groups between 2005 and 2007, said at the time: "These operations here have been successful. But we could not reproduce them in the Kivus. The FDLR and CNDP are much more political animals than the Ituri armed groups."[76]

Geopolitics far from the Congo also had an impact. Only two months before the UN Security Council voted to authorize the military intervention that would become Operation Artemis, the United States invaded Iraq. The critics of that invasion—in particular, the French government that took the lead in Artemis—wanted to provide the case for how a legitimate international intervention under United Nations auspices could have an impact. The United Nations, under fire after a sex abuse scandal among peacekeepers and for their inaction in Bukavu, then also wanted to showcase how military force could be used to protect civilians, bolstering commanders like Cammaert who wanted to take a more aggressive posture.

In an effort to make Ituri a case study for successful stabilization, donors complemented the military and diplomatic efforts with humanitarian and development aid. A regional pilot program for the national demobilization and reintegration program was deployed in September 2004, the Disarmament and Community Reintegration (DCR) program. Over 15,000 combatants, including 4,525 children, were demobilized through the program.[77] At the same time, donors funded a set of local peacebuilding projects intended to boost employment, reconciliation, and the local economy.

The final acts of Ituri's main conflict were played out in The Hague, in front of the judges of the International Criminal Court. Thomas Lubanga was eventually sentenced to fourteen years in prison for war crimes, while German Katanga—the leader of the largely Ngiti FRPI—received a twelve-year sentence. Bosco Ntaganda is also under arrest at the International Criminal Court for crimes committed in Ituri, while Jerome Kakwavu and Chief Kahwa were found guilty and sentenced by Congolese military courts.

Conclusion

The UPC's short life span—a mere three years—and the forces that precipitated its disintegration illuminate the differences between Ituri and the Kivus. Most armed groups in Ituri were never given the opportunity to develop deep local roots. Armed mobilization there did not begin until 1999, six years after the initial large-scale mobilization in the Kivus, and society was not as militarized as it was further south, where the massive influx of Rwandan refugees in 1994 and the wars of the AFDL and RCD deeply transformed societies, creating conflict economies and militarized networks that would prove difficult to erase.

Ituri's geopolitical position also played an important role in this story. At no time did the Ugandan or Rwandan governments perceive Ituri as indispensable to their strategic interests in the region, as was the case for Rwanda in the Kivus. For Uganda, by 2002 its involvement in the Congo was primarily a means for the presidency to distribute patronage to military officers, while Rwanda was mostly interested in provoking Uganda. By 2003, the Ugandan and Rwandan governments, under considerable pressure from their donors, had realized that the proxy wars they were fighting in Ituri were detrimental to their mutual interests. They cut the UPC loose.

The involvement of outsiders and the internal weakness of the Ituri armed groups were only part of the story. Local constituencies also pushed back against insecurity in ways they could not in the Kivus. While Hema landowners were initially deeply involved in backing the UPC, the armed group's more abusive and less responsive actions eventually disenchanted them. This contrasted starkly to the response in the areas around Beni, Butembo, and Goma, where two decades of conflict incrementally produced a new class of politicians and entrepreneurs invested in conflict and where local civil society and business were overwhelmed by the larger regional and political forces that opposed them. By 2005, when the MRC attempted to revive armed group activism in Ituri, the mood had soured, especially among the wealthy class of businesspeople and landowners who depended heavily on stability for cattle herding, cash crops, and long-distance trade.

Not all the news from Ituri is good. While most armed groups demobilized or were forcibly dismantled, the FRPI has persisted, the provincial administration is still weak, and tensions over land and customary boundaries remain. As of this writing in early 2021, the province (it was transformed from a district to a province in 2015) was experiencing renewed violence between armed groups rooted in the Hema and Lendu communities. Arguably, despite the short-term gains in stability, the various stakeholders had not been able to address the root conflicts over land and mining wealth, the lack of durable employment for many the demobilized, or the weakness of the state administration.

Nonetheless, the differences between Ituri and the Kivus are instructive. Despite regional interference, a weak state, natural resources, and communal tensions, Ituri's conflict in the 1999–2007 period, involving multiplying militias and extreme violence, was brought under control relatively quickly. As I argue in the final chapter, the Ituri experience highlights the importance of reining in armed conflict before it becomes self-perpetuating, as it has in the Kivus. It also shows the importance of elites—in this case, regional and national, military and civilian—in perpetuating the conflict.

9

Peacemaking and the Congo

The sick Congolese state and the confused international community
are strategic partners. They manage Congo's problems together. They
support each other in maintaining their hegemonies or momentarily
fall out with each other to distract a people who are dying to see
something other than hypocritical games.

—LUTTE POUR LE CHANGEMENT
(CONGOLESE YOUTH MOVEMENT), 2018

THIS BOOK DELVES into a thicket of Congolese politics, featuring an
alphabet soup of rebel acronyms and complex relationships among dozens of local, national, and regional actors. Can we disentangle this knot
of narratives, with dozens of actors driven by layered interests, into
something simpler, to allow us to assess the failures of peacemaking
during this period? While historians have the luxury of detail and nuance, policymakers have to make decisions about how to structure a
peacebuilding strategy. Policy memos are rarely more than a few pages
long—not several hundred.

This chapter is not intended to be a comprehensive evaluation of
donor engagement in the Congo; that would take many volumes. Instead, I draw on the preceding chapters to discern flaws in peacebuilding
since 2003, when the peace deal entered into force. I argue that the main
mistake of peacemakers in the Congo was not that they missed one

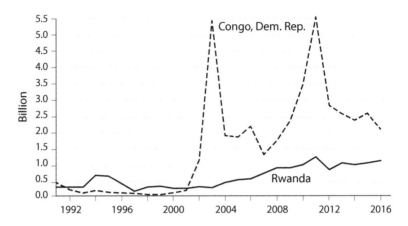

FIGURE 9.1. Overseas development aid to Congo and Rwanda (World Bank Open Data, available at data.worldbank.org, accessed December 10, 2020)

variable, one facet of the conflict, as has been argued by scholars and activists who have emphasized local conflicts over land and identity or who have pointed to the importance of "conflict minerals."[1]

Rather, the main mistakes were of an epistemological and geopolitical nature. Outsiders were blinkered by their own preconceptions as well as by their interests. Donors and diplomats failed to fully understand the main actors in the conflict and their interests, leading to key structural flaws in the peace process. They should have then acknowledged and dealt with the Rwandan meddling in the eastern Congo, on the one hand, and the perverse interests of the Congolese government to sustain conflict, on the other. Their failures are all the more striking given the dependence of the region on Western donors; over half of the budgets of Rwanda and the Congo during this time came from foreign donors who failed to use their considerable leverage. This support was not politically neutral but aided and abetted the entrenchment of conflict.

What caused this flawed approach? I argue that donors framed the conflict in terms of peacemaking models that privilege technocracy over politics and abstract institutions over lived reality. This was possible because, despite donors' huge sway in the Congo, there was no domestic constituency in their own countries to push for real change. The Congo was a peripheral interest for global powers; what interests they

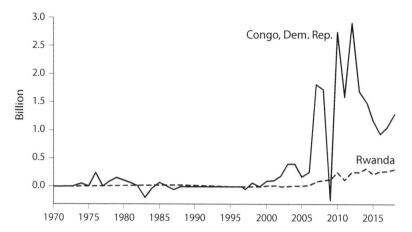

FIGURE 9.2. Foreign direct investment in the Congo and Rwanda, in billions of US dollars (World Bank Open Data, available at data.worldbank.org, accessed December 10, 2020)

did have in mining or humanitarian concern were either not enough to change or not in contradiction with the violent status quo. This allowed the UN Security Council to approve the transition to a technocratic stabilization mission, declare the war over, and throw its weight behind the Congolese government even though violence was escalating, and the dysfunctional state was part of the problem.

This technocratic approach coincided with other, economic and ideological trends. The liberal peacebuilding model triggered the rapid privatization of state assets, in particular mining concessions, allowing the ruling elite to illegally accumulate massive resources in a short period of time without having to employ the kind of taxation that could have rendered the state more accountable to its citizens. The trappings of democracy and administrative efficiency became sideshows, albeit important ones, as the important power politics took place in a shadowy economic realm that international policymakers either disregarded or were complicit in. By the time the World Bank and the International Monetary Fund began paying serious attention to economic malfeasance and conditioned their support, almost all of the country's major mining concessions had been sold to private investors, at great loss to the Congolese state.

The Flaws of the Peace Deal

The logic of peacemaking in the Congo followed the conventional steps laid out by United Nations doctrine: bring an end to the conflict, foster negotiations between warring sides, and produce a durable political settlement built on a respect for human rights and the rule of law.[2] In its early days, this was liberal peacebuilding at its best, remarkably successful in achieving its formal goals, albeit after many delays. It unfurled as follows:

- A first agreement of principles through the 1999 Lusaka Agreement, which led to the creation of MONUC, the first UN peacekeeping mission and initiated mediation between the belligerents;
- The signing of the 2002 Global and Inclusive Agreement, which spelled out the concrete terms of a power-sharing deal between the main belligerents, for which MONUC and an international support group were the guarantors;
- The creation of a transitional government between 2003 and 2006 and the forging of democratic, decentralized institutions through a new constitution that ushered in national and provincial parliaments, checks on executive power, and an independent judiciary;
- A series of national and provincial elections in 2006 and 2007 that marked the end of the transitional government and the inauguration of the Third Republic.

To implement this plan, which required belligerents to lay down their weapons and accept that elections would make some of them lose power, donors devised a political strategy. According to Howard Wolpe, who was US special envoy to the African Great Lakes Region during this period, "The peace process was built on the premise of reducing outside intervention. Once we could get the Rwandans and Ugandans to withdraw their support, it would be easier to force their allies to the table and to accept a deal."[3] Using both financial leverage and diplomatic pressure, donors brokered the Pretoria Agreement and the

Luanda Agreement in 2002, the first leading to the withdrawal of Rwandan troops and the second to the withdrawal of Ugandan troops from the Congo.[4]

While on the surface this approach was politically neutral, it inherently favored the incumbent president, Joseph Kabila. Part of this was simply through inertia: as pointed out in chapter 3, he refused to extend power sharing to his presidential guard, the intelligence service, and important parastatals. Perhaps more important, since real power resided in the presidency and its informal networks, power sharing in formal institutions did not change Kabila's functional hold on power. And since Kabila was the internationally recognized head of state, while his challengers were rebels, he had an edge on his rivals. As Filip Reyntjens has observed, "The recognition of juridical, rather than empirical, statehood . . . allowed Kabila to 'play state' and to create an impression of legal/institutional normality."[5]

It is unclear whether the peace brokers intended for Kabila to be able to dominate the transitional government, or whether this simply resulted from Kabila's leverage in negotiations. It is also important to remember—this is difficult in hindsight, given his tarnished reputation later—that the young president was popular, especially in the East, where he was seen as the response to Rwandan occupation. This dominance allowed Kabila to control the direction of the peace process and entrench his patronage networks, and it prevented other parts of Congolese society from demanding greater accountability. When I asked why donors did not push for a non-partisan, civil society leader to head the transition or at least for a more equitable sharing of power, diplomats from major embassies argued that this would not have been possible, suggesting that Kabila was in too strong a position.[6] This seems strange, for Rwandan troops had almost captured Lubumbashi, the country's mining hub, in December 2000; Joseph Kabila himself had taken over a very shaky government following his father's assassination in January 2001; and the Congolese government was deeply dependent on foreign military support. Below, I try to imagine what an alternative approach could have looked like.

The Failure to Transform the Congolese State

When it comes to civil wars, there is a tendency in the media and even among scholars to focus on the rebel side of the conflict, as I have done in the last three chapters, probing their motives, portraying them as ideological freedom fighters, greedy bandits, and extremists. This is perhaps because we are attracted to the romantic allure of rebellion, or because we are disposed to accept authority and normality but are excited by those who challenge these traits. The Congo confirms this tendency to focus on those opposing the state. There have been hundreds of studies on armed groups and their structure, their motives, and their underlying drivers. Very few since 2003 have focused on understanding the structure and interests of the state security apparatus.

This focus is misplaced. The main failings of donors involved state actors, in particular the Congolese government. If that government had wanted to address the conflict, it would have created disciplined, meritocratic security forces with parliamentary oversight and an apolitical system of military justice. It would have extended its demobilization and reinsertion program, integrating it into community-based development initiatives. It would have tried to transform the local economy of the eastern Congo to generate revenue and alleviate poverty by investing in agriculture and artisanal mining instead of focusing on industrial extraction of natural resources. And it would have worked more urgently to promote equitable land reform and agricultural development.

An obvious response to that kind of idealism is: That's crazy! Even a strong and efficient state would have had a hard time doing this, to say nothing of the patronage-riddled and weak Congolese administration. Yes, and reforms in neopatrimonial states come with costs for regimes and can, *in extremis*, lead to their demise if they crack down on the vested interests of power brokers. However, as I have highlighted throughout these pages, even low-cost, low-risk initiatives—setting up a demobilization plan, investing in public diplomacy, instructing local officials to engage in community reconciliation efforts—were neglected. There was little attempt by the government to reform, and it gradually became complicit—in particular through its notable apathy—in the persistence and escalation of conflict in the east of the country.

These missed opportunities were underscored by the arrival of Félix Tshisekedi in the presidency in January 2019. Within eighteen months and facing remarkably little backlash from either political or military elites, Tshisekedi marginalized Kabila and many of his close associates. While he has not, as of this writing, forged much greater accountability or efficiency, this suggests that patronage networks can be displaced and even dismantled without the kind of broad destabilization that many diplomats worried about.

The complicity of donors and peace-brokers in these dynamics took two main forms: focusing on technocratic reforms, rather than addressing the inequalities built into the structure of the Congolese state, and ignoring parallel developments in the private sector that dramatically entrenched the political elites in charge of the state. In doing so, wittingly or unwittingly, these donors and diplomats rendered themselves complicit to the conflict and extraction of resources.

Technocratic Solutions to Political Problems

Many of the donors working on the Congo have a deep appreciation of how the state works. Of the thirty-seven donors and diplomats I interviewed in my research, most of them articulated a frustration with the Congolese state and understood full well that the main interests of the Congolese state were not aligned with the imperatives of efficiency, transparency, and accountability. And yet, donor policy all too often ended up shoring up the Congolese state, providing enough resources to prevent it from collapsing but unable to bring about substantial reforms.

In part, this is due to internal dysfunctions of their own donor bureaucracy. "We understand that the state does not want to truly reform. We build new accounting systems for them, but that just means they steal money from elsewhere," one diplomat told me about the reforms they had supported in the management of civil servants. "However, our capital tells us we need to support this, because the Congo is an important place for us to be."[7] A World Bank official told me: "Nobody wants to be the [World] Bank director who shuts down a country program. Our internal incentives are to spend money. We are a bank, after all."[8] As studies of donors have shown elsewhere, the actions of donors were often shaped not by policy debates but by the demands of their own bureaucracies and the need to maintain relationships.[9]

These bureaucratic incentives then often create a way of framing the problems facing the Congo in abstract technocratic terms that strip away politics.[10] In general, a large part of donor policy interpreted state weakness and conflict as a dysfunction that needed to be fixed instead of an architecture set up to serve the interests of political elites.

This technocratic approach congealed following the elections of 2006.[11] In the conflict-ridden East, its main manifestations were the International Security and Stabilization Support Strategy (I4S, the main vehicle donors have used for conflict resolution in the eastern Congo), a demobilization program, and various attempts to reform the army and the police. At the national level, the World Bank, the South African government, the African Development Bank, the European Union, and the IMF have focused on improving the financial system, the state administration, regulation of the private sector, and the customs agency.

This transition to a stabilization framework was built on the problematic, implicit assumption that the Congolese government wanted to create efficient, disciplined institutions instead of privileging the cultivation of patronage networks and political survival. An Oxfam evaluation of the initial 2009–2012 phase of the I4S, for example, concluded that it suffered from the absence of government ownership.[12] Roads were built that were not maintained, and new police stations were constructed whose staff was not paid. All diplomats I interviewed who were involved in this initial phase of the I4S agreed with that assessment. Even when donors offered to fund a new demobilization plan in 2015, the Congolese government showed little interest. It was unable to provide the approximately 10 percent of the $90 million budget it had proposed; in the meantime, it invested at least $285 million in a chimerical and short-lived agro-industrial park in Bukanga Lonzo, of which $200 million went missing.[13] Indeed, between 2015 and 2020, there was no impetus for the creation of a new demobilization program, despite the thousands of combatants who self-demobilized across the country following the inauguration of President Félix Tshisekedi in 2019. Similarly, when the commander of a large Mai-Mai group, William Amuri Yakutumba, was brought to Kinshasa in 2007, ostensibly to persuade him to abandon his rebellion, he was left more or less to his own devices in the capital for six months. "It's as if our government just doesn't care," went the analysis of one of his commanders.[14]

The transformation in 2010 of the UN peacekeeping mission—from MONUC to MONUSCO—was also part of this stabilization logic, which entailed not questioning the underlying assumption that the government was a willing partner. The Security Council declared its three objectives: to conduct military operations in the East, to help reform Congolese security forces, and to consolidate state authority.[15] The UN mission, which had been relatively successful at midwifing the 2002 peace deal and in shepherding through the transitional government, the high-water mark of its political involvement, suddenly found itself politically marginalized. Despite the insistence by UN policymakers on the "primacy of the political," from 2007 onwards the mission stayed largely on the sidelines of the negotiations between the government and armed groups.[16] Negotiations with the CNDP and the M23 were bilateral, with the Congolese government largely insisting on keeping the peacekeeping mission in the dark; there were some efforts at local peacebuilding with other armed groups, but here as well the government mostly refused to empower the UN to become an official mediator. Without being able to play intermediary with the government, the UN often had little to offer these groups. In the end, the mission, outside of a few exceptions, found itself largely confined to what it does least well: the military protection of civilians in imminent danger. In the meantime, and despite the steady increase in violence since 2006, there has been no political process through which to deal with the conflict.

UN protection of civilians in the Congo often took place through joint operations with the FARDC, which were conducted sporadically since the early days of the transition in 2003. According to UN commanders and civilian leaders, these operations were above all useful in reducing the human rights violations of the FARDC and helped make progress against armed groups. However, these operations also sparked criticism from numerous sides. By backing the FARDC, MONUSCO became party to the conflict, undermining principles of impartiality in peacekeeping operations. It was also obliged to reconcile its support for the Congolese army—and to a lesser degree, for the police—with its mandate to protect civilians and the human rights principles of the United Nations.[17]

As highlighted throughout this book, the Congolese government's abuses range from its security services' abuse of civilians, to complicity with militia and armed groups, to inaction and passivity. Since 2013 the UN has tried to limit its complicity in this abuse through the Human Rights Due Diligence Policy, but given the complex nature of the government's involvement, this has proven difficult. For example, during their Sukola II operations against the FDLR in late 2015 and early 2016, the FARDC collaborated with local proxies, in particular the NDC-R and the Mai-Mai Mazembe, against the Rwandan rebels. This exacerbated local ethnic conflict, as the NDC-R and the Mazembe draw support from the Nyanga and Nande populations, respectively, and the FDLR collaborated with Nyatura, militia from the Congolese Hutu community. While MONUSCO did not back these militia or condone these operations, its backing of other aspects of Sukola II operations undermined its ability to publicly criticize these dynamics and compromised its impartiality in the eyes of the population. Similarly, the FARDC has been accused of being involved in the massacres around Beni in the 2014–2016 period; the FARDC commander of these operations, General Akili Mundos, was later sanctioned by the United Nations for his role in these killings. Nonetheless, MONUSCO provided support to some of Mundos's commanders during this period.

Finally, during the repression of peaceful protests that marked the prolonged 2015–2018 electoral season, police in Goma could be seen using motorcycles emblazoned with "Gift of MONUSCO" and youth activists complained that police trucks received fuel from MONUSCO gas stations before going out to disperse protesters. MONUSCO

FIGURE 9.3. Police motorcycle marked "Gift of MONUSCO" used
during repression of LUCHA demonstrations in Goma

officials have argued that this support allows them to influence police
officers and restrain human rights abuses.

When presented with this criticism of stabilization, some of the donors and diplomats I interviewed pushed back, arguing that they understood the internal politics of the Congolese state perfectly well and that
their approach was deeply political, even if it was not presented as such.
According to this logic, the only way to render the Congolese state more
accountable was to create greater accountability from within the state
as well as from other sectors in society. This has been the justification
for donor support to parliament, the courts, auditing bodies, and regulatory agencies. Drawing on liberal peacebuilding theory, donors have
backed civil society organizations, media outlets, and the private sector,
counting on them to hold the government accountable. State reform
and democratization, they argue, is a long-term process.

There is some truth to this. Reforms under the Third Republic,
many of which were backed by donors, have improved some aspects of
governance and have forged greater accountability, especially through
the electoral process. There is no question that public discourse has

been influenced by the activism of civil society and that the courts have been able to try and convict hundreds of abusers, often with the support of donors. The importance of elections has been upheld by a broad coalition of civil society organizations, resulting in parliamentary elections in 2006 and 2011 in which large numbers of incumbents were defeated.

However, eighteen years after the peace deal, this approach has not been successful in pushing the government to focus on reforming its security services, demobilizing armed groups, or finding lasting solutions to the problems of local governance and community reconciliation. Armed conflict looks very different today than in 2003—it does not, with the exception of Beni, threaten major urban centers or divide the country, but seen in terms of displacement and deaths, the situation was arguably worse in 2020. The private sector is still largely in the thrall of the state, and while committed civil society organizations regularly denounce government abuses and inaction, these calls do not seem to have had a measurable impact on government action, either in terms of policies implemented or in terms of a decrease in conflict.

Even in the areas of governance, the record is ambiguous. In the elections of 2011 and 2018 we can see how donors have provided real political constraints to the ruling class but also how they have backed down at key moments. Late in the run-up to the 2011 elections, Western donors realized that the elections would be deeply flawed and suspended their support. After condemning "seriously flawed polls"[18] that were "were not credible in the light of numerous irregularities and fraud witnessed during the electoral process,"[19] these same donors largely continued with their support in the Congo. Shortly after the elections debacle, the French government endorsed the holding of the global Francophonie Summit in Kinshasa, attended by French president François Hollande himself. Time and again, short-term goals trumped the deeper structural reforms that were necessary.

The run-up to the 2018 elections, which was supposed to herald the first democratic transfer of executive power in the country's history, was even more contentious. Serious protests erupted when Joseph Kabila's government considered changing the constitution to allow the incumbent to prolong his stay in office, as many other presidents on the continent had done. A powerful coalition of civil society actors, youth movements, and the Catholic Church emerged, backed at key moments by Western diplomats. This impressive mobilization had a clear impact: Kabila was prevented from changing the constitution and, after a long delay, elections were held in December 2018. By most accounts, Kabila was forced to retreat from his preferred outcome of imposing his hand-picked successor Ramazani Shadary, since election results showed him as losing the presidential election by a landslide.[20]

When elections came, however, they were still rigged. Kabila's coalition struck a deal with the runner-up, Félix Tshisekedi, to say that the latter had won, despite evidence that handed that distinction to another opposition figure, Martin Fayulu. In return, Kabila's coalition would be allowed to dominate the national assembly and most of the twenty-six provincial governments. This time, the United States endorsed this result—saying in private that it was the best possible outcome—and most other donors accepted it, also intimating that there was no better option.[21] "We know the elections were rigged," a Western ambassador told me in February 2019. "But they cost over a billion dollars—asking them to do them again is a non-starter. So we just make the best out of this situation."[22]

It is more likely, however, that donors and diplomats are not engaged in a process of constantly reviewing their theory of change, of trying to understand the main actors and their interests and then debating how best to attain their stated goals of democracy, development, and stability. These discussions, to the degree that they do take place—some major donors told me that these kinds of internal fora are rare and relatively exclusive—are constrained by bureaucratic imperatives and ideological frames. "I honestly do not think that MONUSCO's presence will be able to improve security. I think we should talk more seriously about shutting down the mission, but nobody wants to do that," one senior UN official said to me.[23] A European official told me, along similar lines: "We provide support to the national assembly, to other accountability bodies here in the Congo. But for every euro we spend, two euros are stolen, sometimes in complicity with banks and other companies based in Europe. It's a fool's game [*un jeu de dupes*]. But those are not discussions we are having."[24]

While foreign assistance has thus been able to support greater political accountability, it has proved to be insufficient to bring about systemic change, propping up and improving but not transforming governance. Most important for this book, donors have been unable to have much impact on conflict dynamics in the eastern Congo, providing billions in much-needed humanitarian aid but failing to reduce conflict.

The International Economic Stakes of the Congolese Peace Process

The second major flaw in how donors approaches the conflict was evident in how the economy was managed. The rapid liberalization of the Congolese economy during this period brought about dramatic growth but also compromised the peace process and helped entrench conflict dynamics related to the predatory state. Donors and diplomats were complicit, as they implemented policies based on preconceived templates of peacebuilding and refrained from enforcing stricter regulatory guidelines and conditionalities.

At the beginning of the transition in 2003, the Congolese economy was tiny, around $9 billion in terms of real GDP, and state revenues were only $730 million—as a comparison, the budget of my employer, New York University, in 2020 was $3.6 billion. The size of the Congolese economy, however, soon grew, as the peace process brought about the privatization of many of the country's most valuable mining and oil concessions, which Mobutu had nationalized. This privatization process rapidly and dramatically enriched the new governing elite. Global trends, driven by a booming demand in electronics and construction, reinforced the influx of foreign capital: copper prices grew from $0.65 per pound in 2001 to a peak $4.50 per pound in 2011, a 592 percent increase over ten years. Cobalt prices also roughly doubled in this period.

This privatization was backed and encouraged by donors who believed that private investment would not undermine the peace process but bolster it. This is a central tenet of liberal peacebuilding, which assumes that a rights-based democracy and a market-oriented economy are the best foundations for sustained and equitable peace.[25]

When the World Bank helped draft the 2002 mining law and helped reform state-run companies, and foreign embassies encouraged private business development, they chose not to scrutinize too closely the close connection between politics and business. Some of the investments in mining, for example, were extremely questionable, made far beneath market prices by shadowy offshore companies. Estimates for losses of just a few of these deals range between $1.36 billion and $5.5 billion.[26] One of the players in these deals, Israeli businessman Dan Gertler, was reportedly worth around $1.2 billion, based on wealth amassed almost solely in the Congo.[27]

While most mediatized, this large-scale theft by small operators was arguably a smaller problem than transfer pricing and tax evasion by reputable multinationals. Since the Congolese government's main tax for mining companies is on profits, many declare losses for their local subsidiaries while transferring the profits to a more lenient tax jurisdiction. For example, a study of Glencore, the largest mining company in the Congo, found that its Congolese subsidiary Kamoto Copper Company declared losses of hundreds of millions of dollars between 2009 and 2013. During this same period, Glencore's Canadian subsidiary Katanga Mining Ltd. ran at a net profit of over $400 million, resulting in a $150 million loss to Congolese state coffers.[28] Civil society organizations have made similar criticisms of other multinationals.[29]

This transfer pricing, along with the squirrelling away of corruption money by elites, led to massive flows of money out of the country. According to one calculation, $25.6 billion left in the Congo in capital flight between 1996 and 2010, $4.2 billion of which came during the three years of the transitional government.[30] That is almost as much as the entire government revenue for this period; much of this money went to Europe or North America. While the World Bank did not support most of these deals directly—although it did provide risk insurance to some—it invested billions in loans and grants to the Congo during this period and was intimately involved in supporting the reform of the public mining sector.

During this period, the country's economy grew rapidly, quadrupling in size between 2003 and 2015 as foreign investment poured into the mining, banking, and telecommunication sectors. It is difficult to clarify how this income was distributed, as tax records are not publicly available and household surveys tend to not capture the incomes of the very wealthy. Anecdotally, however, it appears clear that the enormous wealth that accrued to the ruling elite during this period solidified their hold on power and undermined democracy. Interviews with parliamentarians suggest that they are often paid *"avec des enveloppes"* for their votes on bills, and judges have reported similar pressure for sensitive cases.[31]

Other examples abound. Indirect elections for governors and senators became deeply corrupt, as it was fairly easy to bribe several dozen provincial legislators. Every round of these indirect elections saw stories in the media of votes being sold for up to $50,000, suggesting that some governors would have to spend millions of dollars to win.[32] Even direct elections were costly, as campaigning across the country was expensive. According to sources within their respective campaigns, the 2006 presidential election cost Joseph Kabila at least $10 million, and the 2011 campaign for Étienne Tshisekedi, an opposition candidate of relatively modest means, cost $5 million.[33] In 2017, the ruling coalition changed the electoral law, such that political parties had to win 1 percent of votes in the legislative election in order to take a seat in the national assembly. It is estimated that fielding candidates in all national elections will now cost a political party $1 million in non-refundable deposits, not counting the cost of the campaign itself. These conditions clearly favor those with access to state resources and power.

Donors did eventually adjust their approach slightly, focusing less on institutional reforms and more on corruption. After years of providing billions in loans, the International Monetary Fund suspended its program in 2012 over governance concerns, while the World Bank scaled back its support around the same time.[34] By 2016, many of the major Western-backed institutional reform projects had ground to a halt. "There is no reason we should spend millions of dollars on programs that die as soon as we stop funding them," a senior American aid official told me. "We have shifted our resources almost entirely away from supporting state reforms," a senior British aid official concurred, "into the private sector and to NGOs, as the government just doesn't have the political will to carry out these reforms."[35]

Was the liberalization of the Congolese economy a plan orchestrated by Western elites? Such theories are popular in the Congo, particularly the notion that MONUSCO and the peace process are part of a concerted strategy of Western countries—in particular the United States, France, and the United Kingdom—to loot the Congo's natural resources and balkanize the country.[36] In 2012 and 2013, during the M23 rebellion, *Le Potentiel*, a leading newspaper in Kinshasa, ran a large banner across to top of the front page for many months saying: *"Non à la balkanization!"*

In many of my interviews with combatants and civil society members alike, the premise that the Congo was intentionally being kept poor and conflict-ridden to benefit foreigners kept cropping up. An army officer in rural Walikale told me: "I went to law school. They taught us a principle: *Cui bono?* Who benefits from the crime? In the case of the war in the Congo it is foreign companies, foreign NGOs, foreign journalists. Even you! Certainly not us."[37]

There is some evidence of this from the early days of the transition. In particular, the US government played a critical role in obtaining one of the crown jewels of the mining concessions: Tenke Fungurume. According to numerous sources, as well as my own observations at the time, the US embassy in Kinshasa was actively engaged in making sure that Freeport McMoran, a company based in Arizona, obtained the concession, over protests from members of the Congolese government and civil society over a lack of transparency and contractual flaws.[38] The first political secretary at the US embassy, Melissa Sanderson, left soon thereafter to take a lead role at Freeport McMoran. Other diplomats also lobbied for companies based in their countries to obtain critical assets during this period.

However, in the long run, the liberalization of the economy did not resemble a centrally controlled strategy by a select number of countries. Rather, donors and diplomats acted uncritically in accordance with the belief that privatization and foreign investment would bring greater prosperity and stability in the Congo. Once the floodgates of private investment were open, international capital then moved with little control by political elites in individual countries. For example, profits from the sale of Congolese mining assets were not confined to a single Western country. At the time of writing, the largest owner of Congolese mining assets is Glencore PLC, which has its headquarters in Switzerland, is registered in the island of Jersey, and is listed on the London and Johannesburg stock exchanges. Several of the country's largest mines are owned by the Eurasian Natural Resources Corporation, which is headquartered in Luxembourg and was listed on the London Stock Exchange before coming under scrutiny by regulators and delisting in 2013. The company was renamed Eurasian Resources Group; it is now privately owned and based in Luxembourg, with the Kazakh government retaining 40 percent of its shares.

Chinese investment in the Congo has grown dramatically since a 2007 deal with the Congolese government. In 2016, Tenke Fungurume was sold to China Molybdenum, which is owned by the Chinese government and private shareholders. Between 2012 and 2017, Chinese mining companies—some private, some publicly traded, some state-owned—spent more than $10 billion purchasing or investing in mining projects in Katanga.[39] Chinese investors now own many of the large mining companies in the Congo.

In other words, if there is a conspiracy to keep the Congo poor and weak, the economic evidence suggests that it would not be either only Western or piloted by governments. Rather, the liberal peacebuilding approach opened to Congo up to private capital, which obtained mining deals for bargain prices, taking advantage of the poor regulatory framework in the Congo and the opacity of the international financial system. This ended up creating few jobs for Congolese and leaving little profit in the country. And while multinational capital has benefited considerably from the peace process in the Congo, there is also little evidence that these companies engineered it or that they benefit from continued violence in the country.

Ironically, the public focus during much of this period was not on industrial mining but on "conflict minerals," which NGO activists have linked to the conflict in the eastern Congo. Organizations such as the Enough Project and V-Day were able to galvanize enormous attention for the Congolese conflict by focusing on two themes: sexual violence and conflict minerals. Weaving these two together, they explained the conflict in a more readily digestible fashion, at the same time linking it to American consumers and their use of electronics containing Congolese tin, tungsten, and tantalum. They crafted slogans like, "Don't want your cell phone to fuel war in the Congo? Tell Obama!"

The crisis attracted bipartisan support in the United States, with former senators Russ Feingold and Sam Brownback traveling several times to the region; a freshman senator named Barack Obama even sponsored a Congo-focused bill. Lisa Shannon, a photography producer from Portland, Oregon, was personally affected when she saw a description of the conflict on *The Oprah Winfrey Show* and founded A Thousand Sisters, which has raised over $11 million in support of Congolese women. In 2009, these efforts were joined by actor Ben Affleck, who founded the Eastern Congo Initiative, and over the past few years a stream of other celebrities have become involved in Congo, including Ryan Gosling, Angelina Jolie, Robin Wright Penn, and Javier Bardem. These initiatives eventually led to the passing of the Congo Minerals Act in 2010, requiring companies to report on their efforts to avoid trading in conflict minerals from the Congo. The Organisation for Economic Cooperation and Development (OECD) and the European Union followed suit, issuing slightly different guidelines and regulations in 2011 and 2017, respectively.

While these minerals do form important parts of the local conflict economy in the Kivus, they present minor stakes for the state and the broader economy. Tin, tungsten, and tantalum, the three main "conflict minerals," amounted to less than 2 percent of total Congo mineral exports in 2012 and 2013,[40] most of it mined artisanally and not amenable for rents that could be extracted by elites in Kinshasa.

Even in the Kivus, the importance of conflict minerals was never straightforward and was almost always mediated by other factors. How artisanal mining affects Congolese society depends on the regulatory framework, the way miners are ruled by local customary or political authorities, the position of the Congo in the global economy, and the interactions among the miners, administrators, combatants, businessmen, and politicians involved in the trade. For example, in Shabunda territory in South Kivu, many artisanal miners were drawn into armed groups in 2011 when the Congolese army withdrew from the area and protection rackets shifted to the FDLR. Elsewhere, minerals have been an enabler but not a cause of conflict—the Nyatura commanders of Kalehe territory in South Kivu defected from the Congolese army due to perceived mistreatment. Only after they arrived in rural Kalehe did they become invested in tin and gold mining. As Christopher Cramer puts it: "[T]he roots of conflict do lie in political economy, but . . . this involves investigating the changes in social relations and material conditions within which individuals act."[41]

The CNDP is another case in point. Minerals did play an important role in the CNDP's formation as well as during a brief period in 2004. During the 1998–2003 war, business in Goma and the surrounding areas was controlled by the RCD, members of the Rwandan military establishment, and businessmen affiliated with them. With the end of the RCD rebellion, these business networks were threatened, and some evidence suggests that the formation of the CNDP occurred, in part, as a reaction to those threats.[42] In December 2004, however, the ex-RCD officers were pushed out of the main mining areas they controlled. While Nkunda's men would control smaller tantalum mines in Masisi territory intermittently between 2005 and 2008, the taxation of mining pits no longer constituted a major part of their internal financing.[43] Other important sources of CNDP revenues included millions of dollars in illegal taxes and extortion from local trade.[44]

Former members of the CNDP have observed that the minerals trade, while important, should be seen as just one of several motives for maintaining control over parts of the Kivus: "You can always make money—it can be smuggling, taxation, cannabis, or charcoal. Minerals were important. But the main objective was just to have influence and control. The rest will follow."[45]

His conclusion is bolstered by the fact that many businessmen in Goma formerly affiliated with the Rwandan government or the RCD switched allegiances during this period and began working with the Kabila government.[46] There is, in other words, no inherent connection between business and rebellion.

The fact that the marginalization of the RCD produced conflict only in one small part of the areas under their control in the 1998–2003 period suggests that natural resources resulted in conflict when only they combined with other factors, in particular the interests of a small Tutsi military in the southern part of North Kivu. It is telling that natural resources were equally prevalent in Ituri district and eastern Maniema province, but armed group activity in those areas decreased between 2007 and 2017.

In sum, artisanal mining in the Kivus was rarely the main trigger of conflict, although it has often been a factor in the persistence of armed groups. Reforming the mining sector in the eastern Congo and making it more transparent and accountable are good things, there is no doubt. But haste can cause unintended consequences—the focus on conflict minerals led to an initial ban on exports of minerals in 2010, leaving many miners out of a job. When trade started up again the following year, the due diligence requirements created a quasi-monopoly in the tin trade for a certification scheme managed by an industry body, the International Tin Research Institute (ITRI), which was in turn criticized for being expensive and untransparent.[47] While there are signs that over the following decades these due diligence laws and guidelines produced greater accountability, they—initially, at least—also led to difficult economic times for the vulnerable pick-and-shovel miners and their families. Meanwhile, while some armed groups have lost access to some mines, others have diversified their extortion rackets—one can certainly not say that the eastern Congo has become a more stable place since 2010.

Donors and activists have been very proactive in reforming the governance of artisanal mining in the East, but they have been much less focused on the much more lucrative industrial mining sector. While that sector was not directly linked to armed groups, it played a large role in providing the resources necessary for the central government to sustain itself and its patronage networks during this period.

Alternative Realities: What Could Have Been Done Differently

The challenge of rebuilding "failed states" has come to international prominence in the past fifteen years, not least due to US wars in Iraq and Afghanistan. Most scholars agree that a critical factor in the success of such efforts is the ability to forge agreement among key stakeholders about the structure and nature of political institutions and how power will be shared in politics, society, and the economy. This understanding of postconflict political orders is commonly referred to as "political settlement analysis"; it has become an important framework for policy-making in the UK government, the Organisation for Economic Co-operation and Development (OECD), and the World Bank.[48] In the Congo, this language is particularly noticeable among British diplomats and aid officials, who have funded research and drafted policy analysis based on this concept.[49] This language has been prominent in recent flagship conflict prevention reports—such as the World Bank's 2011 *World Development Report* or the joint World Bank/United Nations *Pathways to Peace* report from 2018.

Political settlement analysis builds on scholarship on state formation, which argues that in order for states to be stable and resilient, there must be inclusive elite bargains. A seminal report drafted for the World Bank by scholars of institutional development argues that the first step toward the development of institutions is the creation of a dominant coalition that can centralize rents and monopolize violence.[50] Similarly, Alex de Waal, using the metaphor of a political marketplace, argues that "the best patrimonial solution is a robust and inclusive buy-in. This generates genuine political good for the country in question."[51]

My analysis here suggests, however, that there is no inherent link between elite deals and stability. By most accounts, the Congolese peace deal did end up forging a fairly broad political settlement supported by a significant injection of capital and funds from international multinationals. However, as described in chapters 3 and 4, the Congolese bargain created a small elite of politicians and military officers who have been able to capture the main sources of revenue from the national economy and have remained either apathetic toward or actively invested in the continuation of conflict and instability. And instead of conflict resulting from a settlement that locked out other elites, who then employ violence as means to be included in the bargain, much of the violence in the Congo has been the result of bargaining *within* the ruling elite and a means of distributing patronage. By 2015, even armed groups in the Kivus were mostly deploying violence not in a bid to be bought off but in order to survive and maintain their fiefdoms. In other words, political settlements in some circumstances do not end conflict but instead require it.

So if the core flaw of the peace process was not a lack of inclusion, then what was it? Imagining alternative realities can help us to lose the feeling of inevitability this history can elicit. In 2006, Kabila could have harnessed the overwhelming international good will that then existed for a genuine reform of the security sector and demobilization. There is no reason to believe that there was a fundamental contradiction between his survival and the creation of a more efficient, less abusive security sector. While the CNDP rebellion was largely out of his hands, Kabila could have reassured the Congolese Tutsi community instead of allowing his commanders to antagonize it.[52] Instead of using militias as proxies against the CNDP, the government could have punished that behavior and reformed the army. It would have been impossible to get rid of corruption and patronage overnight, but key reforms would have been feasible, such as slashing the size of the army and confining most troops to barracks while raising their pay and living conditions.

Meanwhile, donors and diplomats could have maintained their political engagement and not shifted to a technocratic approach after the 2006 elections. Some members of the international community were pushing in this direction—in 2006, the World Bank and the UNDP developed a "Governance Compact" that was supposed to provide terms for future engagement by donors in the Congo, including mutual accountability.[53] After the elections, however, the compact was quickly jettisoned. The country opened to business, and each major donor pursued its own goals. This was fine with the Congolese government, which steadfastly rejected any attempts to coordinate major reform projects. Reforms in the security sector was a good example of this, as Belgium, South Africa, the United States, France, and Angola each trained different parts of the army, without coordinating conditions or the overarching framework.

There could have been coordinated multilateral engagement on reforms in the security sector, justice, and administration, conditioned on clear ownership demonstrated by the Congolese. Donors could have demanded more accountability and governance, including through greater support to parliament and regulatory bodies, to political parties, to civil society, and to the electoral process. Instead of seeing political pressure as a potential spoiler in its relations with the Congolese government, the UN peacekeeping mission could have seen political reforms as a prerequisite for further engagement. The kind of short-termism evident in the grudging acceptance of electoral fraud in 2011 and 2018 could have been replaced with a more principled, long-term engagement.

Aid makes little sense if the ruling elite can siphon billions from public coffers, particularly through mining contracts and other forms of direct foreign investment. Given the involvement of the World Bank in drafting a new mining code and of all donors in promoting international investment, there should have been much closer scrutiny of the activities of multinational corporations, especially those involved in extractive industries—mining, timber, and oil—with profit margins of sufficient magnitude to make the risky environments of a postconflict setting worthwhile. Such additional scrutiny should also have included the banking sector, which is critical in gaining access to international capital, and to laundering and offshoring illicit proceeds. After all, many of these companies were initially, in the early years following the peace deal, based in the major donor countries or listed on their stock exchanges.

Additional scrutiny did come belatedly with investigations launched by the Department of Justice and the Department of the Treasury in the United States and by the Serious Fraud Office in the United Kingdom, culminating in US sanctions on Dan Gertler in 2017 and a guilty verdict against the US hedge fund Och-Ziff in 2016. By then, however, it may have been too late, for by that point much of the money lost by the Congolese state was unrecoverable. In general, mechanisms could have been put in place, managed by the World Bank or the United Nations, to allow closer scrutiny of private investments following 2002 and to enforce punishment of violations.

One of the most striking features of donor intervention was not just the poor outcomes but the process as well. There was strikingly little public discussion of the broad structural approach needed to transform the Congolese state. The focus was programmatic and short-term—reminiscent of the "anti-politics machine" described by James Ferguson in Lesotho in the 1980s—with most donor officials not staying longer than three or four years in the post.[54] The Poverty Reduction Strategy Papers, which formed the basis of donor strategy between 2001 and 2015, were comprehensive and coherent plans to boost economic growth and create more accountable governance, but they were apolitical. They did not provide a theory for why corruption and violence had become so entrenched and how donor assistance could uproot them.[55] Nor did they address capital flight, the dramatic inequality in land and other sources of wealth in the Congo, or the lack of revenues generated by the extractives sector.

When a theory of change does shine through it is usually this: over time, free markets will lead to a growing middle class, which, coupled with a strong media environment, elections, and civil society, will forge more accountable government, creating a virtuous cycle of growth and good governance. There is, unfortunately, little evidence of this trajectory taking hold. As in much of Africa, the liberalization of markets has led to growth but also to rampant inequality, which in turn has undermined democratic politics and elite accountability.[56]

Rwanda's Continued Interference

Perhaps the most glaring flaw in foreign engagement was with regard to Rwanda. What would the Congolese conflict have looked like if Rwanda had cut off its support to armed groups in its neighbor entirely with the

Pretoria Agreement in 2002? There could have been different gradations of this—it could have actively clamped down on support networks, denied safe haven to armed groups, and encouraged its former RCD allies to pursue their political ambitions peacefully.

Even a modest engagement in peacemaking by Kigali would have rendered the creation of the CNDP difficult, if not impossible. As outlined in chapter 4, Nkunda's refusal to join the FARDC was in part due to pressure from Kigali, whose officials launched a campaign among their RCD allies against the Kabila government. The Bukavu mutiny of 2004, a precursor to the CNDP, was fomented by Rwanda's nomination of a governor and senior military officers who were accused of having killed President Kabila's father. The critical alliance between Nkunda and Eugène Serufuli, governor of North Kivu, was also unlikely to have come about without Rwandan pressure, as one of Serufuli's close advisors admitted to me.[57] Finally, it is unlikely that Bosco Ntaganda and his colleagues from Ituri would have joined the CNDP without prompting by the Rwandan government. Without these interventions, and despite persistent tensions between the CNDP and Kigali, it is difficult to imagine the creation of the CNDP.

It is even clearer that the M23 could not have emerged without Rwandan backing. The Rwandan Defense Forces propped up every large-scale offensive carried out by the M23, including those on Bunagana and Rutshuru in July 2012 and on Goma in November 2012. In addition, the RDF supplied weapons, ammunition, medical care, recruitment, and free passage for troops and politicians throughout the M23's existence. According to diplomats and M23 officers, once the Rwandan government decided to cease their support, the movement quickly collapsed.

The Reasons for Donor Complacency and Complicity

Given the importance of Rwandan meddling, why did the donor community do so little to counteract it? The paradox is striking: the same donors who were providing almost half of Rwanda's budget during the 2006–2013 period paid for the bulk of the humanitarian response the crisis caused, in part by the Rwandan government in neighboring

Congo. I argue that the reason for this lies in donors' investment in the narrative of the Rwandan success story, guilt and compassion for the genocide, a lack of understanding of Rwandan involvement in the Congo, and bureaucratic dysfunction.

Rwanda is a beacon of success in development aid. According to the government, more than a million people were lifted out of poverty in Rwanda—a country of 11 million—between 2006 and 2016, with some estimates putting the number even higher.[58] Under-five mortality dropped by 70 percent between 2000 and 2013, and maternal mortality decreased by 50 percent between 2000 and 2010.[59] These statistics have been contested by close followers of Rwandan development.[60] For those who have agreed with the data, however, this makes Rwanda an exception in a landscape in which development aid is often questioned. "When we spend money here, we know it goes to good use," a senior British aid official told me.[61] The British government reportedly concluded that aid to Rwanda offered the best value for taxpayers' money in the world.[62]

Perhaps this admiration clouded donors' vision, preventing them from acknowledging the link between donor backing to Rwanda and the Congolese conflict. In addition, Rwanda's support to armed groups in the Congo was a matter of speculation to most diplomats until the M23 crisis, and without certainty there was little appetite to undermine what for many donors were flagship aid programs.

This uncertainty was accentuated by a "labor of confusion" led by the Rwandan government.[63] Rwandan diplomats aggressively challenged their critics. Steve Hege, the author of a United Nations report on support to the M23, for example, was threatened, vilified in the Rwandan press, and labeled a genocide denier. Following Rwandan lobbying, he was reportedly blocked from consultancies at the United Nations.[64] I faced aggressive criticism after my publications on the M23, as did Ida Sawyer, the lead researcher for Human Rights Watch.[65] Given that almost all of our work was based on eyewitness testimony, the strategy was to discredit our legitimacy and that of our sources. Important opinion leaders with whom the Rwandan government had close ties could also be relied on to back them up. Jendayi Frazier, the former US assistant secretary of state for Africa, appeared on television, rejecting any

Box 9.1. Perceptions of the Rwandan Patriotic Front by Western diplomats

"We heard about abuses carried out by the Rwandans in the eastern Congo, but we were not sure. We didn't have good information."

—HOWARD WOLPE, US SPECIAL ENVOY TO THE AFRICAN
GREAT LAKES (1997–2001), IN A 2008 INTERVIEW.

"I am fed up with people criticizing the Rwandan government. They have every right to be concerned about the FDLR threat from the Congo. These *genocidaires* are just waiting to finish the job they began in 1994."

—CINDY COURVILLE, SENIOR DIRECTOR FOR AFRICA,
US NATIONAL SECURITY COUNCIL, IN A 2006 INTERVIEW.

"We did the right thing with Rwanda. We needed to help them rebuild after the genocide. We engaged and challenged them over human rights abuses, but they also had genuine security concerns."

—SUE HOGWOOD, UK AMBASSADOR TO RWANDA (2001–2004),
IN A 2008 INTERVIEW.

"Yes, we think the Rwandan government is involved in the eastern Congo. But we also have to understand the impact that cutting aid will have on successful programs here."

—SENIOR DUTCH EMBASSY OFFICIAL IN RWANDA, IN A 2012 INTERVIEW

Rwandan support to the M23. When Bill Clinton visited Kigali in the middle of the M23 fracas in September 2012, he studiously avoided the subject of the conflict in the neighboring Congo in media interviews and praised President Paul Kagame.

Even for those who believed that Rwanda was involved wondered whether intervention could be legitimate or whether the risks of cutting aid could outdo the benefits. In an opinion piece in February 2013, Tony Blair and Howard Buffett (the son of billionaire Warren Buffett) suggested that the M23 may be justified, as it was formed to "defend the Tutsi minority in eastern Congo." They continued:

> Slashing international support to Rwanda ignores the complexity of the problem within DRC's own borders and the history and circumstances that have led to current regional dynamics. Cutting aid does nothing to address the underlying issues driving conflict in the region, it only ensures that the Rwandan people will suffer—and risks further destabilizing an already troubled region. Cutting aid to

Rwanda also risks undoing one of Africa's great success stories. In the last five years, Rwanda has lifted 1 million people out of poverty, created 1 million new jobs, and is poised to meet most of the U.N. Millennium Development Goals.[66]

Buffett even hired a former CIA analyst to discredit Hege's UN report on the M23. Similarly, the US ambassador to the UN, Susan Rice—another long-standing supporter of Paul Kagame—focused blame on the Congolese government. She reportedly told fellow diplomats at the United Nations: "This is the DRC. If it weren't the M23 doing this, it would be some other group."[67]

But the M23 emerged at an exceptional moment when Rwandan interference in the Congo had become apparent, and their justifications had started to lose credibility. "During the Nkunda years, we heard rumors and speculation, we were never quite sure, certainly not sure enough to cut aid programs. During the M23 we knew," one veteran State Department official remembered.[68]

A Different Approach to Rwanda

Rwanda's interference in the eastern Congo constitutes a significant failure of peacemaking. There were no critical national security or economic interests that could have led any of the world or regional powers to back Kigali's ventures in the eastern Congo. Nor was it a matter of a lack of leverage: as noted above, foreign donors contributed around half—and in some years more—of Rwanda's budget. Norms of sovereignty would have allowed diplomats to sway regional countries, where Rwanda had few allies during this period, as well as more recalcitrant members of the UN Security Council to pressure Kigali.

There is little evidence that the failure of the international community to act on Rwandan intervention was because of a US-backed conspiracy against the Congo. Such a conspiracy would require both a motive and protagonists. The allegations that the United States wanted to plunder minerals there does not hold up: the Congo makes up only around 1 percent of global tin production, and that tin is mined artisanally. While tantalum production in Rwanda and the Congo in 2015 made up over half of the global consumption, it was only around 5 percent of global consumption during the critical 2005–2008 period.[69] While it is entirely plausible that individual mining companies had an interest in maintaining their supply chains, if countries like the United States had been swayed by corporate interests, they would have probably tried to generate the kind of political stability required for the industrial extraction of minerals.

The conclusion here is in some ways grimmer. Instead of an international conspiracy, the diplomatic failings were driven by a lack of interest and engagement. Policy was guided more by personal relationships and preconceived assumptions than facts. The presumption of a threat posed by FDLR, which had not launched a significant incursion into Rwanda since April 2001, was not questioned, and the allegations of significant RDF backing to the CNDP were not critically scrutinized. Instead, donors built up an image of a resurgent Rwanda surmounting incredible odds to rebuild in the wake of genocide. Despite high funding levels for development and humanitarian programming, few resources were invested in uncovering Rwandan actions in the Congo between 2002, the year the Rwandan army officially withdrew, and 2013, when the M23 fell apart.

This conclusion is gleaned from personal experience. In 2008, I led a UN Group of Experts tasked with uncovering illegal backing of armed groups in the eastern Congo. There were only five of us, and we had few resources—I was forced to use an insecure Yahoo! email account and we had no security training. Despite a UN Security Council mandate, France, the United Kingdom, and the United States did not provide us with any substantive responses to our requests for information about specific bank and email accounts linked to armed groups. When we briefed officials from those countries, it was clear that they had relatively superficial information about the security situation in the Kivus. An analysis of US State Department cables during this period leaked by WikiLeaks reveals a good understanding of politics in Kinshasa by the embassy there, as well as deep suspicions of Rwanda, but no actionable intelligence on Rwandan backing of the CNDP.

A more serious approach would have invested more diplomatic and intelligence resources in gathering information, which then should have informed conversations in capitals and could have deconstructed the stereotypes of Congolese state dysfunction and Rwanda victimhood. Such an approach would also have provided significant resources to the UN peacekeeping mission on the ground, as well as to the UN Group of Experts.

Policy did shift, but not until 2012, when the M23 collapsed and Rwanda was forced to intervene much more obviously to back up its ally. Russ Feingold—a former senator and then the well-connected US envoy to the region—armed with reporting from the UN Group of Experts, Human Rights Watch, and US intelligence, played a critical role within the Obama administration and in talks with the Rwandan government, while other countries also took action by cutting their aid to Rwanda, eventually causing the RDF to pull their backing of the M23.

Conclusion

Stability is not likely to return to the eastern Congo soon. In Ituri, we saw that if action is taken quickly, even within the context of a weak state and an abundance of natural resources, the dynamics of armed mobilization can be nipped in the bud. Even there, there have been signs since 2017 that the stability could crumble if state institutions are not strengthened. In the Kivus, armed mobilization never ceased; it is now well into its third decade and is deeply entrenched in the local economy and society.

It did not have to be this way. During the early days of the Congolese transition, armed groups demobilized *en masse*, and internal displacement dropped to historic lows. Diligent scrutiny of and firm pressure on the Rwandan government could have prevented the birth of the CNDP, which, in turn, could have staved off the creation of dozens of other armed groups, the massive deployment of FARDC troops to the Kivus, and the fostering of the *pompier-pyromane* that has become a cornerstone of Congolese politics.

Conflict would not have ceased altogether. The nascent FARDC was unlikely to have been successful in dismantling all armed groups, and the massive demobilization of 130,000 soldiers would have certainly produced malcontents and recycled rebels. However, without the powerful fulcrum of Rwandan-backed aggression, it would have been possible to focus earlier on getting rid of the FDLR, which would have weakened other armed groups. Conflict would likely have been an order of magnitude smaller, and that would have prevented army officers from becoming so involved in institutionalizing disorder.

Today, however, foreign governments, especially Rwanda, are much less involved than in the past, and simple solutions are harder to come by. The conflict has transformed trade networks, social hierarchies, mentalities, and political structures—there is no one strand of this cat's cradle that can be tugged to collapse it. Now, despite the complexity and multipolarity of Congo's conflict, it is difficult to imagine a lasting transformation of the conflict ecosystem that does not involve the state. Only the state can provide durable incentives—either the carrots of demobilization or army integration, or the harsh stick of military operations. National institutions are inevitably involved in addressing the root causes of local grievances, ranging from land tenure to customary rule and development. And while the state has never lived up to its Lumumbist, postcolonial promise, it continues to occupy the center of Congolese political imagination: it is the ultimate prize to be controlled, reformed, or overthrown.

As I hope this book has made clear, the challenges facing Congolese are generational. At the local level, they will have to contend with the demobilization of hundreds of armed groups and the psychological and social scars of decades of war. At the national level, they will have to battle a political elite that has become less accountable and more corrupt as massive investment has flowed into the country. Meanwhile, on the international scene, they will have to contend with a relatively apathetic Africa community of states and a Western donor community that has done little to constrain international capital and often fails to live up to its high-minded human rights rhetoric. These are not technical battles but rather struggles for power, for control over local and national politics.

The messages, like the one at the beginning of this chapter, coming from many Congolese recognize this, pointing the way toward a different kind of engagement. The youth movement, LUCHA, was created in 2011 by youths in Goma as a new form of mobilization. It refused foreign financial support, created a flat organizational structure with consensual decision-making, and focused on the bread-and-butter issues of governance: water, electricity, and security. Their main actions were visible, popular protests in front of state institutions. While these protests were rarely much larger than a hundred youths, the organization quickly rose to the forefront in criticism of the Congolese state and embodied a new kind of political engagement. "We want to show people that politics is not about access to power, that it is about serving others, about caring," Luc Nkulula, one of their leaders who shortly afterwards died tragically in a fire, told me.[70]

Others share this vision, as well, albeit in different ways. Over the past seventeen years, I have come to know General Prosper Nabyolwa well. With over forty years of experience in the army, he was the commander of South Kivu province and is now deputy chief of staff of the FARDC in Kinshasa. In 2013, when donors and NGOs were undergoing a major push to promote security sector reform, Nabyolwa told me: "This is all fine. But the problem of the Congolese army is not about training some battalions and building new barracks. You have to reform *l'homme congolais* [the Congolese man]. We are supposed to become soldiers to protect other Congolese, to give our lives for them. Where has that spirit gone?"

A Congolese human rights lawyer—one of the leaders of the boom in civil society activity in the 1990s—Pascal Kambale, over the series of many debates, has persuaded me that the spirit exists, stifled under layers of incrusted elites. "Yes, our political leaders are sick with corruption, and violence is far too acceptable," he says. "But that's the surface. Look below that surface and you will find a Congolese society bustling with dynamism, eager to criticize and defy its own leaders, eager to transform their own country. We just need to give them a voice. Our day will come."

In 2017, I conducted a poll with a local polling institute that confirmed Pascal's premonition. It revealed an electorate disgusted by its leaders, yet strangely attached to democracy. One of the many questions we asked was whether they wanted elections, security, or development. Fully 86 percent either said, "elections" or "all three go together," rejecting an argument proffered by some government officials that the people wanted food on their plate, not elections. This was astounding: even provinces with endemic violence, such as Sud-Kivu (43%), and those that were very poor, such as Mai-Ndombe (72.4%) saw elections as the absolute priority. For a population struggling to make ends meet, and facing pervasive insecurity, these results were remarkable.

Those figures confirm my experience of Congolese politics over the past nineteen years tend to confirm this: it is noisy, messy, and vibrant. This provides hope.

ACKNOWLEDGMENTS

THIS BOOK has been a long time in the making, drawing on twenty years of research and travels in the Democratic Republic of the Congo. It could not have been possible without the support, advice, and help of many. It is my family that deserves my greatest gratitude, for suffering my prolonged absences, my late nights at work, and my quirky and quixotic passions for all things Congo. Lusungu, Baye, and Masha: *Asanteni sana, matondo mingi*. Mom, Dad, Justin—you have been an anchor throughout this journey.

Since first setting foot in Bukavu in 2001, I have been hosted, taught, and accompanied by a multitude of kind, generous people. Raphael Wakenge, Kizito Mushizi—*grand frère, koko bwenene à toute la famille*—Christian Mukosa, Balzac Buzera, Berthe Misabiko, Tshivu Ntite, Sumbu Mambu, *toute la famille* Aziz, Willy Mikenye, and *bandugu bote ba* DDR (*nzagaruka!*). This warm welcome then extended to Kinshasa, where I would not have been able to survive without the warm guidance and support of Michel Losembe, Djo Munga, Thomas Luhaka, Patrick Muyaya, Nickson Kambale, Jean-Luc Mutokambali, and many others.

The research for this book relied on the help of many, especially Blaise Karege, Willy Mikenye, Lievain Mukingi, Juvenal Twaibu, Remy Ngabo, Judith Verweijen, Gillian Mathys, and Henning Tamm. Zachariah Mampilly, Kwame Ato Onoma, Alex de Waal, Koen Vlassenroot, Pascal Kambale, and Joshua Walker gave me valuable, patient feedback. My PhD advisor Elisabeth Wood was generous, challenging, and above all kind. To my friends at the Rift Valley Institute—especially Michel Thill, Kit Kidner, and John Ryle—which supported much of this research: *Shukran*.

Many others contributed to this project as sources, researchers, or by opening their houses, kitchens, and address books to me. Some of them I cannot name for reasons of confidentiality, but I warmly thank Serge Muhima, Johan Peleman, Federico Borello, Francesca Jannotti, Christian Pay-Pay, Prosper Nabyolwa, Christian Deschryver, Peter Kaodi, Robert Seninga, Felicien Miganda, and Enoch Ruberangabo. Tragically, Serge Maheshe, Luc Nkulula, Blaise Ngabo, Alison Desforges, and Pascal Kabungulu did not live to see the publication of this book—I remain in their debt.

At some point in this journey, we launched the Congo Research Group, which then became a *carrefour* for the cross-fertilization of thoughts and energies that are expressed here. This would not have been possible with the help of Richard Gowan, Sarah Cliffe, and many others at the Center of International Cooperation at New York University. I am deeply grateful to those who have made the CRG grow and become a real thing: *grand prêtre* Pascal, Ida Sawyer, Jean Omasombo, Jean Kenge, Nickson Kambale, Nissé Mughendi, Fred Bauma (*panda ebuteli mon cher*), tatu Joshua, Trésor Kibangula, Pierre Boisselet, Donatella Rostagno, Christoph Vogel, Michael Kavanagh (papa Diego), Sonia Rolley, Francesca Bomboko, *et tout le reste de l'équipe. Dua la kuku litaroga mwewe mishowe.*

Finally, I thank my editors at Princeton University Press for their time and efforts.

NOTES

Chapter 1: Introduction

1. Interview #189A.

2. Interview #133A.

3. Kapend, Bijak, and Hinde, "Democratic Republic of the Congo Armed Conflict 1998–2004"; Coghlan et al., "Update on Mortality in the Democratic Republic of Congo."

4. This news scan was conducted with Nexis Uni, using the keyword "Congo."

5. See Pham, "To Save the Congo, Let It Fall Apart"; Herbst and Mills, "There Is No Congo."

6. Violence in Ituri did pick up again in December 2017, but it is unclear what the trend there will be, and levels of displacement had remained relatively low for the previous decade.

7. Walter, "Bargaining Failures and Civil War"; Blattman and Miguel, "Civil War"; Cederman, Wimmer, and Min, "Why Do Ethnic Groups Rebel?"; Kalyvas, "Civil Wars."

8. Mac Ginty and Richmond, "Local Turn in Peace Building"; Autesserre, *Trouble with the Congo.*

9. The aid statistics including official development aid (ODA) and other official flows (OOFs). Development Initiatives, data.devint.org. The number of international NGOs comes from the DRC INGO Forum, www.ongirdc.org, accessed May 2, 2018.

10. Conrad, *Heart of Darkness,* 38.

11. Gettleman, "Rape Epidemic Raises Trauma of Congo War."

12. Kristof, "Orphaned, Raped, and Ignored."

13. Interview #157A.

14. Kaldor, *New and Old Wars.*

15. Bennett and Checkel, "Process Tracing: From Philosophical Roots to Best Practices."

16. Bennett, "Process Tracing: A Bayesian Approach."

Chapter 2: The Historical Background

1. This chapter draws extensively on Stearns, Mercier, and Donner, "L'ancrage social des rébellions congolaises."

2. Wickham-Crowley, *Guerrillas and Revolution in Latin America,* 131–38; Debos, "Living by the Gun in Chad."

3. Stearns, Mercier, and Donner, "L'ancrage social des rébellions congolaises."

4. Vlassenroot and Huggins, "Land, Migration, and Conflict in Eastern DR Congo"; Mac-Gaffey, "Policy of National Integration in Zaire."

5. Mamdani, *Citizen and Subject.*

6. Turner, "'Batetela,' 'Baluba,' 'Basonge.'"

7. These immigrations were mainly linked to political dynamics in the Rwandan and Rundi kingdoms. The first settlement of Barundi in the Ruzizi Plain, the area of the border between today's Congo and Burundi, dates to the end of the eighteenth century, when a son of Mwami Ntare, the king of Burundi, arrived in search of grazing land for cattle. The origins of the first immigrants of Rwandan descent in South Kivu, a community that came to be known as the Banyamulenge, are less well established; most written sources agree that a significant number of them arrived in South Kivu at the end of the nineteenth century. See Loons, *Histoire du territoire d'Uvira*; Depelchin, "From Pre-Capitalism to Imperialism"; Weis, *Le pays d'Uvira*.

8. The lower estimate follows figures provided by Bucyalimwe, who provides official figures for immigration as follows: 17,902 between 1928 and 1936; around 100,000 between 1937 and 1945; and around 22,000 for the 1949–1956 period. Bucyalimwe suggests that these figures are an underestimate. Working backwards from Pabanel, who states that in all of North Kivu there were 464,182 people of Rwandan descent in 1990, we could come to a similar figure, especially considering high birth rates and the further waves of immigration around Rwandan independence. However, Léon de Saint Moulin states that a total of 300,000 Rwandans immigrated before independence. See Bucyalimwe, "Land Conflicts in Masisi, Eastern Zaire"; Pabanel, "La question de la nationalité au Kivu"; Saint Moulin, "Mouvements récents de population dans la zone de peuplement dense de l'est du Kivu."

9. The MNC split into two factions in 1959 as a result of disagreements between Patrice Lumumba and those led by Albert Kalonji, who pushed for greater federalism.

10. Tull, *Reconfiguration of Political Order in Africa*, 75.

11. I am leaving out here the two invasions of the far south of the country, in Shaba (Katanga) province by Angolan-backed Front for the National Liberation of the Congo (FNLC) in 1977 and 1978.

12. In a similar fashion, the central government pitted "indigenous" Katangans against Luba migrants in the cities of Lubumbashi, Likasi, and Kolwezi during this period.

13. Reyntjens, *Great African War*, 22.

14. Office of the UN High Commissioner for Human Rights, "Democratic Republic of the Congo, 1993–2003," 58–60.

15. Jackson, "Sons of Which Soil?"

16. This coalition included Burundi, Ethiopia, and Tanzania.

17. This figure is conservative. Between 2003 and 2006, 130,000 soldiers were demobilized, and a similar number remained in the national army. The Congolese police has another 110,000–150,000 members, many of whom are former soldiers. A large number of all of these men and women come from the eastern Congo, although exact numbers are not available.

18. Interview #344B.

19. Most notably, the various Local Defense Forces. There were various such forces set up by members of the RCD political elite as a way of bolstering their stature: Governor Eugène Serufuli of North Kivu created the most notorious Local Defense Forces; his South Kivu counterpart Norbert Katintima created an eponymous group; and similar forces were set up in Luhwindja (Mwenga territory), Lemera (Uvira territory), and the High Plateau of Kalehe territory. The Mudundu 40 in Walungu territory played a similar role.

20. The main Rwandan group was the *Forces Démocratiques de Libération du Rwanda* (FDLR). The Burundian rebels were the *Forces de Libération National* (FNL) and the *Conseil National pour la Défense de la Démocratie–Forces de Défense de la Démocratie* (CNDD-FDD).

21. Vlassenroot, "Making of a New Order."

Chapter 3: Explaining the Congolese Conflict

1. The Multi-Country Demobilization and Reintegration Program (MDRP), which managed the basket of funds for demobilization, estimated that 102,148 soldiers had been demobilized by 2008, in addition to 30,219 children. World Bank, "Demobilization and Reintegration in the Democratic Republic of Congo (DRC)."

2. International Monetary Fund, "Press Release: IMF Approves US$750 million PRGF Arrangement for the Democratic Republic of the Congo," June 13, 2002; World Bank, "DR Congo Country Brief," http://web.worldbank.org/archive/website00286B/WEB/CD_CTRY _.HTM, accessed October 18, 2019. A small World Bank project was launched in 2001, with more funding to follow after the signature of the peace deal in 2002.

3. Paris, "Peacebuilding and the Limits of Liberal Internationalism."

4. Interview with diplomat in Kinshasa, May 16, 2006. At that time the author was an analyst for the International Crisis Group.

5. Poverty data from World Bank Data (data.worldbank.org), accessed May 18, 2020; International Crisis Group, "Escaping the Conflict Trap," 5.

6. International Rescue Committee, *"Mortality in the Democratic Republic of Congo."*

7. Weiss and Carayannis, "Reconstructing the Congo"; Congo Research Group and BERCI, "Impasse in the Congo."

8. They eventually were held in June and December 2006. The RCD presidential candidate Azarias Ruberwa won 1.69 percent of the vote. The party won 3 percent of seats in the national assembly, and 6.5 percent of seats in the senate.

9. International Crisis Group, "Congo's Transition Is Failing."

10. Interview with Azarias Ruberwa in Kinshasa, January 13, 2013.

11. On the CNDP and M23 and the dynamics leading up to the escalation of violence, see chapter 6.

12. Interview #148A.

13. Integrated Regional Information Networks, "DRC."

14. Interview #104.

15. Stearns, "From CNDP to M23."

16. The name *Mai-Mai* referred to most armed groups that did not emerge out of the Congolese Kinyarwanda-speaking communities. The latter often defined themselves as "local defense." Since 2011, however, new names have flourished. Many groups now brandish political party-style acronyms, the Raia Mutomboki often consciously define themselves as not being Mai-Mai, while many groups in the Hutu community call themselves *Nyatura* ("hit hard").

17. Interview #819D.

18. This included Dunia Lwendama, Rubaruba Zabuloni, Delphin Mbaenda, and Kapopo Alunda.

19. Baaz and Verweijen, "Volatility of a Half-Cooked Bouillabaisse."

20. Berghezan, "Forces armées de RDC."

21. Interview #814A.

22. Interview #207A.

23. For documentation regarding these figures, see Stearns, "PARECO"; Stearns et al. [Verweijenm], *Mai-Mai Yakutumba*; United Nations, "Final Report," S/2008/773, December 12, 2008; United Nations, "Final Report," S/2010/596, November 29, 2010; United Nations, "Final Report," S/2011/738, December 2, 2011; United Nations, "Interim Report," S/2012/348, June 21, 2012.

24. Centre Indépendant des Recherches et d'Etudes Stratégiques au Kivu (CIRESKI), "Étude analytique sur la milice 'FAL,'" 2014, report on file with the author; Stearns et al. [Verweijenm], *Mai-Mai Yakutumba*.

25. These included the FDLR-Soki, the Mai-Mai Shetani, the Mouvement populaire d'autodéfense (MPA, Popular Self-defense Movement), and the Forces pour la défense des intérêts du peuple congolais (FDIPC, Forces for the Defense of the Interests of the Congolese People). Increased mobilization also resulted from efforts by the M23 and its allies in Rwanda to forge alliances or create new groups throughout the east such as the Alliance pour la libération de l'est du Congo (ALEC, Alliance for the Liberation of East Congo) in Uvira and the Force oecuménique pour la libération du Congo (FOLC, Ecumenical Force for the Liberation of Congo), led by FARDC deserter Hilaire Kombi in the Beni area in northern North Kivu.

26. United Nations. "Final Report," S/2012/843, November 15, 2012, paras. 19–27.

27. United Nations, "Midterm Report," S/2013/433, July 19, 2013, paras. 13–15.

28. Congo Research Group, "Mass Killings in Beni Territory."

29. The FARDC reportedly allied with the NDC-Guidon and the UPDI, while the FDLR partnered with a variety of Nyatura groups, which were local militias that recruit among the Congolese Hutu community.

30. Stearns and Vogel, "Landscape of Armed Groups in Eastern Congo."

31. Pierre Benetti and Joan Tilouine, "Mbusa Nyamwisi ou le retour d'un chef de guerre dans le bourbier congolais," *Le Monde*, January 30, 2018.

32. Stearns and Vogel, "Landscape of Armed Groups."

33. Cunningham, "Veto Players and Civil War Duration."

34. Collier and Hoeffler, "Greed and Grievance in Civil War."

35. Cederman, Wimmer, and Min, "Why Do Ethnic Groups Rebel?"

Chapter 4: The Role of the Congolese and Rwandan States

1. See Mowoe, *Performance of Soldiers as Governors*, 485; Joris, *Dans van de luipaard*, 395.

2. See Stedman, "Spoiler Problems in Peace Processes."

3. Schmitt, *Concept of the Political*, 26.

4. Nepstad, *Nonviolent Revolutions*; Wickham-Crowley, *Guerrillas and Revolution in Latin America*; Paige, "Revolution and the Agrarian Bourgeoisie in Nicaragua"; Arjomand, *Turban for the Crown*.

5. Goldstone, "Toward a Fourth Generation of Revolutionary Theory."

6. Reno, *Warlord Politics and African States*; Bayart, *L'État en Afrique*.

7. During this time, Katumba was secretary-general of Kabila's ruling coalition and parliamentarian, but neither position gave him an official role in the executive.

8. The initial size of the army was declared to be 360,000 soldiers in 2003. After a census conducted with the support of the European Union, there were 120,000 soldiers registered.

9. The following paragraphs draw from Stearns, Verweijen, and Baaz, *National Army and Armed Groups in the Eastern Congo*.

10. Interview #828A.

11. Baaz and Olsson, "Feeding the Horse."

12. Internal FARDC document on file with the author; see also United Nations, "Final Report," S/2011/738, December 2, 2011, 82.

13. Hogg and Stoddard, "Insight."

14. Interview #824A.

15. Interview #811A.

16. Interview #133.

17. Interview #101C.

18. Peemans, *Le Congo-Zaïre au gré du XXème siècle*.

19. Carter Center, *Elections présidentielle et législatives République Démocratique du Congo, 28 Novembre 2011*. The list of 2018 political parties was accessed at www.ceni.cd on May 26, 2020.

20. Interviews #833A, #834B, #839.

21. Interview #902A.

22. Interview #902D.

23. Gettleman, "Interview with Joseph Kabila."

24. As of this writing, a process was underway to split the country into twenty-six provinces from the previous ten. This process was expected to take several years.

25. Interview #832.

26. Bollag, "Public Expenditure Review of the Education Sector in the Democratic Republic of Congo."

27. Van Lerberghe, *DR Congo*.

28. Olsson, Baaz, and Martinsson, "Fiscal Capacity in 'Post'-Conflict States."

29. This argument builds on other scholars of the Congo. Vlassenroot and Raeymaekers, "New Political Order in the DR Congo?" Thomas Callaghy saw the Zairian state as a "lame Leviathan," aspiring to the total domination of society but desperately limited in its capacities. Callaghy, *State-Society Struggle*.

30. Butler, *Frames of War*, 51.

31. These interviews were conducted by myself and my research team in person between January 2012 and April 2016 in Kinshasa, Goma, and Bukavu. I conducted additional interviews over the phone between April 2016 and December 2019. They were all semi-structured and open-ended and conducted confidentially.

32. Interview #731A.

33. Interview #733B.

34. Interview #178A.

35. Interviews #179A, #190B, and #180B.

36. Interview #134D; LUCHA is a Congolese social movement; its formal name is Lutte pour le changement.

37. Interview #147A.

38. Interview #168A; Boisbouvier, "Le mystère Kabila"; International Crisis Group, "Katanga," 6.

39. Interview #151A.

40. Interview #117C.

41. In 2008, Amisi was promoted from commander of North Kivu to become commander of the FARDC land forces. In 2012, following the fall of Goma to the M23, he was suspended from the land forces, only to be promoted to become head of one of three national defense zones in 2014.

42. Interview #802C.

43. Interview #183A.

44. Interview #176A.

45. Interview #801A.

46. Moshonas, "Political Economy of Human Resource and Payroll Management in the Democratic Republic of the Congo," 4.

47. Verheijen and Mulumba, "Democratic Republic of Congo."

48. Interview #159B.

49. Interview #113A.

50. Interview #811A.

51. Interview #810A.

52. Interview #821A.

53. Interview #852B.

54. Interview #812A.

55. Interview #104B.

56. These depictions of military life as squalor and suffering have been confirmed by Maria Eriksson Baaz and Maria Stern's interviews with 171 FARDC soldiers in 2005 and 2006. Baaz and Stern, "Making Sense of Violence."

57. Interview #811A.

58. Congo Research Group, "For the Army, With the Army, Like the Army?"

59. Interview #157A.

60. The World Integrated Trade Solution, https://wits.worldbank.org/CountryProfile/en/Country/RWA/Year/LTST/TradeFlow/EXPIMP/Partner/by-country, accessed on May 27, 2020.

61. Allison and Zelikow, *Essence of Decision*.

62. Ripley, "Psychology, Foreign Policy, and International Relations Theory."

63. Reyntjens, *Political Governance in Post-Genocide Rwanda*; Jones, "Murder and Create"; Verhoeven, "Nurturing Democracy or into the Danger Zone?"; Shahabudin McDoom, "Rwanda's Exit Pathway from Violence"; Booth and Golooba-Mutebi, "Developmental Patrimonialism?"

64. Interview #116B.

65. Interviews #169A and #172A.

66. Interview #146A.

67. Interview #122B.

68. Kayumba Nyamwasa was the army commander, Patrick Karegeya was the director of external intelligence, Frank Rusagara was the special advisor to the president, and Théogène Rudasingwa was Kagame's chief of staff.

69. Jones, "Murder and Create," 297–99.

70. Interviews #122 and #104.

71. Interview #122.

72. Interview #172A.

73. United Nations, "Final Report," S/2010/596, November 29, 2010, 45.

74. Interviews #113 and #104.

75. Prunier, "Rwandese Patriotic Front"; Verhoeven, "Nurturing Democracy or into the Danger Zone?"

76. Interview #125B.

77. Interview #160.

78. Interview #161.

79. Interview #192; see also Fair, *Fighting to the End.*

80. Speech uploaded to YouTube at https://www.youtube.com/watch?time_continue =69&v=HYgAQAPlIaE, accessed on May 26, 2020.

81. Longman and Rutagengwa, "Memory, Identity, and Community in Rwanda."

82. Waldorf, "Revisiting Hotel Rwanda."

83. Interview #104B.

84. Interview #125B.

85. Clark, "After Genocide," 310.

86. Van Evera, "Cult of the Offensive and the Origins of the First World War."

87. Interview #116C.

88. Interview #142A.

89. Interview #192A.

90. De Failly, "Coltan"; Global Witness, "Under-Mining Peace." According to Global Witness, a kilogram of tin was being sold for $6 in Goma in 1998 when the world coltan price was hovering around $60 per kilogram for refined tantalum. Coltan sold in Goma usually included around 20 to 40 percent tantalum.

91. United Nations, "Report of the Panel of Experts," S/2001/357, April 12, 2001.

92. Interviews #159 and #107.

93. Marysse and André, "Guerre et pillage économique en République démocratique du Congo."

94. Willum, "Foreign Aid to Rwanda."

95. United Nations, "Report of the Panel of Experts," S/2001/357, April 12, 2001, 27.

96. Interviews #162 and #159.

97. Interview #162.

98. Interview #150.

99. Interview #162.

100. Interview #159.

101. Interviews #107 and #164.

102. Interviews #171 and #170.

103. Global Witness, "'The Hill Belongs to Them,'" 10.

104. United Nations, "Final Report," S/2014/42, January 23, 2014.

105. Interviews #113, #159, and #122; United Nations, "Final Report," S/2010/596, November 29, 2010; United Nations, "Final Report," S/2011/738, December 2, 2011. Official tax policy also played a role. Until late 2011, the Congo's export tax on gold was more than triple that of Uganda or Burundi.

106. Exports peaked in 2013 at $226 million before declining to $169 million in 2016. There were declines in 2009 and 2014, the years following the dismantling of the CNDP and M23, respectively, but those years also coincided with steep declines the world tin prices, which is more likely to be the explanation for the fluctuation.

107. World Bank Group, *Rwanda Economic Update, January 2021*, 9.

108. United Nations, "Final Report," S/2018/531, June 4, 2018, 21, 23.

109. Rwanda Trade Statistics, https://wits.worldbank.org/CountryProfile/en/RWA, accessed April 4, 2018.

110. Kabona, "Rwanda in Talks to Export Chicken, Eggs, Beef to DRC."

111. Behuria, "Between Party Capitalism and Market Reforms."

112. Interview #172A.

113. Interviews #125 and #116.

114. Sundaram, "The Other War"; interview #125B.

115. Newbury, "Irredentist Rwanda."

116. Interview #113.

117. Interviews #104, #112, and #113.

118. Interview #105.

119. Geertz, *Interpretation of Cultures*, 29.

Chapter 5: The Theory: Involution, Fragmentation, and a Military Bourgeoisie

1. The name has been changed to protect his identity.

2. Baaz and Olsson, "Feeding the Horse."

3. Kaldor, *New and Old Wars*.

4. Chabal and Daloz, *Africa Works*; Reno, *Warfare in Independent Africa*; Keen, *Conflict and Collusion in Sierra Leone*.

5. Fearon, "Rationalist Explanations for War."

6. Kalyvas, *Logic of Violence in Civil War*; Wood, "Social Processes of Civil War."

7. Daly, "Organizational Legacies of Violence."

8. Bateson, *Order and Violence in Postwar Guatemala*.

9. Paige, *Agrarian Revolution*.

10. Wolf, *Peasant Wars of the Twentieth Century*.

11. Richards, *Fighting for the Rain Forest*.

12. Ellis, "War in West Africa"; Stearns, "PARECO."

13. There are exceptions to this, especially among the CNDP and M23, where one could find large numbers of urban, well-educated cadres. By 2013, however, most of these figures had demobilized, gone into exile, or joined the national army. This preponderance of rural youths contradicts Mkandawire, "Terrible Toll of Post-Colonial 'Rebel Movements' in Africa."

14. Baaz and Stern, "Making Sense of Violence."

15. The Multi-Country Demobilization and Reintegration Program (MDRP), which managed the basket of funds for demobilization, estimated that 102,148 soldiers had been demobilized by 2009, in addition to 30,219 children (http://www.mdrp.org/PDFs/MDRP_DRC_FS _0309.pdf, accessed March 27, 2014). A recent census of the national army in 2012 established that it had 105,000 members, in addition to whom around 18,000 that had not received ID cards and perhaps 10,000 new recruits. Stearns, Verweijen, and Baaz, *National Army and Armed Groups in the Eastern Congo*. The new Congolese demobilization program estimates that there were 11,000 members of armed groups in the eastern Congo in 2013 (http://desc-wondo.org /wp-content/uploads/2014/01/Plan-Global-de-DDR-III.pdf, accessed March 27, 2014). These numbers do not take into account soldiers who had spontaneously demobilized or had gone through smaller programs not funded by the MDRP.

16. See the various UN Group of Experts reports at https://www.un.org/sc/suborg/en /sanctions/1533/work-and-mandate/expert-reports. Laudati, "Beyond Minerals"; Verweijen and Marijnen, "Counterinsurgency/Conservation Nexus"; Nest, Grignon, and Kisangani, *Democratic Republic of Congo*.

17. Kasfir, "Introduction," 5.

18. Sklar, "The Nature of Class Domination in Africa"; Diamond, "Class Formation in the Swollen African State."

19. Pinaud, "South Sudan."

20. Pinaud, "South Sudan," 590.

21. These numbers come from the respective annual reports of the United Nations Joint Human Rights Office, available at https://monusco.unmissions.org/en/human-rights.

22. International Peace Information Service, "Roadblock Rebels."

23. Interview #824A.

24. Vinck and Pham, "Searching for Lasting Peace."

25. Geffray, *La cause des armes au Mozambique*, 165–66. The translation is my own.

26. Cunningham, "Veto Players and Civil War Duration."

27. Verweijen and Iguma, "Understanding Armed Group Proliferation in the Eastern Congo."

28. Interview #804A.

29. Interview #139A.

30. Jackson, "'It Seems to Be Going.'"

31. Geertz, *Agricultural Involution*, 81.

32. Interview #802D.

33. De Waal, "When Kleptocracy Becomes Insolvent," 349–50.

34. Barkey, *Bandits and Bureaucrats*.

35. Christensen, Nguyen, and Sexton, "Strategic Violence during Democratization"; Trejo and Ley, *Votes, Drugs, and Violence*.

36. Keohane, "International Institutions"; Wendt, *Social Theory of International Politics.*

37. Norms are collective expectations for the proper behavior of actors within a given identity. They are constructed collectively and draw on moral and ideological conceptions of what is appropriate or good behavior. Ideas can be simple concepts, such as a monetary union, or they can be a more complex assembly of concepts such as communist ideology. Habits are unconscious and automatic scripts and schemas that we carry out in reaction to stimuli or as part of a traditional routine. Identity is "a set of attributes, beliefs, desires, or principles of action that a person thinks distinguish her in socially relevant ways." Fearon, "What is Identity (as We Now Use the Word)."

38. See also Baaz and Stern, "Making Sense of Violence."

39. Interview #811B.

40. Cohen, "Female Combatants and the Perpetration of Violence," 383.

41. Interview #633A.

42. Interview #820A.

43. Interview #810B.

44. This is based on an analysis of keyword searches for "attaque," "violence," and "groupe armé" in the *Le Potentiel* archives through LexisNexis. The results were sorted to retain only those that referred to specific attacks. Multiple articles on the same attacks were counted as one.

45. Interview #187A.

46. Jackson, "Culture, Identity, and Hegemony."

47. Kapferer, *Legends of People, Myths of State.*

48. Zulaika, *Basque Violence.*

49. Evans and Glenn, "'TIA—This Is Africa'"; Leung and Huang, "Paradox of Journalistic Representation of the Other."

50. Ellis, *Mask of Anarchy*; Richards, *Fighting for the Rain Forest*; Beneduce et al., "Violence with a Purpose"; Jourdan, Vlassenroot, and Raeymaekers, "Being at War, Being Young"; Hedlund, "Exile Warriors."

51. Interview #218B.

52. Human Rights Watch, "D.R. Congo: M23 Rebels Committing War Crimes"; United Nations, "Report of the Group of Experts," S/2005/30, January 25, 2005, 44; United Nations, "Final Report," S/2008/773, December 12, 2008, 15.

53. Stearns et al., "Congo's Inescapable State."

54. Interview #204B.

55. Congo Research Group and BERCI, "Impasse in the Congo."

56. Clapham, *African Guerrillas.*

57. Reno, *Warfare in Independent Africa.*

58. Bøås and Dunn, "From Liberation Struggles to Warlordism and International Terrorism?" 85.

59. Menkhaus, "Elite Bargains and Political Deals Project."

60. Bøås and Torheim, "Trouble in Mali," 1285.

61. Walter, "Why Bad Governance Leads to Repeat Civil War."

62. Debos, "Living by the Gun in Chad."

63. Day and Reno, "In Harm's Way."

64. UCDP GED Dataset, accessed June 22, 2020.

65. Debos, "Living by the Gun in Chad."

66. Vigh, "Conflictual Motion and Political Inertia."

67. Achille Mbembe emphasizes the centrality of *homo ludens*, the comical and the grotesque. These observations, based largely on Cameroon and Kenya in the 1980s and 90s, certainly ring true in the Congo. Mbembe, "Provisional Notes on the Postcolony," 25.

68. Food and Agriculture Organization, "Ending Extreme Poverty in Rural Areas," 8.

69. Straus, "Wars Do End!"

70. Omotola, "From Political Mercenarism to Militias," 91; Asuni, *Understanding the Armed Groups of the Niger Delta*.

71. Bøås and Torheim, "Trouble in Mali."

72. Geschiere and Nyamnjoh, "Capitalism and Autochthony."

73. Keen, "Liberalization and Conflict."

74. Bryceson and Jamal, eds., *Farewell to Farms*.

75. Masters et al., "Urbanization and Farm Size in Asia and Africa."

76. Bayart and Ellis, "Africa in the World."

77. Hagmann, *Stabilization, Extraversion, and Political Settlements in Somalia*.

78. Mampilly and Stearns, "New Direction for US Foreign Policy in Africa."

79. Tull and Mehler, "Hidden Costs of Power-Sharing."

80. De Waal, "Mission without End?"

81. Geenen and Cuvelier, "Local Elites' Extraversion and Repositioning"; Omeje, "Oil Conflict in Nigeria."

82. According to ACLED, www.acled.org, accessed January 18, 2021.

83. R. J. Reinhardt, "Nigerians Head to Polls with Stronger Faith in Elections, Gallup," February 6, 2019.

84. Kalyvas, "Civil Wars"; Wood, "Social Processes of Civil War."

85. Finnemore and Sikkink, "International Norm Dynamics and Political Change."

86. Hopf, *Social Construction of International Politics*; Weldes, *Constructing National Interests*.

Chapter 6: The CNDP and the M23

1. This chapter draws extensively on a report I authored for the Usalama Project, a Rift Valley Institute project. Stearns, "From CNDP to M23."

2. Pierson, "Increasing Returns, Path Dependence, and the Study of Politics."

3. Since 2014, the Rwandan FDLR and the Ugandan ADF have been targets of military campaigns, although only sporadically and with ambiguous returns.

4. Interview #165.

5. Scott, *Laurent Nkunda et la rébellion du Kivu*; interview #103A.

6. Interviews #103A and #100A.

7. Human Rights Watch, "War Crimes in Kisangani."

8. Confidential cable from US embassy in Kinshasa to State Department (posted on Wikilieaks). "Wanted: Leadership at DRC's Helm." November 28, 2003.

9. Interview with Azarias Ruberwa, Kinshasa, November 11, 2012.

10. Interviews #103A, #113C, and #104A.

11. Interview #104A.

12. Interviews #105B, #124A, and #113A.

13. Interview #105B.

14. The names of these brigades were changed in 2005—early in the transition they kept their RCD titles: the 5th, 11th, and 12th brigades.

15. The RCD named Xavier Chiribanya and Déogratias Mirindi governor and regional commander, respectively, shortly before the beginning of the transition. It took months to set up a transfer of power following the inauguration of the transitional governmental in June 2003, so Chiribanya and Mirindi maintained effective control over parts of South Kivu administration and military into 2004.

16. Interview with Azarias Ruberwa, Kinshasa, November 11, 2012; interview with civil society activist in Bukavu, October 2002.

17. Human Rights Watch, "D.R. Congo: War Crimes in Bukavu."

18. Interview #109; Department of Peacekeeping Operations, "MONUC and the Bukavu Crisis 2004."

19. Interview #191A.

20. International Crisis Group, "Congo's Transition Is Failing."

21. Munyamulenge is singular, Banyamulenge plural.

22. Human Rights Watch, "Burundi: The Gatumba Massacre."

23. Press report, on file with the author.

24. Interview #111A.

25. International Crisis Group, "Congo's Transition Is Failing."

26. Stearns, "PARECO"; Bucyalimwe Mararo, "Le TPD à Goma (Nord-Kivu)."

27. Interviews #113C, #112A, #201A, and #207.

28. Interview #154C.

29. United Nations Office of the High Commissioner for Human Rights (UNOHCR), "Democratic Republic of the Congo, 1993–2003," 79–118.

30. That antipathy had deep roots in some places but was subject to regional variations. In the eastern part Rutshuru territory, for example, the local Hutu population—called the Banyabwisha—had historical ties to Hutu in western Rwanda, where President Juvénal Habyarimana's main support base was. This area had also suffered from massacres and abuse by the Rwandan army during the 1996–1997 war. In contrast, Hutu from Masisi had different concerns, as most were descendants of Rwandan immigrants from the 1930–1960 period and often allied with local Tutsi interests to defend their land and citizenship rights against other communities.

31. Interview with Eugène Serufuli, Goma, October 9, 2012.

32. Interviews #112B and #132A.

33. "North Kivu Daily Report," MONUC, December 16, 2004. Confidential document, on file with the author.

34. Interview with Robert Seninga, Goma, May 16, 2012.

35. Interviews #103B and #144A.

36. Interview #155B.

37. "Analyse de Laurent NKUNDA sur la situation en RD du Congo," August 25, 2005. Document on file with the author.

38. The arrest warrant was not dated, but according to UN reporting, was issued on this date. See "North Kivu Daily Report," MONUC, September 9, 2012.

39. Interview #117A.

40. Interviews #118, #117, and #120.

41. Three incidents were reported by UN and local officials that could be construed as ethnically motivated: Kasikila had a local man, probably a Hutu, removed from the hospital in Rutshuru in December 2005 and beaten in public, accusing him of banditry. Around the same time, Kasikila's brigade chased out pro-Nkunda troops from a defunct niobium mine, allegedly as part of a takeover of the mine by a German company. Lastly, Kasikila reportedly arrested some bandits, also probably Banyarwanda, who had participated in the killing of a church minister and handed them over to a mob that lynched them. "North Kivu Weekly Report, December 3–9, 2005," MONUC; interviews #113A, #121, and #122.

42. Interview #103B.

43. Interview #144B.

44. He did keep the promise in some provincial governments, such as Bas-Congo and Kasai-Occidental, where he needed the support of RCD provincial MPs. This deal may have been the reason why Nkunda appeared to give preferential treatment to Kabila's coalition for campaigning in his territory.

45. The one Tutsi elected, Dunia Bakarani, came from Masisi, but was not close to the CNDP; he was elected as a member of Jean-Pierre Bemba's Mouvement pour la libération du Congo (MLC).

46. Interviews #144 and #113.

47. "North Kivu Weekly Report, November 26–December 1, 2012," MONUC.

48. Interview #144.

49. Personalities matter. Numbi had been a close associate of James Kabarebe, the Rwandan commander who later became minister of defense in Rwanda, during the 1996–1997 AFDL war. During this time, he had also come to know Laurent Nkunda.

50. The brigades were called Alpha, Bravo, Charlie, Delta, Echo, and Foxtrot.

51. Interview #113D.

52. The document in question was an outline of the payroll for the CNDP. I was able to see and take note of the relevant amounts but was not able to obtain a copy of the document.

53. Interview #144C.

54. Interview with Laurent Nkunda, Bwiza, June 25, 2006.

55. Interview #104B.

56. The Congolese army strategically positioned units led by Hutu officers Colonel Smith Gihanga and Colonel David Rugayi to encourage defections. According to CNDP deserters, Nkunda began to clamp down on deserters, issuing orders to deal harshly and even kill them. One such deserter is mentioned in "North Kivu Weekly Report, August 11–17, 2012," MONUC.

57. Interviews #144 and #124.

58. In Buramba, for example, following an FDLR ambush on his vehicle, CNDP Colonel Sultani Makenga carried out a reprisal attack against local civilians, killing at least fifteen people.

In another attack several days earlier, CNDP soldiers shot dead a parish priest in Jomba, close to the Ugandan border.

59. Interview with General Mayanga wa Gishuba, Kinshasa, March 21, 2012.

60. Interview #201.

61. The CNDP claim that they surprised the army in the middle of drunken festivities, catching officers in some cases literally with their pants down. It is difficult to confirm this apocrypha, but it is likely that incompetence and not treason—as some army officers claim—was the source of the defeat.

62. Minister of Interior Denis Kalume, along with National Assembly President Vital Kamerhe, were reportedly backers of this idea, as were numerous foreign diplomats.

63. Interview #104B.

64. Interviews #124 and #122.

65. United Nations, "Final Report," S/2008/773, December 12, 2008, para. 66.

66. Interviews #104 and #144.

67. United Nations, "Final Report," S/2008/773, December 12, 2008, paras. 61–68; Gettleman, "Rwanda Stirs Deadly Brew of Troubles in Congo."

68. Interview #113D.

69. Human Rights Watch, *You Will Be Punished*, 42.

70. Interview #144. The official government list put the number at 6,006 soldiers, but CNDP officers say they got paid for far more than that for months during the integration process.

71. United Nations, "Final Report," S/2009/603, November 23, 2009. According to the United Nations Group of Experts, the CNDP handed over 2,542 personal weapons, seven PKM machine guns, one MAG machine gun, seven RPG-7s, four 60-mm mortars, one 82-mm mortar, six 75-mm recoilless guns, two SPG-9 recoilless guns, and four multiple rocket launchers.

72. I was shown the names of several of these individuals by a CNDP officer in an official, confidential document. See also United Nations, "Final Report," S/2009/603, November 23, 2009, 45.

73. United Nations, "Final Report," S/2009/603, November 23, 2009, 54–75.

74. Interview #117.

75. Interview #121.

76. Interview #138A.

77. United Nations, "Final Report," S/2011/738, December 2, 2011.

78. Interviews #139 and #140.

79. Interview #140; United Nations, "Final Report," S/2011/738, December 2, 2011. In September and October of 2010, Ntaganda held several meetings in Minova, on Lake Kivu, with PARECO officers, suggesting that they had been unfairly marginalized by a corrupt group of Congolese generals, but that he would be able to help them out. Three senior PARECO officers—Col. Edmond "Saddam" Ringo, Col. Kifaru Nyiragiye, Lt. Col. Mwendangabo Nsabimana—were co-opted by Ntaganda, along with the group's president Sendugu Museveni, and given high-ranking positions. In one Congolese intelligence officer's analysis: "Ntaganda took advantage of the weak members of PARECO"—Nsabimana was a civilian, Kifaru was accused of mass rape, and Saddam had defected from the army. Nsabimana had been the

spokesperson for PARECO in South Kivu and was then named a colonel during integration, Saddam defected from the army in March 2010 when he didn't get the position he wanted, and Kifaru was accused of the mass rape of women in Nakiele (Fizi territory) in June 2011.

80. Interviews #139, #141, and #121.

81. Interview #140.

82. Interviews #145 and #146.

83. Interview #147.

84. Interview #105.

85. Interview #121.

86. Interviews #138 and #142.

87. The troops sent belonged largely to the 811th regiment. Nine hundred and fifty of its 1,200 soldiers had refused to desert, even though they were mostly ex-CNDP and under the command of Colonel Innocent Zimurinda, who had joined Ntaganda. Now under the command of ex-CNDP Lieutenant-colonel Bahati Mulonda, they were sent to Kananga, in the province of Kasai Occidental.

88. Interview #125.

89. Interview #121C.

90. Interview #113C.

91. The alliances included the FDC in southwestern Masisi and Sheka Ntaberi's Mai-Mai group in Walikale, both of which had received military support from Ntaganda during anti-FDLR operations in 2011. Another alliance was struck with Colonel Albert Kahasha, who defected from the Congolese army in January 2012, ironically in protest against excessive ex-CNDP power in the military. In April, Kahasha joined with General Sikuli Lafontaine to form the Union des patriotes congolais pour la paix (UPCP). Kahasha later traveled to M23 bases in Rutshuru to coordinate operations with the M23, claiming that they had the same enemies. Ironically, the UN Group of Experts suggests that Kahasha collaborates with Ralliement pour l'unité et la démocratie (RUD), an FDLR splinter faction. United Nations, "Interim Report," S/2012/348, June 21, 2012, 31–32.

92. Kimenyi, "DRC Should Stop Playing the Victim—Mushikiwabo."

93. Mwenda, "Don't Save Congo."

94. In Ituri, a new alliance of armed groups called Coalition des groupes armés de l'Ituri (Cogai) reportedly sent a delegation to Kigali in late May 2012 to speak with Gen James Kabarebe. However, this group is still small and has little support from leaders of the Hema or Lendu communities. United Nations, "Addendum to the Interim Report," S/2012/348/Add.1, June 27, 2012, 15; interviews in Ituri in August, 2012. In Fizi, the M23 have reached out to Gen. Amuli Yakutumba's Mai-Mai group, and there have been some meetings, but no firm commitments.

95. The donors who suspended aid included the United States, the United Kingdom, the Netherlands, and Germany. The largest suspensions in aid came from the African Development Bank, the European Union, and the World Bank. However, most of the aid was released during the first half of 2013, as Rwanda claimed it was using its influence to keep the M23 at the negotiating table.

96. Kabeera, "Ex-M23 Combatants Seek Refugee Status in Rwanda."

97. Interviews #148 and #100A. Chiribanya, as noted, was sentenced in absentia for helping to kill Laurent Kabila. He was named governor of South Kivu in 2003, shortly before the transition began, by the Rwandan government, which did not consult the RCD leadership. Nzabirinda had been a schoolteacher before Rwandan security officials asked him to join the RCD. Kamanzi and Gasana were both named as parliamentarians for the RCD during the transition but refused to take up their positions. Ntare was the chief of staff of the governor of North Kivu before the latter fell out with the Rwandan government.

98. Interview #103B.

99. Interview #104B.

100. Academics have made diverging estimates for the Banyarwanda population living in the Kivus. A 1970 government census suggested there were 335,000 Rwandan immigrants living in the Congo. Jean-Pierre Pabanel (1990) put the number for North Kivu at 464,000, perhaps 15 to 30 percent of whom were Tutsi. If we take higher mortality into account over the following decade, due to the various spates of violence, that population may have grown to 800,000 to a million by 2007.

101. Interview #103A.

102. Interviews #103, #113, #144, and #143.

103. Telephone interview with Patrick Karegeya, September 11, 2012.

104. These were Xaxier Chiribanya and Col. Déo Mirindi, respectively. Both had been sentenced to death in absentia for the assassination of President Laurent Kabila. While the military trial was deeply flawed, many of their fellow officers suggest that they were probably involved in the conspiracy.

105. Interviews #105 and #204.

106. Interviews #144C and #201.

107. Interviews #143 #103, and #113. This included Innocent Kaina and Salongo Ndekezi.

108. United Nations, "Final Report," S/2008/773, December 12, 2008, paras. 61–68; United Nations, "Report of the Group of Experts," S/2006/525, July 18, 2006.

109. Interviews #121, #144, and #103.

110. United Nations, "Final Report," S/2008/773, December 12, 2008, para. 66; interviews #140, #121, and #147.

111. Interview #105.

112. Interviews #172A and #146B.

113. Interviews #199, #146C, #147E, and #151A.

114. Prendergast, "New Face of African Conflict." Thanks to Laura Seay for the reference.

115. United Nations, "Final Report," S/2008/773, December 12, 2008, 11.

116. Ngezayo also has extensive ranches in the area under CNDP occupation, which may have been a factor in his support.

117. Interview #148.

118. Mamdani, "Invention of the Indigène"; Autesserre, "Only Way to Help Congo."

119. Interviews #144, #104, #122, and #113.

120. Interview #153A; Jean-Claude Willame, *Banyarwanda et Banyamulenge: Violences ethniques et gestion de l'identitaire au Kivu* (Brussels and Paris: Institut Africain-CEDAF and L'Harmattan, 1997).

121. Interview #144B.

122. Human Rights Watch, "D.R. Congo: M23 Rebels Committing War Crimes"; United Nations, "Report of the Group of Experts," S/2005/436, July 26, 2005, 44; United Nations, "Final Report," S/2008/773, December 12, 2008, 15.

123. Interview #154.

124. According to the terms of the deal, the four vice presidents were supposed to represent the MLC, the RCD, Kabila's government, and the political opposition. However, during the peace talks, Kabila was able to co-opt the representative of the opposition, Arthur Zahidi N'Goma.

125. Four of these seats were allocated to customary chiefs.

126. Julien Paluku was first elected as a member of the RCD-K-ML party, a former rebellion that became close to Kabila during the 1998–2003 war. Paluku then left the RCD-K-ML to found his own party and has remained a close ally of Kabila.

127. Interviews #107, #108, #113, and #103.

128. Interview #105.

129. Interview #124.

130. This included about a hundred Tutsi soldiers in the Kamina military camp (Katanga province), eighty in the Kananga camp (Kasai-Occidental), 133 Tutsi civilians around the town of Kalima (Maniema), dozens in Kisangani (Province Orientale), seventy in cities of southern Katanga, seventy in Kalemie (Katanga), forty in Moba (Katanga), and about a hundred soldiers in military camps in Kinshasa. Office of the UN High Commissioner for Human Rights, "Report of the Mapping Exercise Documenting. . . ."

131. Interview #100C.

132. Interview #120.

133. Interview with Laurent Nkunda, Bwiza, June 24, 2006.

134. Prominent examples of Tutsi from North Kivu are Déo Rugwiza, who would go on to lead the customs agency; Tharcisse Habarugira, who was vice minister of defense during the transition; Colonel Willy Bonane, who would command the 4th integrated brigade; General Obed Rwibasira, who in 2005 would leave North Kivu to command the 5th military region; General Jean Bivegete, who would become a leading military prosecutor in Kinshasa. There are also many examples of Banyamulenge, who played a less prominent role in the CNDP and M23.

135. Interview with Laurent Nkunda, Kitchanga, December 20, 2006.

136. Interview #103.

137. United Nations, "Report of the Group of Experts," S/2004/551, July 15, 2004; United Nations, "Report of the Group of Experts," S/2005/436, July 26, 2005, 44–45; US State Department, *DR Congo Human Rights Country Report* (Washington, D.C.: US Department of State, 2012).

138. United Nations, "Final Report," S/2011/738, December 2, 2011, paras. 86–89.

139. Interviews #113 and #104.

140. Interview #113.

141. Interview #105.

142. Hoffmann et al., "Violent Conflict and Ethnicity in the Congo."

Chapter 7: The Raia Mutomboki

1. The Raia Mutomboki appeared briefly in a small area in 2005, but then quickly disappeared. The 2011 emergence was much longer and widespread.

2. This list of Raia Mutomboki groups includes some that have not been active in some time. It was compiled in collaboration with the Kivu Security Tracker, www.kivusecurity.org.

3. Interview #702B; "Situation Report, March 2005," MONUC, on file with the author.

4. Until 2000, the FDLR was called Alliance pour la libération du Rwanda (ALIR).

5. Interview #823A.

6. International Crisis Group, "Congo's Transition Is Failing."

7. US State Department, *Human Rights Report: Democratic Republic of the Congo* (Washington, D.C.: US State Department, 2006).

8. *Musumbu* means "spirit" in Kirega, the local language.

9. Interviews #704A and #705A; MONUSCO Report #13.

10. The state administration of the DRC is organized hierarchically in the following fashion: province, territory, *chefferie* (sector), *groupement*, *localité*, and village. The last three levels are often, although not always, led by customary authorities.

11. Interviews #704B and #705A; MONUC Threat Assessments #21–#43.

12. In the UN's weekly internal threat reports, which monitor major developments across the country, the name Raia Mutomboki only appeared fifteen times in a two-year period, clustered in late 2005 and early 2007, and mostly in relation to efforts to demobilize a group by that name in southern Maniema province. Analysis of 107 MONUC reports, on file with the author.

13. Interview #706A.

14. Interviews #704 and #706.

15. Interview #702B.

16. Biebuyck, *Lega Culture*, 46–50.

17. Interview #706A.

18. Interviews #139D and #702.

19. Interview #711A; MONUSCO Report #14.

20. MONUSCO Report #9.

21. Football teams provide powerful political platforms in the DRC. Muungano is popular among Rega, while Bukavu Dawa is seen to represent the Shi community.

22. Interview #704B.

23. Interviews #702A and #709.

24. Interview #711D.

25. Interview #709A.

26. United Nations, "Final Report," S/2011/738, December 2, 2011, 81–90.

27. Interview #703B.

28. "Special Report on MONUC Bukavu (PAS) mission to Shabunda and Lulingu (South Kivu) on 29–30 November 2007," internal MONUC report, on file with the author.

29. Interview #713A. This account was confirmed by two other sources, interviews #715A and #706A.

30. Interviews #706, #702, and #704.

31. Interview #702A. Alternative accounts suggest that Eyadema obtained his first batch of *dawa* from the Mai-Mai of Amuli Yakutumba in Fizi territory.

32. Interview #713A.

33. Interview #717A.

34. Interview #717A.

35. Interview #702B.

36. Interview #139D.

37. Office of the UN High Commissioner for Human Rights, "Report of the Mapping Exercise Documenting. . . . ," 89–92, 182–84.

38. Interview #709A.

39. Interviews #709C, #710A, and #719A.

40. Interview #720A.

41. Interviews #702A, #139B, and #704E; MONUSCO Report #15.

42. Interview #721A.

43. Hoffmann and Vlassenroot, "Armed Groups and the Exercise of Public Authority."

44. Interview #730A.

45. In early 2012, the FDLR attacked several villages around Nzofu after they had learned that the Raia Mutomboki had left the area to track down the FDLR in Kalehe. FDLR elements from Kalonge and Kalehe wanted to teach the Nzofu population a lesson for its support to the Raua Mutomboki and, on 1 January, killed eight people in Mugabilo village, nine people in Mpamba village, and six people in Luyuyu village. The next day, eleven people were killed in Ngolombe village; this last killing happened close to an FARDC camp, which for the population was further proof that the FARDC was not trying to protect them.

46. Office of the UN High Commissioner for Human Rights, "Report of the Mapping Exercise Documenting the Most Serious Violations of Human Rights. . . ."

47. Stearns, "North Kivu."

48. Interview #725A.

49. Interview #726B.

50. Interview #727A.

51. Interview #725A.

52. Interview #728A.

53. Office of the UN High Commissioner for Human Rights, "Report of the United Nations Joint Human Rights Office. . . ."

54. Stearns, "PARECO," 39–43.

55. Office of the UN High Commissioner for Human Rights, "Report of the United Nations Joint Human Rights Office. . . ."

56. United Nations, "Interim Report," S/2012/348, June 21, 2012.

57. Interview #731A.

58. Interview #714A.

59. Interview #737A.

60. Interview #721A.

61. Interview #733A.

62. Interview #718A.

63. Interview #736A.

64. Interview #727A.

65. Interviews #413 and #414.

66. Interview #710D.

67. Interviews #723D and #739A.

68. Interview #740A.

69. Interview #724A.

70. Interview #746A.

71. Interview #709.

72. Interview #713B.

73. Hoffmann and Vlassenroot, "Armed Groups and the Exercise of Public Authority"; Vogel, "Contested Statehood, Security Dilemmas, and Militia Politics."

74. Interviews #705A and #706B.

75. Interview #713B.

76. Weinstein, *Inside Rebellion*.

77. Interviews #719A, #722A, #743A, and #713A.

78. Ostrom, "Behavioral Approach to the Rational Choice Theory of Collective Action: Presidential Address, American Political Science Association, 1997."

79. Interview #710B.

80. Fortes and Evans-Pritchard, eds., *African Political Systems*.

81. Staniland, *Networks of Rebellion*.

82. Interview #734A.

83. Interview #712B.

84. Interview #735A.

85. Jackson, "Sons of Which Soil?"

86. Mamdani, *Understanding the Crisis in Kivu*; Willame, *Banyarwanda et Banyamulenge*.

87. Interviews #737B, #720A, #728A, #729A, #720A, and #740A.

88. Interviews #737A and #729A.

Chapter 8: Ituri and the UPC

1. The chapter is based largely on Tamm, *UPC in Ituri*. This was part of the Usalama Project that I managed for the Rift Valley Institute.

2. Human Rights Watch, "UPC Crimes in Ituri (2002–2003)."

3. The following three paragraphs draw the following sources: Pottier, "Displacement and Ethnic Reintegration in Ituri, DR Congo"; Pottier, "Representations of Ethnicity in the Search for Peace"; Fahey, "Rethinking the Resource Curse."

4. Interview #86.

5. While there were also similar land conflicts in Irumu, many interviewees, both Hema and Lendu, pointed to this difference between the two territories. Interview #86; Pottier, "Displacement and Ethnic Reintegration in Ituri, DR Congo."

6. Interview #87.

7. Pottier, "Representations of Ethnicity in the Search for Peace," 433.

8. Interviews #4, #19, and #54.

9. Fahey, "Rethinking the Resource Curse."

10. United Nations Secretariat, "Special Report on the Events in Ituri, January 2002–December 2003"; interview #58.

11. Unless otherwise referenced, the following paragraphs and quotes in this section draw on interviews #65, #66, and #67. On Uganda's involvement, see Human Rights Watch, "Uganda in Eastern DRC," 35–39.

12. Human Rights Watch, "Uganda in Eastern DRC."

13. Human Rights Watch, "Uganda in Eastern DRC," 16, 44.

14. Porter, *Final Report*, section 44.2.

15. *Chui* in Swahili means "leopard."

16. "Bunia Team Makes Contact," *The New Vision* (Kampala), August 7, 2000.

17. This may be the reason for the oft-repeated but false claim that he is Lotsove's nephew.

18. "UN Finds Congo Child Soldiers," BBC News, February 21, 2001.

19. Interviews #54, #60, #61, and #62.

20. Interviews #84 and #82.

21. International Criminal Court (ICC), *Prosecutor v. Thomas Lubanga* (Judgment pursuant to Article 74 of the Statute: Public), ICC-01/04–01/06–2842 (2012), para. 1031.

22. Ngonga, "'La Républiquette de l'Ituri' en République Démocratique du Congo"; Human Rights Watch, "Uganda in Eastern DRC," 20–22.

23. Interview #85.

24. Interview #82.

25. "Mayombo Wants UPDF to Quit Congo," *The Monitor* (Kampala), August 2, 2002.

26. Interviews #3 and #34.

27. Interviews #83 and #82.

28. Interview #901.

29. Between March and April 2002, Lompondo negotiated with Lendu militias from Walendu-Bindi.

30. United Nations Secretariat, "Special Report on the Events in Ituri, January 2002–December 2003," para. 22.

31. ICC, *Prosecutor v. Thomas Lubanga Dyilo* (Judgment pursuant to Article 74 of the Statute: Public), ICC-01/04–01/06–2842 (2012), para. 1089; interview #51.

32. Interview #16.

33. ICC, *Prosecutor v. Thomas Lubanga Dyilo* (Decision on the Confirmation of charges: Public Redacted Version with Annex I), ICC-01/04–01/06–803 (2007), para. 173.

34. Interview #85.

35. United Nations Secretariat, "Special Report on the Events in Ituri, January 2002–December 2003" para. 29; Human Rights Watch, "Ituri: 'Covered in Blood'"; interviews #83 and #81.

36. "Ugandan Troops Take Control of Bunia, Northeastern DR Congo," Agence France Presse, August 11, 2002.

37. ICC, *Prosecutor v. Thomas Lubanga Dyilo* (Judgment pursuant to Article 74 of the Statute: Public), ICC-01/04–01/06–2842 (2012), para. 90 fn 217.

38. United Nations Secretariat, "Special Report on the Events in Ituri, January 2002–December 2003."

39. Interview #20; Human Rights Watch, "Ituri: 'Covered in Blood.'"

40. Like Lonema and Lubanga, Angaika had studied psychology in Kisangani; see his testimony in the Lubanga trial, April 7, 2011, http://www.icc-cpi.int/iccdocs/doc/doc1053174.pdf.

41. Nilotic is actually a linguistic reference, although many have endowed it with racial overtones. Neither Kihema nor Kinyarwanda are Nilotic languages. Interviews #34, #39, #50, #52, and #53.

42. Interview #16; Human Rights Watch, "Ituri: 'Covered in Blood.'"

43. The numbers and incidents in this paragraph are drawn from Human Rights Watch, "Ituri: 'Covered in Blood.'"

44. Human Rights Watch, *Curse of Gold*, 24.

45. Human Rights Watch, "Ituri: 'Covered in Blood'"; Human Rights Watch, *Curse of Gold*.

46. Interview #60.

47. United Nations Secretariat, "Special Report on the Events in Ituri, January 2002–December 2003" para. 29; Human Rights Watch, *Curse of Gold*, 24.

48. Interviews #91 and #99.

49. "Fears of War in Bunia Town," *The East African* (Nairobi), February 17, 2003.

50. ICC, *Prosecutor v. Thomas Lubanga Dyilo* (Judgment pursuant to Article 74 of the Statute: Public), ICC-01/04–01/06–2842 (2012), para. 554.

51. United Nations Secretariat, "Special Report on the Events in Ituri, January 2002–December 2003" 29.

52. Interviews #16, #29, #43, and #52. Estimates of the UPC-K's strength varied widely, ranging from 500 to 4,500. In early 2005, Kisembo was eventually appointed General in the FARDC and most of his combatants were integrated. Lubanga's rebellion, however, continued, albeit in a weakened form. Interview #70.

53. Interview #81.

54. While the UPC effectively ceased to exist as an armed group with the creation of the MRC in June 2005 and Bosco's departure to North Kivu at the end of that year, some of its former combatants continued their fight. In 2008, FRPI, PUSIC and UPC remnants formed the Front populaire pour la justice au Congo (FPJC, Popular Front for Justice), which fell apart in 2010. In May 2012, other former UPC combatants re-emerged as members of the Coalition des groupes armés de l'Ituri (COGAI, Coalition of Ituri's Armed Groups), an attempt to unite several smaller militias with the mostly FRPI of Cobra Matata. However, COGAI never gained any real momentum. As a result of this failure, several COGAI members created another group in August 2012, the Mouvement de résistance populaire au Congo (MRPC, Popular Resistance Movement in the Congo). By mid-2013, however, under substantial military pressure from the Congolese army and the United Nations and lacking local or regional support, the MRPC collapsed.

55. Fahey, "Rethinking the Resource Curse"; Pottier, "Roadblock Ethnography."

56. Interview #65.

57. Interviews #66 and #67.

58. Interview #65.

59. United Nations Secretariat, "Special Report on the Events in Ituri, January 2002–December 2003," 6.

60. ICC, *Prosecutor v. Thomas Lubanga Dyilo* (Witness Transcript Filed During Trial Phase), ICC-01/04–01/06-T-168 (2009), 25.

61. Interview #901.

62. ICC, *Prosecutor v. Thomas Lubanga Dyilo* (Witness Transcript Filed During Trial Phase), ICC-01/04–01/06-T-346 (2011), 36.

63. Interview #901.

64. Tamm, *UPC in Ituri.*

65. Interview #99A.

66. Interview #91.

67. Human Rights Watch, "Ituri: 'Covered in Blood,'" 47.

68. ICC, *Prosecutor v. Thomas Lubanga Dyilo* (Witness Transcript Filed During Trial Phase), ICC-01/04–01/06-T-168 (2009), 55.

69. Interview #115E.

70. ICC, *Prosecutor v. Thomas Lubanga Dyilo* (Judgment pursuant to Article 74 of the Statute: Public), ICC-01/04–01/06-2842 (2012), para. 255.

71. Human Rights Watch, *Curse of Gold*, 27; ICC, *Prosecutor v. Thomas Lubanga Dyilo* (Judgment pursuant to Article 74 of the Statute: Public), ICC-01/04–01/06-2842 (2012), paras. 255–56.

72. United Nations, "Report of the Panel of Experts," S/2001/357, April 12, 2001, para. 180.

73. Office of the UN High Commissioner for Human Rights, "Report of the Mapping Exercise Documenting. . . . ," 246.

74. Daily Press Briefing by the Office of the Spokesman for the Secretary-General, June 2, 2004.

75. Interview #94.

76. Interview #93.

77. Amnesty International, *Democratic Republic of Congo.*

Chapter 9: Peacemaking and the Congo

1. The argument regarding land and identity can be found in Autesserre, *Trouble with the Congo*; I discuss this argument in Stearns, "Trouble with the Congo." The argument regarding conflict minerals is epitomized in Prendergast, "To Understand the Congo Conflict, Follow the Money," which echoes arguments made in Collier and Hoeffler, "Greed and Grievance in Civil War."

2. Department of Peacekeeping Operations, *UN Peacekeeping Operations.*

3. Interview with Howard Wolpe in Bukavu, February 27, 2009.

4. A key moment, according to diplomats, was the abstention of the US government from a vote on renewing IMF loans to Rwanda in 2002.

5. Reyntens, *Great African War,* 232.

6. Interviews #904A and #907B.

7. Interview #892.

8. Interview #893.

9. Mosse, *Cultivating Development*.

10. Ferguson, *Anti-Politics Machine*.

11. A similar argument is made in Trefon, *Congo Masquerade*.

12. Oxfam, "'For Me, but Without Me, Is Against Me.'"

13. Radio Okapi, "Kinshasa: 'Le projet agricole de Bukanga Lonzo a été un échec planifié dans sa conception,'" November 19, 2020.

14. Interview #613A.

15. United Nations Security Council Resolution 1925.

16. United Nations, "Report of the High-Level Panel," S/2015/446, June 17, 2015s. See also Congo Research Group, "The Art of the Possible—MONUSCO's New Mandate," March 2018.

17. Rhoads, *Taking Sides in Peacekeeping*.

18. Hillary Clinton, press statement, Supreme Court Decision Confirming Results of the Presidential Election in the DR Congo, December 20, 2011.

19. "EU Says DRC Vote Results Not Credible," Agence France Presse, March 29, 2012.

20. Tom Wilson, David Blood, and David Pilling, "Congo Voting Data Reveal Huge Fraud in Poll to Replace Kabila," *Financial Times,* January 15, 2019; Congo Research Group, "Who Really Won the Congolese Elections?" New York University, 2019.

21. Interview #897A.

22. Interview #894A.

23. Interview #889B.

24. Interview #890A.

25. Paris, "Peacebuilding and the Limits of Liberal Internationalism"; Richmond, *Liberal Peace Transitions*.

26. "Equity in Extractives: Stewarding Africa's Natural Resources for All," African Union, Africa Progress Panel, Addis Ababa, 2013; "Congo Asset Sales Lose State Billions of Dlrs: UK MP," Reuters, November 19, 2011.

27. For more on Gertler, see "#2378," Forbes, 2021, available at https://www.forbes.com/profile/dan-gertler/#995505d348df, accessed September 16, 2020. His wealth in 2014 was estimated at $2.5 billion; it is not clear why his wealth decreased by half since then.

28. Peyer, Feeney, and Mercier, "PR or Progress?"

29. Carter Center, "Improving Governance of Revenues from the Mining Industry," February 2017.

30. The calculation was by subtracting the entire capital flight for the 1970–1996 period in the DR Congo (see Boyce and Ndikumana, "Is Africa a Net Creditor?" 38), adjusted for 2010 currency; from the estimate for capital flight between 1970–2010 in the DR Congo (see Ndikumana, Boyce, and Ndiaye, "Capital Flight from Africa," 48). The estimates for government revenue come from World Bank, "Democratic Republic of Congo." Additional data on capital flight for 2003–2006 comes from Kar et al., "Capital Flight from the Democratic Republic of the Congo."

31. Interviews #178A, #815B, #207A, and #177A.

32. Kodi, "Corruption and Governance in the DRC," 39; Stanislas Bujakera, "Sénatoriales en RDC: des candidats dénoncent la corruption et retirent leur candidature," *Jeune Afrique*, February 18, 2019.

33. Interview #922A.

34. The IMF suspension was due to the failure of the Congolese government to disclose mining contracts. The trigger was the Comide mining contract, which is in part owned by the Kabila family.

35. Interviews #910A and #943B.

36. Mbaya and Nsenda, "La République Démocratique du Congo face au complot de balkanisation et d'implosion."

37. Interview #748A.

38. McGregor, "Ending Corporate Impunity," 469.

39. This figure doesn't include the $3.2 billion invested in Sicomines, part of the 2007 deal between the Congo and China, or a five-project deal between China Nonferrous Metal Mining (Group) Co., Ltd. and Gécamines, easily worth billions, none of whose details have been made public.

40. US Geological Survey, 2012 and 2013 Minerals Yearbook, available at www.minerals.usgs .gov. This excludes gold, which is also taxed by armed groups, and does not account for the large amounts of minerals that are smuggled across the border.

41. Cramer, "*Homo Economicus* Goes to War," 1857.

42. For example, Tribert Rujugiro, a co-owner of Mining and Processing Congo (MPC), a company with interests in the Bisie mine in Walikale, was an early supporter of the CNDP, and men loyal to Nkunda or the RCD maintained control over major Walikale mining sites between 2003–2004. Global Witness, "Under-Mining Peace," 15–16; United Nations, "Final Report," S/2008/773, December 12, 2008. During this period, there was allegedly strong complicity between the Rwandan army and ex-RCD officers close to Nkunda as they tried to maintain control of mineral exports that at the height of the tin boom in 2004 were valued $50,000 in daily exports from Walikale. Global Witness, "Under-Mining Peace," 16.

43. Numerous sources, however, suggested that the new military networks that controlled Walikale mining sites, while deeply hostile toward Nkunda, were linked to General Gabriel Amisi, who in turn had cordial relations to Nkunda. These same sources suggest that Amisi was maintained as the regional commander of North Kivu—and then as the commander of all land forces—as a means of comprimise with Nkunda's backers.

44. United Nations, "Final Report," S/2008/773, December 12, 2008.

45. Interview #101A.

46. They included Alexis and Modeste Makabuza, Eugène Serufuli, Antoine Musanganya, and Vany Bishweka.

47. Jeroen Cuvelier et al., "Analyzing the Impact of the Dodd-Frank Act on Congolese Livelihoods."

48. For summaries of this approach, see Kelsall, "Thinking and Working with Political Settlements"; Dressel and Dinnen, "Political Settlements."

49. For example, a British strategy document from 2012 argues: "On the regional level, the key goal is the normalisation of regional relationships, most importantly between Kinshasa and Kigali. . . . Provincial and national interventions should be focused on supporting the sustainability of local level agreements and protecting them from external manipulation, including reducing the influence of predatory political actors in Kinshasa." Internal policy document, on file with the author.

50. Douglass et al., *Limited Access Orders in the Developing World.*

51. De Waal, "Mission without End?"

52. Several of the commanders Kabila deployed against the nascent CNDP were known for their anti-Tutsi rhetoric. Kabila also never reassured the Tutsi community in public, there was never any conciliatory rhetoric.

53. International Crisis Group, "Escaping the Conflict Trap."

54. Ferguson, *Anti-Politics Machine.*

55. The USAID country strategy for 2014–2019 was more explicit about the political obstacles to reform, but does not put forward a comprehensive strategy for dealing with these.

56. Oxfam, "A Tale of Two Continents."

57. Interview #201B.

58. World Bank, "Rwanda."

59. "Success Factors for Women's and Children's Health," Rwandan Ministry of Health, Kigali, 2015.

60. An Ansoms et al., "Statistics versus Livelihoods."

61. Interview #173A.

62. "Rwanda: A Painful Dilemma," *The Economist,* August 4, 2012.

63. Auyero and Swistun, "Social Production of Toxic Uncertainty."

64. Interview #199.

65. Interview #147.

66. Blair and Buffett, "Stand with Rwanda."

67. Cooper, "U.N. Ambassador Questioned on U.S. Role in Congo Violence."

68. Interview #146A.

69. Most world production came from industrial mines in Brazil in Australia that shut down due to the fall in demand causes by the 2008 financial crisis.

70. Interview #963A.

BIBLIOGRAPHY

Allison, Graham, and Philip Zelikow. *Essence of Decision: Explaining the Cuban Missile Crisis.* New York: Longman, 1999.

Amnesty International. *Democratic Republic of Congo: Disarmament, Demobilization, and Reintegration (DDR) and Reform of the Army.* London: Amnesty International, 2007.

Ansoms, An, Esther Marijnen, Giuseppe Cioffo, and Jude Murison. "Statistics versus Livelihoods: Questioning Rwanda's Pathway out of Poverty." *Review of African Political Economy* 44, no. 151 (2017): 47–65.

Arjomand, Said Amir. *The Turban for the Crown: The Islamic Revolution in Iran.* New York: Oxford University Press, 1988.

Asuni, Judith Burdin. *Understanding the Armed Groups of the Niger Delta.* Council on Foreign Relations, New York, 2009.

Autesserre, Séverine. "The Only Way to Help Congo." *New York Times,* June 22, 2012.

———. *The Trouble with the Congo: Local Violence and the Failure of International Peacebuilding.* Cambridge Studies in International Relations, vol. 115. New York: Cambridge University Press, 2010.

Auyero, Javier, and Debora Swistun. "The Social Production of Toxic Uncertainty." *American Sociological Review* 73, no. 3 (2008): 357–79.

Baaz, Maria Eriksson, and Ola Olsson. "Feeding the Horse: Unofficial Economic Activities within the Police Force in the Democratic Republic of the Congo." *African Security* 4, no. 4 (2011): 223–41.

Baaz, Maria Eriksson, and Maria Stern. "Making Sense of Violence: Voices of Soldiers in the Congo (DRC)." *Journal of Modern African Studies* 46, no. 1 (2008): 57–86.

Baaz, Maria Eriksson, and Judith Verweijen. "The Volatility of a Half-Cooked Bouillabaisse: Rebel-Military Integration and Conflict Dynamics in the Eastern DRC." *African Affairs* 112, no. 449 (2013): 563–82.

Barkey, Karen. *Bandits and Bureaucrats: The Ottoman Route to State Centralization.* Ithaca: Cornell University Press, 1994.

Bateson, Regina. *Order and Violence in Postwar Guatemala.* New Haven: Yale University, 2014.

Bayart, Jean-François. *L'Etat en Afrique: La Politique Du Ventre.* Paris: Fayard, 2006.

Bayart, Jean-François, and Stephen Ellis. "Africa in the World: A History of Extraversion." *African Affairs* 99, no. 395 (2000): 217–67.

Behuria, Pritish. "Between Party Capitalism and Market Reforms: Understanding Sector Differences in Rwanda." *Journal of Modern African Studies* 53, no. 3 (2015): 415–50.

Beneduce, Roberto, Luca Jourdan, Timothy Raeymaekers, and Koen Vlassenroot. "Violence with a Purpose: Exploring the Functions and Meaning of Violence in the Democratic Republic of Congo." *Intervention* 4, no. 1 (2006): 32–46.

Bennett, Andrew. "Process Tracing: A Bayesian Approach." In *Oxford Handbook of Political Methodology*, edited by Janet Box-Steffensmeier, Henry Brady, and David Collier, 703–21. Oxford: Oxford University Press, 2008.

Bennett, Andrew, and Jeffrey T. Checkel. "Process Tracing: From Philosophical Roots to Best Practices." In *Process Tracing in the Social Sciences: From Metaphor to Analytic Tool*, edited by Andrew Bennett and Jeffrey T. Checkel. Cambridge: Cambridge University Press, 2014.

Berghezan, Georges. "Forces armées de RDC: Le chaos institutionnalisé?" Groupe de recherche et d'information sur la paix et la sécurité (GRIP), January 9, 2014.

Biebuyck, Daniel P. *Lega Culture: Art, Initiation, and Moral Philosophy among a Central African People*. Berkeley: University of California Press, 1973.

Blair, Tony, and Howard Buffett. "Stand with Rwanda." *Foreign Policy,* February 21, 2013.

Blattman, Christopher, and Edward Miguel. "Civil War." *Journal of Economic Literature* 48, no. 1 (2010): 3–57.

Bøås, Morten, and Kevin Dunn. "From Liberation Struggles to Warlordism and International Terrorism?" In *Routledge Handbook of African Security,* edited by James J. Hentz, 85–95. London: Routledge, 2013.

Bøås, Morten, and Liv Elin Torheim. "The Trouble in Mali—Corruption, Collusion, Resistance." *Third World Quarterly* 34, no. 7 (2013): 1279–92.

Bollag, Burton. "Public Expenditure Review of the Education Sector in the Democratic Republic of Congo: An Efficiency, Effectiveness, and Equity Analysis. Report No. ACS14542." World Bank, 2015.

Booth, David, and Frederick Golooba-Mutebi. "Developmental Patrimonialism? The Case of Rwanda." *African Affairs* 111, no. 444 (2012): 379–403.

Boyce, James K., and Léonce Ndikumana. "Is Africa a Net Creditor? New Estimates of Capital Flight from Severely Indebted Sub-Saharan African Countries, 1970–96." *Journal of Development Studies* 38, no. 2 (2001): 27–56.

Bryceson, Deborah Fahy, and Vali Jamal, eds. *Farewell to Farms: De-Agrarianisation and Employment in Africa.* Aldershot: Ashgate, 1997.

Bucyalimwe Mararo, Stanislas. "Le TPD à Goma (Nord-Kivu): Mythes et realités." In *L'Afrique des Grands Lacs, Annuaire 2003–2004,* edited by Filip Reyntjens and Marysse Stefaan, 139–70. Paris: L'Harmattan, 2004.

Callaghy, Thomas M. *The State-Society Struggle: Zaire in Comparative Perspective.* New York: Columbia University Press, 1984.

Campioni, Maddalena, and Patrick Noack, eds. *Rwanda Fast Forward: Social, Economic, Military and Reconciliation Prospects.* London: Palgrave Macmillan, 2012.

Carter Center. *Elections présidentielle et législatives République Démocratique du Congo, 28 Novembre 2011.* Atlanta: The Carter Center, 2012.

Cederman, Lars-Erik, Andreas Wimmer, and Brian Min. "Why Do Ethnic Groups Rebel: New Data and Analysis." *World Politics* 62, no. 1 (2010): 87–119.

Chabal, Patrick, and Jean-Pascal Daloz. *Africa Works: Disorder as Political Instrument.* Oxford: James Currey, 1999.

Christensen, Darin, Mai Nguyen, and Renard Sexton. "Strategic Violence during Democ-ratization: Evidence from Myanmar." *World Politics* 71, no. 2 (2019): 332–66.

Clapham, Christopher S. *African Guerrillas*. Oxford: James Currey, 1998.

Clark, Phil. "After Genocide: Democracy in Rwanda, 20 Years On." *Juncture* 20, no. 4 (2014): 308–11.

Coghlan, Benjamin, Pascal Ngoy, Flavien Mulumba, Colleen Hardy, Valerie Nkamgang Bemo, Tony Stewart, Jennifer Lewis, and Richard J. Brennan. "Update on Mortality in the Demo-cratic Republic of Congo: Results from a Third Nationwide Survey." *Disaster Medicine and Public Health Preparedness* 3, no. 2 (2009): 88–96.

Cohen, Dara. "Female Combatants and the Perpetration of Violence: Wartime Rape in the Sierra Leone Civil War." *World Politics* 65, no. 3 (2013): 383–415.

Collier, Paul, and Anke Hoeffler. "Greed and Grievance in Civil War." *Oxford Economic Papers* 56, no. 4 (2004): 563–95.

Congo Research Group. "For the Army, With the Army, Like the Army? The Rise of Guidon Shimiray and the NDC-Rénové in Eastern Congo." Center on International Cooperation, New York University, 2020.

———. "Mass Killings in Beni Territory: Political Violence, Cover Ups, and Cooptation." In-vestigative Report No. 2, September 2017.

Congo Research Group and Bureau d'études, de Recherches, et de Consulting International (BERCI). "Impasse in the Congo: Results from a National Public Opinion Poll." Center on International Cooperation, New York, October 2016.

Conrad, Joseph. *Heart of Darkness*. Cambridge: Cambridge University Press, 2018.

Cooper, Helene. "U.N. Ambassador Questioned on U.S. Role in Congo Violence." *New York Times*, December 9, 2012.

Cramer, Christopher. "*Homo Economicus* Goes to War: Methodological Individualism, Rational Choice, and the Political Economy of War." *World Development* 30, no. 11 (2002): 1845–1864.

Cunningham, David E. "Veto Players and Civil War Duration." *American Journal of Political Science* 50, no. 4 (2006): 875–92.

Cuvelier, Jeroen, Steven Van Bockstael, Koen Vlassenroot, and Claude Iguma. "Analyzing the Impact of the Dodd-Frank Act on Congolese Livelihoods." Social Science Research Council, November 2014.

Daly, Sarah Zukerman. "Organizational Legacies of Violence: Conditions Favoring Insurgency Onset in Colombia, 1964–1984." *Journal of Peace Research* 49, no. 3 (2012): 473–91.

Day, Christopher R., and William S. Reno. "In Harm's Way: African Counter-Insurgency and Patronage Politics." *Civil Wars* 16, no. 2 (2014): 105–26.

Debos, Marielle. "Living by the Gun in Chad: Armed Violence as a Practical Occupation." *Journal of Modern African Studies* 49, no. 3 (2011): 409–28.

Department of Peacekeeping Operations. *MONUC and the Bukavu Crisis 2004*. Best Practices Unit. New York: United Nations, 2005.

———. *UN Peacekeeping Operations: Principles and Guidelines*. New York: United Nations, 2008.

Depelchin, Jacques M. François. "From Pre-Capitalism to Imperialism: A History of Social and Economic Formations in Eastern Zaire (Uvira Zone, c. 1800–1965)." Stanford University, PhD dissertation, 1974.

de Waal, Alex. "Mission without End? Peacekeeping in the African Political Marketplace." *International Affairs* 85, no. 1 (2009): 99–113.

———. "When Kleptocracy Becomes Insolvent: Brute Causes of the Civil War in South Sudan." *African Affairs* 113, no. 452 (2014): 347–69.

Diamond, Larry. "Class Formation in the Swollen African State." *Journal of Modern African Studies* 25, no. 4 (1987): 567–96.

Dressel, Björn, and Sinclair Dinnen. "Political Settlements: Old Wine in New Bottles?" Development Policy Centre, Canberra, February 2012.

Ellis, Stephen. *The Mask of Anarchy: The Destruction of Liberia and the Religious Dimension of an African Civil War*. Updated edition. New York: NYU Press, 2006.

———. "War in West Africa." *Fletcher Forum of World Affairs* 25, no. 2 (2001): 33–39.

Evans, Martha, and Ian Glenn. "'TIA—This Is Africa': Afropessimism in Twenty-First-Century Narrative Film." *Black Camera: An International Film Journal (The New Series)* 2, no. 1 (2010): 14–35.

Fahey, Dan. "Rethinking the Resource Curse: Natural Resources and Polywar in the Ituri District, Democratic Republic of the Congo." PhD dissertation, University of California at Berkeley, 2011.

Fair, C. Christine. *Fighting to the End: The Pakistan Army's Way of War*. New York: Oxford University Press, 2014.

Fearon, James D. "Rationalist Explanations for War." *International Organization* 49, no. 3 (1995): 379–414.

———. "What Is Identity (as We Now Use the Word)." Unpublished manuscript. Stanford University, Palo Alto, California, 1999.

Ferguson, James. *The Anti-Politics Machine: "Development," Depoliticization, and Bureaucratic Power in Lesotho*. Cambridge: Cambridge University Press, 1990.

Finnemore, Martha, and Kathryn Sikkink. "International Norm Dynamics and Political Change." *International Organization* 52, no. 4 (1998): 887–917.

Food and Agriculture Organization. "Ending Extreme Poverty in Rural Areas: Sustaining Livelihoods to Leave No One Behind." Rome, 2018.

Fortes, Meyer, and Edward Evan Evans-Pritchard, eds. *African Political Systems*. 1940; repr. London: Routledge, 1987.

Geenen, Sara, and Jeroen Cuvelier. "Local Elites' Extraversion and Repositioning: Continuities and Changes in Congo's Mineral Production Networks." *Extractive Industries and Society* 6, no. 2 (2019): 390–98.

Geertz, Clifford. *Agricultural Involution: The Process of Ecological Change in Indonesia*. Vol. 11. Berkeley: University of California Press, 1963.

———. *The Interpretation of Cultures*. New York: Basic Books, 1973.

Geffray, Christian. *La cause des armes au Mozambique: Anthropologie d'une guerre civile*. Paris: Karthala, 1990.

Geschiere, Peter, and Francis B. Nyamnjoh. "Capitalism and Autochthony: The Seesaw of Mobility and Belonging." *Public Culture* 12, no. 2 (2000): 423–52.

Gettleman, Jeffrey. "An Interview with Joseph Kabila." *New York Times*, April 3, 2009.

———. "Rape Epidemic Raises Trauma of Congo War." *New York Times*, October 7, 2007.

———. "Rwanda Stirs Deadly Brew of Troubles in Congo." *New York Times*, December 3, 2008.

Global Witness. "'The Hill Belongs to Them': The Need for International Action on Congo's Conflict Minerals Trade." December 2010.

———. "Under-Mining Peace: Tin: The Explosive Trade in Cassiterite in Eastern DRC." June 2005.

Goldstone, Jack A. "Toward a Fourth Generation of Revolutionary Theory." *Annual Review of Political Science* 4, no. 1 (2001): 139–87.

Hagmann, Tobias. *Stabilization, Extraversion, and Political Settlements in Somalia.* Nairobi: Rift Valley Institute, 2016.

Hedlund, Anna. "Exile Warriors: Violence and Community among Hutu Rebels in the Eastern Congo." PhD dissertation, Lund University, 2014.

Herbst, Jeffrey, and Greg Mills. "There Is No Congo." *Foreign Policy,* March 18, 2009. Available at https://foreignpolicy.com/2009/03/18/there-is-no-congo/, accessed March 24, 2021.

Hoffmann, Kasper, and Koen Vlassenroot. "Armed Groups and the Exercise of Public Authority: The Cases of the Mayi-Mayi and Raya Mutomboki in Kalehe, South Kivu." *Peacebuilding* 2, no. 2 (2014): 202–20.

Hoffmann, Kasper, Koen Vlassenroot, Tatiana Carayannis, and Godefroid Muzalia. "Violent Conflict and Ethnicity in the Congo: Beyond Materialism, Primordialism and Symbolism." *Conflict, Security, and Development* 20, no. 5 (2020): 539–60.

Hopf, Ted. *Social Construction of International Politics: Identities and Foreign Policies, Moscow, 1955 and 1999.* Ithaca: Cornell University Press, 2002.

Human Rights Watch. "Burundi: The Gatumba Massacre: War Crimes and Political Agendas." Human Rights Watch Briefing Paper, September 2004. Available at https://www.hrw.org/legacy/backgrounder/africa/burundi/2004/0904/burundi0904.pdf, accessed May 20, 2021.

———. *The Curse of Gold: Democratic Republic of Congo.* New York: Human Rights Watch, 2005. Available at https://www.hrw.org/sites/default/files/reports/drc0505_0.pdf, accessed May 20, 2021.

———. "D.R. Congo: M23 Rebels Committing War Crimes." 2012. Available at https://www.hrw.org/news/2012/09/11/dr-congo-m23-rebels-committing-war-crimes#, accessed May 20, 2021.

———. "D.R. Congo: War Crimes in Bukavu." Human Rights Watch Briefing Paper, June 12, 2004. Available at https://www.hrw.org/report/2004/06/12/dr-congo-war-crimes-bukavu/human-rights-watch-briefing-paper-june-2004, accessed May 20, 2021.

———. "Ituri: 'Covered in Blood': Ethnically Targeted Violence in Northeastern DR Congo." July 2003. Available at https://www.hrw.org/reports/2003/ituri0703/DRC0703full.pdf, accessed May 20, 2021.

———. "Uganda in Eastern DRC: Fueling Political and Ethnic Strife." March 1, 2001. Available at https://www.hrw.org/sites/default/files/reports/drc0301web.pdf, accessed May 20, 2021.

———. "UPC Crimes in Ituri (2002–2003)." November 8, 2006. Accessed https://www.hrw.org/report/2006/11/08/upc-crimes-ituri-2002-2003/summary, accessed May 20, 2021.

———. "War Crimes in Kisangani: The Response of Rwandan-backed Rebels to the May 2002 Mutiny." August 2002. Accessed https://www.hrw.org/reports/2002/drc2/, accessed May 20, 2021.

———. *You Will Be Punished: Attacks on Civilians in Eastern Congo*. New York: Human Rights Watch, 2009. Available at https://www.hrw.org/sites/default/files/reports/drc1209web wcover2.pdf, accessed May 20, 2021.

Integrated Regional Information Networks. "DRC: Rebel Group Guilty of Kisangani Massacres." *The New Humanitarian*, July 17, 2002. Available at https://reliefweb.int/report/democratic -republic-congo/drc-rebel-group-guilty-kisangani-massacres, accessed April 7, 2021.

International Crisis Group. "The Congo's Transition is Failing: Crisis in the Kivus." Africa Report No. 91, March 30, 2005. Available at https://www.crisisgroup.org/africa/central-africa /democratic-republic-congo/congos-transition-failing-crisis-kivus, accessed May 20, 2021.

———. "Escaping the Conflict Trap: Promoting Good Governance in the Congo." Africa Report No. 114, July 20, 2006. Available at https://www.crisisgroup.org/africa/central-africa /democratic-republic-congo/escaping-conflict-trap-promoting-good-governance-congo, accessed May 20, 2021.

———. "Katanga: The Congo's Forgotten Crisis." Africa Report No. 103, January 9, 2006. Available at https://www.crisisgroup.org/africa/central-africa/democratic-republic-congo/katanga -congo-s-forgotten-crisis, accessed May 20, 2021.

International Peace Information Service. "Roadblock Rebels: IPIS Maps Important Mechanism of Conflict Funding in Central Africa." December 7, 2017.

International Rescue Committee. "Mortality in the Democratic Republic of Congo: An Ongoing Crisis." New York, May 1, 2007. Available at https://www.rescue.org/report/mortality -democratic-republic-congo-ongoing-crisis, accessed May 21, 2021.

Jackson, Richard. "Culture, Identity, and Hegemony: Continuity and (the Lack of) Change in US Counterterrorism Policy from Bush to Obama." *International Politics* 48, no. 2 (2011): 390–411.

Jackson, Stephen. "'It Seems to Be Going': The Genius of Survival in Wartime DR Congo." In *Hard Work, Hard Times: Global Volatility and African Subjectivities*, edited by Anne-Maria Makhulu, Beth Buggenhagen, and Stephen Jackson, 48–68. Berkeley: University of California Press, 2020.

———. "Sons of Which Soil? The Language and Politics of Autochthony in Eastern D.R. Congo." *African Studies Review* 49, no. 2 (2006): 95–123.

Jones, Will. "Murder and Create: State Reconstruction in Rwanda since 1994." PhD dissertation, Oxford University, 2014.

Joris, Lieve. *Dans van de luipaard*. 2001; repr. Amsterdam, Atlas Contact, 2012.

Jourdan, Luca, Koen Vlassenroot, and Timothy Raeymaekers. "Being at War, Being Young: Violence and Youth in North Kivu." In *Conflict and Social Transformation in Eastern DR Congo*, edited by Koen Vlassenroot and Timothy Raeymakers, 157–76. Gent: Academia Press, 2004.

Kabeera, Eric. "Ex-M23 Combatants Seek Refugee Status in Rwanda." *The New Times* (Kigali), May 1, 2013.

Kabona, Esiara. "Rwanda in Talks to Export Chicken, Eggs, Beef to DRC." *The East African*, September 26, 2017.

Kaldor, Mary. *New and Old Wars: Organised Violence in a Global Era*. London: John Wiley & Sons, 2013.

Kalyvas, Stathis N. "Civil Wars." In *Oxford Handbook of Comparative Politics*, edited by Carles Boix and Susan Stokes, 416–34. New York: Oxford University Press, 2007.

———. *The Logic of Violence in Civil War*. Cambridge: Cambridge University Press, 2006.

Kapend, Richard, Jakub Bijak, and Andrew Hinde. "The Democratic Republic of the Congo Armed Conflict 1998–2004: Assessing Excess Mortality Based on Factual and Counter-Factual Projection Scenarios." *Revue Quetelet/Quetelet Journal* 8, no. 1 (2020): 7–35.

Kapferer, Bruce. *Legends of People, Myths of State: Violence, Intolerance, and Political Culture in Sri Lanka and Australia*. New York and Oxford: Berghahn Books, 2011.

Kar, Dev, Ramil Mammadov, Rachel Goodermote, and Janak Upadhyay. "Capital Flight from the Democratic Republic of the Congo." Global Financial Integrity, July 24, 2008.

Kasfir, Nelson. "Introduction: Relating State to Class in Africa." *Journal of Commonwealth and Comparative Politics* 21, no. 3 (1983): 3–8.

Keen, David. *Conflict and Collusion in Sierra Leone*. Oxford: James Currey, 2005.

———. "Liberalization and Conflict." *International Political Science Review* 26, no. 1 (2005): 73–89.

Kelsall, Tim. "Thinking and Working with Political Settlements." Overseas Development Institute, London, November 2018.

Keohane, Robert O. "International Institutions: Two Approaches." *International Studies Quarterly* 32, no. 4 (1988): 379–96.

Kimenyi, Felly. "DRC Should Stop Playing the Victim—Mushikiwabo." *The New Times* (Kigali), September 7, 2012.

Kodi, Muzong. "Corruption and Governance in the DRC." Institute for Security Studies, Pretoria, January 2008.

Kristof, Nicholas D. "Orphaned, Raped, and Ignored." *New York Times,* January 30, 2010.

Laudati, Ann. "Beyond Minerals: Broadening 'Economies of Violence' in Eastern Democratic Republic of Congo." *Review of African Political Economy* 40, no. 135 (2013): 32–50.

Leung, Christine C. M., and Yu Huang. "The Paradox of Journalistic Representation of the Other: The Case of SARS Coverage on China and Vietnam by Western-Led English-Language Media in Five Countries." *Journalism* 8, no. 6 (2007): 675–97.

Longman, Timothy, and Théonèste Rutagengwa. "Memory, Identity, and Community in Rwanda." In *My Neighbor, My Enemy: Justice and Community in the Aftermath of Mass Atrocity*, edited by Eric Stover and Harvey M. Weinstein, 162–82. Cambridge: Cambridge University Press, 2004.

Loons, P. *Histoire du territoire d'Uvira*. Uvira: Archives de La Sous-Région du Sud-Kivu, 1933.

MacGaffey, Wyatt. "The Policy of National Integration in Zaïre." *Journal of Modern African Studies* 20, no. 1 (1982): 87–105.

Mac Ginty, Roger, and Oliver P. Richmond. "The Local Turn in Peace Building: A Critical Agenda for Peace." *Third World Quarterly* 34, no. 5 (2013): 763–83.

Mamdani, Mahmood. *Citizen and Subject: Contemporary Africa and the Legacy of Late Colonialism*. Princeton: Princeton University Press, 2018.

———. "The Invention of the Indigène." *London Review of Books* 33, no. 2 (2011): 1–18.

———. *Understanding the Crisis in Kivu: Report of the CODESRIA Mission to the Democratic Republic of Congo*. Vol. 1. Dakar: African Books Collective, 2001.

Mampilly, Zachariah, and Jason Stearns. "A New Direction for US Foreign Policy in Africa." *Dissent* 67, no. 4 (2020): 107–17.

Marysse, Stefaan, and Catherine André. "Guerre et pillage économique en République démocratique du Congo." In *L'Afrique des Grands Lacs, Annuaire 2000–2001*, edited by Filip Reyntjens and Stefaan Marysse. Paris: L'Harmattan, 2001.

Masters, William A., Agnes Andersson Djurfeldt, Cornelis de Haan, Peter Hazell, Thomas Jayne, Magnus Jirström, and Thomas Reardon. "Urbanization and Farm Size in Asia and Africa: Implications for Food Security and Agricultural Research." *Global Food Security* 2, no. 3 (2013): 156–65.

Mbaya, J. Kankwenda, and F. Mukoka Nsenda. "La République Démocratique du Congo face au complot de balkanisation et d'implosion." Icredes, Kinshasa/Montreal/Washington, D.C., 2013.

Mbembe, Achille. "Provisional Notes on the Postcolony." *Africa* 62, no. 1 (1992): 3–37.

McGregor, Michael A. "Ending Corporate Impunity: How to Really Curb the Pillaging of Natural Resources." *Case Western Reserve Journal of International Law* 42, no. 1 (2009): 469–97.

Meditz, Sandra, and Tim Merill. *Zaire: A Country Study.* Washington, D.C.: Federal Research Division, Library of Congress, 1994.

Menkhaus, Ken. "Elite Bargains and Political Deals Project: Somalia Case Study." Stabilisation Unit, Department for International Development, London, 2018.

Ministère de la Défense Nationale et des Anciens Combattants. *Plan Global De Desarmement Demobilisation et Reintegration (DDRI II).* Democratic Republic of Congo. Kinshasa: Ministère de la Défense Nationale et des Anciens Combattants, 2014.

Mkandawire, Thandika. "The Terrible Toll of Post-Colonial 'Rebel Movements' in Africa: Towards an Explanation of the Violence against the Peasantry." *Journal of Modern African Studies* 40, no. 2 (2002): 181–215.

———. "The Terrible Toll of Postcolonial Rebel Movements: Towards an Explanation of the Violence against the Peasantry." In *The Roots of African Conflicts: The Causes and Costs*, edited by Alfred Nhema and Paul Tiyambe Zeleza, 106–35. Oxford: James Currey, 2008.

Moshonas, Stylianos. "The Political Economy of Human Resource and Payroll Management in the Democratic Republic of the Congo." Working Paper no. 71, Secure Livelihoods Research Consortium (SLRC), March 2019.

Mosse, David. *Cultivating Development.* London: Pluto Press, 2005.

Mowoe, Isaac James. *The Performance of Soldiers as Governors: African Politics and the African Military.* Washington, D.C.: University Press of America, 1980.

Multi-Country Demobilization and Reintegration Program. "MDRP Final Report: Overview of Program Achievements." World Bank, July 2010. Available at https://reliefweb.int/sites/reliefweb.int/files/resources/60A4D1D4EB5BAC5F492577920005E8F0-Full_Report.pdf, accessed May 24, 2021.

Mwenda, Andrew M. "Don't Save Congo." *New York Times,* November 11, 2013.

Ndikumana, Léonce, James K. Boyce, and Ameth Saloum Ndiaye. "Capital Flight from Africa: Causes, Effects, and Policy Issues." In *Capital Flight from Africa: Causes, Effects, and Policy Issues*, edited by S. Ibi Ajayi and Leonce Ndikumana, 15–54. Oxford: Oxford University Press, 2015.

Nepstad, Sharon Erickson. *Nonviolent Revolutions: Civil Resistance in the Late 20th Century.* Oxford: Oxford University Press, 2011.

Nest, Michael Wallace, Francois Grignon, and Emizet F. Kisangani. *The Democratic Republic of Congo: Economic Dimensions of War and Peace.* International Peace Academy Occasional Paper No. 53. Boulder: Lynne Rienner, 2006.

Newbury, David. "Irredentist Rwanda: Ethnic and Territorial Frontiers in Central Africa." *Africa Today* 44, no. 2 (1997): 211–21.

Ngonga, Alphonse Maindo Monga. "'La Républiquette de l'Ituri' en République Démocratique du Congo: Un Far West Ougandais." *Politique Africaine* 89, no. 1 (2003): 181–92.

North, Douglass, John Joseph Wallis, Stephen Webb, and Barry Weingast. *Limited Access Orders in the Developing World: A New Approach to the Problems of Development.* Washington, D.C.: World Bank Publications, 2009.

Office of the UN High Commissioner for Human Rights. "Democratic Republic of the Congo, 1993–2003." August 2010. Available at https://www.ohchr.org/Documents/Countries/CD/DRC_MAPPING_REPORT_FINAL_EN.pdf, accessed May 21, 2021.

———. "Report of the Mapping Exercise Documenting the Most Serious Violations of Human Rights and International Humanitarian Law Committed within the Territory of the Democratic Republic of the Congo between March 1993 and June 2003." Geneva: United Nations High Commission for Human Rights, 2010.

———. "Report of the United Nations Joint Human Rights Office on Human Rights Violations Perpetrated by Armed Groups During Attacks on Villages in Ufamandu I and II, Nyamaboko I and II, and Kibabi Groupements, Masisi Territory, North Kivu Province, between April and September 2012." November 14, 2012. Available at https://reliefweb.int/report/democratic-republic-congo/report-united-nations-joint-human-rights-office-human-rights, accessed May 20, 2021.

Olsson, Ola, Maria Eriksson Baaz, and Peter Martinsson. "Fiscal Capacity in 'Post'-Conflict States: Evidence from Trade on Congo River." *Journal of Development Economics,* vol. 146, September 2020, Article 102506.

Omeje, Kenneth. "Oil Conflict in Nigeria: Contending Issues and Perspectives of the Local Niger Delta People." *New Political Economy* 10, no. 3 (2005): 321–34.

Omotola, J. Shola. "From Political Mercenarism to Militias: The Political Origin of the Niger Delta Militias." In *Fresh Dimensions on the Niger Delta Crisis of Nigeria,* edited by Victor Ojakorotu, 91–124. Bangkok: JAPSS Press, 2009.

Ostrom, Elinor. "A Behavioral Approach to the Rational Choice Theory of Collective Action: Presidential Address, American Political Science Association, 1997." *American Political Science Review* 92, no. 1 (1998): 1–22.

Oxfam. "'For Me, but Without Me, Is Against Me': Why Efforts to Stabilize the Eastern Congo Are Not Working." London, 2011.

———. "A Tale of Two Continents: Fighting Inequality in Africa." London, 2019.

Pabanel, J.-P. "La question de la nationalité au Kivu." *Politique Africaine,* no. 41 (1991): 32–40.

Paige, Jeffery M. *Agrarian Revolution: Social Movements and Export Agriculture in the Underdeveloped World.* New York: Free Press, 1978.

———. "Revolution and the Agrarian Bourgeoisie in Nicaragua." In *Revolution in the World System,* edited by Terry Boswell. New York: Greenwood, 1989.

Paris, Roland. "Peacebuilding and the Limits of Liberal Internationalism." *International Security* 22, no. 2 (1997): 54–89.

Peemans, Jean-Philippe. *Le Congo-Zaïre au gré du XXème siècle: Etat, economie, société 1880–1990.* Paris: L'Harmattan, 1997.

Peyer, Chantal, Patricia Feeney, and François Mercier. "PR or Progress? Glencore's Corporate Responsibility in the Democratic Republic of the Congo." Bread for All, Fastenopfer, and RAID, June 2014.

Pham, J. Peter. "To Save Congo, Let It Fall Apart." *New York Times*, November 30, 2012.

Pierson, Paul. "Increasing Returns, Path Dependence, and the Study of Politics." *American Political Science Review* 1994, no. 2 (2000): 251–67.

Pinaud, Clemence. "South Sudan: Civil War, Predation and the Making of a Military Aristocracy." *African Affairs* 113, no. 451 (2014): 192–211.

Porter, David. *Final Report of the Judicial Commission of Inquiry into Allegations into Illegal Exploitation of Natural Resources and Other Forms of Wealth in the DRC.* Kampala: Government of Uganda, 2002.

Pottier, Johan. "Displacement and Ethnic Reintegration in Ituri, DR Congo: Challenges Ahead." *Journal of Modern African Studies* 64, no. 3 (2008): 427–50.

———. "Representations of Ethnicity in the Search for Peace: Ituri, Democratic Republic of Congo." *African Affairs* 109, no. 434 (2010): 23–50.

———. "Roadblock Ethnography: Negotiating Humanitarian Access in Ituri, Eastern DR Congo, 1999–2004." *Africa* 76, no. 2 (2006): 151–79.

Prendergast, John. "The New Face of African Conflict." *Foreign Affairs*, March 12, 2014.

———. "To Understand the Congo Conflict, Follow the Money." *New York Times*, November 30, 2012.

Reno, William. *Warfare in Independent Africa.* New Approaches to African History Series, Vol. 5. Cambridge: Cambridge University Press, 2011.

———. *Warlord Politics and African States.* Boulder: Lynne Rienner, 1999.

Reyntjens, Filip. *Political Governance in Post-Genocide Rwanda.* Cambridge: Cambridge University Press, 2013.

———. *The Great African War: Congo and Regional Geopolitics, 1996–2006.* Cambridge: Cambridge University Press, 2009.

Rhoads, Emily Paddon. *Taking Sides in Peacekeeping: Impartiality and the Future of the United Nations.* Oxford: Oxford University Press, 2016.

Richards, Paul. *Fighting for the Rain Forest: War, Youth, and Resources in Sierra Leone.* Oxford: James Currey, 1998.

Richmond, Oliver P. *Liberal Peace Transitions: Between Statebuilding and Peacebuilding.* Edinburgh: Edinburgh University Press, 2009.

Ripley, Brian. "Psychology, Foreign Policy, and International Relations Theory." *Political Psychology* 14, no. 3 (1993): 403–16.

Saint Moulin, Léon de. "Mouvements récents de population dans la zone de peuplement dense de l'est du Kivu." *Etudes d'histoire Africaine* 7, no. 10 (1975): 1977–78.

Schmitt, Carl. *The Concept of the Political: Expanded Edition.* Chicago: University of Chicago Press, 2008.

Scott, Stewart Andrew. *Laurent Nkunda et la rébellion du Kivu: Au coeur de la guerre congolaise.* Paris: Karthala, 2008.

Shahabudin McDoom, Omar. "Rwanda's Exit Pathway from Violence: A Strategic Assessment." World Bank, Washington, D.C., 2011.

Sklar, Richard L. "The Nature of Class Domination in Africa." *Journal of Modern African Studies* 17, no. 4 (1979): 531–52.

Staniland, Paul. *Networks of Rebellion: Explaining Insurgent Cohesion and Collapse.* Ithaca: Cornell University Press, 2014.

Stearns, Jason K. "From CNDP to M23: The Evolution of an Armed Movement in Eastern Congo." Rift Valley Institute, London, 2012.

———. "North Kivu: The Background to Conflict in North Kivu Province of Eastern Congo." Rift Valley Institute, London, 2012.

———. "PARECO: Land, Local Strongmen, and the Roots of Militia Politics in North Kivu." Rift Valley Institute, London, 2013. Available at refworld.org/docid/51d2c5304.html, accessed May 21, 2021.

———. "The Trouble with the Congo: Local Violence and the Failure of International Peacebuilding." *Review of African Political Economy* 40, no. 135: 163–67. Review of *The Trouble with the Congo: Local Violence and the Failure of International Peacebuilding* by Séverine Autesserre.

Stearns, Jason, et al. [Judith Verweijen]. *Mai-Mai Yakutumba: Resistance and Racketeering in Fizi, South Kivu.* Rift Valley Institute, London, 2013.

Stearns, Jason, Christine Mercier, and Nicolas Donner. "L'ancrage social des rébellions congolaises." *Afrique Contemporaine* 265, no. 1 (2018): 11–37.

Stearns, Jason, Judith Verweijen, and Maria Eriksson Baaz. *The National Army and Armed Groups in the Eastern Congo: Untangling the Gordian Knot of Insecurity.* London: Rift Valley Institute, 2013.

Stearns, Jason, Koen Vlassenroot, Kasper Hoffmann, and Tatiana Carayannis. "Congo's Inescapable State: The Trouble with the Local." *Foreign Affairs*, March 16, 2017.

Stearns, Jason, and Christoph Vogel. "Landscape of Armed Groups in Eastern Congo." Congo Research Group, December 2015.

Stedman, Stephen John. "Spoiler Problems in Peace Processes." *International Security* 22, no. 2 (1997): 5–53.

Straus, Scott. "Wars Do End! Changing Patterns of Political Violence in Sub-Saharan Africa." *African Affairs* 111, no. 443 (2012): 179–201.

Sundaram, Anjan. "The Other War." *Foreign Policy*, November 21, 2012.

Tamm, Henning. "UPC in Ituri: The External Militarization of Local Politics in North-Eastern Congo." Rift Valley Institute, London, 2013.

Trefon, Theodore. *Congo Masquerade: The Political Culture of Aid Inefficiency and Reform Failure.* London: Zed Books, 2011.

Trejo, Guillermo, and Sandra Ley. *Votes, Drugs, and Violence: The Political Logic of Criminal Wars in Mexico.* Cambridge: Cambridge University Press, 2020.

Tull, Denis M. *The Reconfiguration of Political Order in Africa: A Case Study of North Kivu (DR Congo).* Hamburg African Studies Vol. 13. Hamburg: Institut für Afrika-Kunde, 2005.

Tull, Denis M., and Andreas Mehler. "The Hidden Costs of Power-Sharing: Reproducing Insurgent Violence in Africa." *African Affairs* 104, no. 416 (2005): 375–98.

Turner, Thomas. "'Batetela,' 'Baluba,' 'Basonge': Ethnogenesis in Zaire." *Cahiers d'études africaines* 32, no. 132 (1993): 587–612.

United Nations. "Addendum to the Interim Report of the Group of Experts on the DRC Submitted in Accordance with Paragraph 4 of Security Council Resolution 2021 (2011)." S/2012/348/Add.1, June 27, 2012. Available at https://www.undocs.org/S/2012/348/Add.1, accessed May 20, 2021.

———. "Final Report of the Group of Experts on the DRC Submitted in Accordance with Paragraph 4 of Security Council Resolution 2021 (2011)." S/2012/843, November 15, 2012. Available at https://www.undocs.org/S/2012/843, accessed May 20, 2021.

———. "Final Report of the Group of Experts on the DRC Submitted in Accordance with Paragraph 5 of Security Council Resolution 1952 (2010)." S/2011/738, December 2, 2011. Available at https://www.undocs.org/S/2011/738, accessed May 20, 2021.

———. "Final Report of the Group of Experts on the DRC Submitted in Accordance with Paragraph 18(d) of Security Council Resolution 1857 (2008)." S/2009/603, November 23, 2009. Available at https://www.undocs.org/S/2009/603, accessed May 20, 2021.

———. "Final Report of the Group of Experts on the DRC Submitted in Accordance with Paragraph 18(d) of Security Council Resolution 1807." S/2008/773, December 12, 2008. Available at https://www.undocs.org/S/2008/773, accessed May 20, 2021.

———. "Final Report of the Group of Experts Submitted in Accordance with Paragraph 6 of Security Council Resolution 2360 (2017)." S/2018/531, June 4, 2018. Available at https://www.undocs.org/S/2018/531, accessed May 20, 2021.

———. "Final Report of the Group of Experts Submitted in Accordance with Paragraph 5 of Security Council Resolution 2078 (2012)." S/2014/42, January 23, 2014. Available at https://www.undocs.org/S/2014/42, accessed May 20, 2021.

———. "Final Report of the Group of Experts on the DRC, Submitted in Accordance with Paragraph 6 of Security Council Resolution 1896 (2009)." S/2010/596, November 29, 2010. Available at https://www.undocs.org/S/2010/596, accessed May 20, 2021.

———. "Interim Report of the Group of Experts on the DRC Submitted in Accordance with Paragraph 4 of Security Council Resolution 2021 (2011)." S/2012/348, June 21, 2012. Available at https://www.undocs.org/S/2012/348, accessed May 20, 2021.

———. "Midterm Report of the Group of Experts on the DRC Submitted in Accordance with Paragraph 5 of Security Council Resolution 2078 (2012)," S/2013/433, July 19, 2013. Available at https://www.undocs.org/S/2013/433, accessed May 20, 2021.

———. "Report of the Group of Experts Submitted Pursuant to Resoluton 1533 (2004)." S/2004/551, July 15, 2004. Available at https://www.undocs.org/S/2004/551, accessed May 20, 2021.

———. "Report of the Group of Experts Submitted Pursuant to Resolution 1654 (2006)." S/2006/525, July 18, 2006. Available at https://www.undocs.org/S/2006/525, accessed May 20, 2021.

———. "Report of the Group of Experts Submitted Pursuant to Resolution 1596 (2005)." S/2005/436, July 26, 2005. Available at https://www.undocs.org/S/2005/436, accessed May 20, 2021.

———. "Report of the Group of Experts Submitted Pursuant to Resolution 1552 (2004)." S/2005/30, January 25, 2005. Available at https://www.undocs.org/S/2005/30, accessed May 20, 2021.

———. "Report of the High-Level Panel on United Nations Peace Operations." S/2015/446, June 17, 2015. Available at https://reliefweb.int/report/world/report-high-level-independent -panel-peace-operations-uniting-our-strengths-peace, accessed May 20, 2021.

———. "Report of the Panel of Experts on the Illegal Exploitation of Natural Resources and Other Forms of Wealth of DR Congo." S/2001/357, April 12, 2001. Available at https://www .undocs.org/S/2001/357, accessed May 20, 2021.

United Nations Secretariat. "Special Report on the Events in Ituri, January 2002–December 2003." New York, 2004.

Van Evera, Stephen. "The Cult of the Offensive and the Origins of the First World War." *International Security* 9, no. 1 (1984): 58–107.

Verheijen, T., and J. Mabi Mulumba. "Democratic Republic of Congo: Rebuilding the Public Service Wage System." World Bank, Washington, D.C., 2008.

Verweijen, Judith, and Claude Iguma. "Understanding Armed Group Proliferation in the Eastern Congo." Rift Valley Institute, London, 2015.

Verweijen, Judith, and Esther Marijnen. "The Counterinsurgency/Conservation Nexus: Guerrilla Livelihoods and the Dynamics of Conflict and Violence in the Virunga National Park, Democratic Republic of the Congo." *Journal of Peasant Studies* 45, no. 2 (2018): 300–320.

Vigh, Henrik. "Conflictual Motion and Political Inertia: On Rebellions and Revolutions in Bissau and Beyond." *African Studies Review* 52, no. 2 (2009): 143–64.

Vinck, Patrick, and Phuong Pham. "Searching for Lasting Peace: Population-Based Survey on Perceptions and Attitudes about Peace, Security and Justice in Eastern Democratic Republic of the Congo." Harvard Humanitarian Initiative, December 31, 2014.

Vlassenroot, Koen. "The Making of a New Order: Dynamics of Conflict and Dialectics of War in South Kivu (DR Congo)." PhD dissertation, Ghent University, 2002.

Vlassenroot, Koen, and Chris Huggins. "Land, Migration, and Conflict in Eastern DR Congo." *Eco-Conflicts* 3, no. 4 (2004): 1–4.

Vlassenroot, Koen, and Timothy Raeymaekers. "New Political Order in the DR Congo? The Transformation of Regulation." *Afrika Focus* 21, no. 2 (2008): 39–52.

Vogel, Christoph. "Contested Statehood, Security Dilemmas, and Militia Politics: The Rise and Transformation of Raïa Mutomboki in Eastern DRC." In *L'Afrique des Grands Lacs. Annuaire 2013–2014*, edited by Filip Reyntjens, Stef Vandeginste, and Marijke Verpoorten, 299–324. Paris: L'Harmattan, 2014.

Waldorf, Lars. "Revisiting Hotel Rwanda: Genocide Ideology, Reconciliation, and Rescuers." *Journal of Genocide Research* 11, no. 1 (2009): 101–25.

Walter, Barbara F. "Bargaining Failures and Civil War." *Annual Review of Political Science* 12 (2009): 243–61.

———. "Why Bad Governance Leads to Repeat Civil War." *Journal of Conflict Resolution* 59, no. 7 (2015): 1242–72.

Weinstein, Jeremy M. *Inside Rebellion: The Politics of Insurgent Violence*. Cambridge: Cambridge University Press, 2006.

Weis, Georges. *Le pays d'Uvira*. Brussels: Académie royale des sciences coloniales, 1959.

Weiss, Herbert F., and Tatiana Carayannis. "Reconstructing the Congo." *Journal of International Affairs* 58, no. 1 (2004): 115–41.

Weldes, Jutta. *Constructing National Interests: The United States and the Cuban Missile Crisis.* Minneapolis: University of Minnesota Press, 1999.

Wendt, Alexander. *Social Theory of International Politics.* Cambridge Studies in International Relations No. 67. Cambridge: Cambridge University Press, 1999.

Wickham-Crowley, Timothy P. *Guerrillas and Revolution in Latin America: A Comparative Study of Insurgents and Regimes since 1956.* Princeton: Princeton University Press, 1992.

Willame, Jean-Claude. *Banyarwanda et Banyamulenge: Violences ethniques et gestion de l'identitaire au Kivu.* Brussels and Paris: Institut Africain-CEDAF and L'Harmattan, 1997.

Willum, Bjørn. "Foreign Aid to Rwanda: Purely Beneficial or Contributing to War?" PhD dissertation, Institute of Political Science, University of Copenhagen, 2001.

Wolf, Eric R. *Peasant Wars of the Twentieth Century.* Norman: University of Oklahoma Press, 1999.

Wondo, Jean-Jacques. *Les Armées au Congo-Kinshasa: Radioscopie de la Force publique aux FARDC.* Paris: Monde Nouveau, 2013.

Wood, Elisabeth Jean. "The Social Processes of Civil War: The Wartime Transformation of Social Networks." *Annual Review of Political Science* 11 (2008): 539–61.World Bank Group, *Rwanda Economic Update, January 2021.* Washington, D.C.: World Bank, 2021.

World Bank. "Demobilization and Reintegration in the Democratic Republic of Congo (DRC)." March 11, 2013. Available at https://www.worldbank.org/en/results/2013/03/11/demobilization-and-reintegration-in-the-democratic-republic-of-congo, accessed May 18, 2021.

———. "Democratic Republic of Congo: Public Expenditure Review (PER)." Report No. 42167-ZR, March 2008.

———. "Rwanda: Achieving Food Security, Reducing Poverty, Moving up the Value Chain." July 12, 2016. Available at https://www.worldbank.org/en/results/2016/07/12/rwanda-achieving-food-security-reducing-poverty-moving-up-the-value-chain, accessed May 21, 2021.

Zulaika, Joseba. *Basque Violence: Metaphor and Sacrament.* Reno: University of Nevada Press, 2000.

INDEX

Abandi, René, 138

Accord global et inclusive. *See* Global and Inclusive Agreement

Affleck, Ben, 243

Afghanistan, 110

Aldango, 85–86

Alliance des forces démocratiques pour la libération du Congo-Zaire (AFDL), 32–33, 35, 50, 73–74, 83, 96, 111, 124, 129, 214

Allied Democratic Forces (ADF), 52–53

Amani Leo, 172

Amisi, Gabriel "Tango 4," 61, 70–71

Amuli, Dieudonné, 140–41

anti-valeurs, 67

armed groups: defeating, 15; local, 47, 49, 52, 54–55, 198; maps of and key to, 16–23*f*; proliferation of, 101; ratio of officers to soldiers in, 47

Armée populaire congolais (APC), 199, 201, 204, 207–8, 214

Armée rouge, 171

artisanal mining. *See under* mining

Association coopérative des groupements d'éleveurs du Nord Kivu (ACOGENOKI), 155

autochtonie/autochthony, 30–31, 110, 117

autodéfense groups, 198

bachawi, 168–69

Bagayamukwe, Gustave, 52

Bagonza (UPC commander), 207, 216

Bamako, 114

Banyamulenge, 32

Banyarwanda, 43, 87, 122, 125, 128, 130–31

baraza intercommunautaire, 156

basoeurs. See nuns

Bateson, Gina, 95

battalion cadre, 175

Belgium, 25, 170

belligerents, interests of, 103–13

Bemba, Jean-Pierre, 202–4; territory controlled by, 42*f*

Beni, 49, 52, 69, 100, 148, 158, 200, 202–3, 205, 207, 216, 223, 234

Bidalira, Louis, 26

bijou, 168–69

Bisengimana, Barthélémy, 29–30, 155

Bitakwira, Justin, 49

Bivegete, Jean, 160

Bizimungu, Pasteur, 87

Blair, Tony, 10, 252–53

Bøås, Morten, 114

Bofane, Koli Jean, 67

Bomboko, Justin, 25

Bonane, Mushi, 48

bourgeoisie: military, 12, 34, 96–100; as term, 98; urban, 25–26

Boya, Paul, 117

brassage, 131

Brownback, Sam, 243

Buffett, Howard, 10, 252–53

Bukanga Lonzo, 232

Bukavu, 126–28

Bula Matari ("Breaker of Rocks"), 36, 64

Bulenda, Padiri, 48, 102

bunker mentality, 82

Bunyakiri, 33, 177–78, 181, 183–85, 188, 191
Burhinyi, 103
Butembo, 100, 223
Butler, Judith, 67

Cabral, Amilcar, 96
Cammaret, Patrick, 221
Catholic Church, 42
celebrities, 243
Central African Republic, 118
central government, threat of armed
    violence against, 102
Chabal, Patrick, 66, 94
Chad, 24, 110
chains of command, parallel, 101
Chambucha, FDLR attack on, 180
Chérin, Chéri, 66
China, investment from, 242
China Molybdenum, 242
Chiribanya, Xavier, 126, 148, 155
Chui Mobile Force (CMF), 201
Cisambo, Marcellin, 174
citizenship census, 30
Clapham, Christopher, 113
Clark, Phil, 82
Clausewitz, Carl von, 94
Clinton, Bill, 252
Clooney, George, 5
Coalition nationale pour le peuple et
    la souveraineté du Congo (CNPSC),
    53–54, 76
cobalt, 238
Cohen, Dara, 108
Cold War, 27–29, 94, 116
combatants, interests of, 73–76
Comprehensive Peace Agreement, 98
concessionaires, 214–15
conflict minerals, 243–44
Congo, idea of, 25
Congolese, imaginary, 8–10
Congolese National Movement-
    Lumumba. See Mouvement national
    congolais-Lumumba

Congolese state, 58–59. See also Democratic
    Republic of the Congo
Congo Minerals Act, 243
Congo River, 9, 65
Congo Wars. See First Congo War; Second
    Congo War
Congrès national pour la défense du peuple
    (CNDP), 8, 112, 121–23; backers of, 147–53;
    birth of, 41–45; demise of, 139–40;
    elections and, 133–35; flawed integration
    of, 140–42; forerunner of, 123–26; high
    command members of, 150f; interests
    behind, 157–63; interests of, 146–63; and
    minerals, 244–45; other constituencies of,
    153–57; post-CNDP, 50–56
Conrad, Joseph, 8–9
Conseil militaire pour la defense du peuple
    (CMDP), 133–34
consolidation, disinterest in, 99
Constitutive Act of 2002, 116
convictions, number of, 99
Courville, Cindy, 168, 252
Cramer, Christopher, 244
Cuban Missile Crisis, 119

Daloz, Jean-Pascal, 66, 95
Daly, Sarah, 95
dawa, 164, 168, 176, 180, 183, 192
Day, Christopher, 115
Debos, Marielle, 114–15
democratic elections, consequences of
    introducing, 48–49
Democratic Forces for the Liberation of
    Rwanda (FDLR), 113; Goma Peace Con-
    ference, 138–39; and mixage, 136–37; M23
    mutiny, 142; post-CNDP, 50–53; and
    Raia Mutomboki, 145, 167–69, 173–83,
    191–92; security threats, 80–83; Sukola II
    operations, 234
Democratic Republic of the Congo, 58–59,
    114–15; alternative realities, 246–49;
    armed group proliferation, 101; balkaniza-
    tion, 51; Chinese investment in, 242;

chronology of events in, 38; combatant interests, 73–76; consolidation, 99; defeatism regarding, 5–6; donating to, 8–10; economic/political liberalization, 116–20; estimate of military forces in, 97; explaining conflict in, 37–56; explaining conflict in, 7–8; failure to transform, 230–49; first parliamentary elections, 26–27; foreign direct investment in, 227; foreign invasions in, 32–33; forever war of, 4–7; fragmentation of, 100–103; GDP per capita in, 29; growing economy of, 240; historical background, 24–56; interests of, 66–67; internal displacement in, 4–6; international economic stakes in peacebuilding in, 238–46; lack of tragedy, 94; limits of state power, 64–67; national revenues/grants, 40; overseas development aid to, 226; peacemaking, 225–58; political culture in, 10; political elites, 62–64; political parties in, 63; power informalization, 59–62; private interests, 67–72; private investment in, 242; privatizing, 238–39; rise of political agitation in, 25–28; role of, 57–90; as source of profit, 72; stereotypes from, 8–10; structural transformation, 92–95; structure of, 59–60; tax farming operation, 92; technocratic solutions to, 231–38; under colonialism, 25
"Demoncratie" (painting), 66
Department of Justice, 248
Department of the Treasury, 248
Dhejju, Leonard, 204
Disarmament and Community Reinsertion (DCR), 212, 222
Disorder as a Political Instrument (Chabal), 66
dispo, 72, 92
Dittman, Kyatend, 171
donors, 8, 111, 256; alternative realities involving, 247–49; and artisanal mining, 245–46; complacency of, 250–53; and the Congolese economy, 238, 239, 240–41, 242, 243, 245–46, failings of, 230–31; flaws in, 226

Eastern Congo Initiative, 243
Ebla business, 3
écoles conventionnées, 65
81st Brigade, 133, 135
Eisenhower, Dwight, 106
11th Integrated Brigade, 175
Ellis, Stephen, 111
Enerunga, Anselme, 48
Enough Project, 154
Équateur province, 202
essentialization, 109–10, 111
état major (general staff office), 134
État-major opérationnel intégré (EMOI), 207–8
Ethiopia, political changes in, 114
ethnic identity, 111–12, 162
ethnicity, 110, 111, 141–42, 196–97
Eurasian natural Resources Corporation, 242
Eurasian Resources Group, 242
exceptionalism, framing conflict as, 110

Fataki, 198–99
Fayulu, Martin, 237
Fédération des entreprises du Congo (FEC), 214
Feingold, Russ, 243
First Congo War, 4; trend confluence, 29–36
Fizi, 28, 31, 33, 40, 46, 49, 51, 54, 76
FLC merger, failure of, 202–3
folie, 182
fond secret de renseignement, 71–72
fool's game (*un jeu de dupes*), 237–38
Force de résistance patriotique d'Ituri (FRPI), 209
Forces armées congolaises (FAC), 74, 126
Forces armées de la République démocratique du Congo (FARDC), 34–35, 39, 75, 100, 126, 137, 168; and Mai-Mai, 46–47; and peacemaking, 233–34; post-CNDP, 50–52; power informalization, 60–61; and Raia Mutomboki 168, 172, 175–77, 180—81, 183, 188, 191
Forces armées du peuple congolais (FAPC), 210, 212

Forces armées rwandaises (FAR), 32–33, 129
Forces Armées Zaïroises (FAZ), 60
Forces d'autodéfense locales et légitimes (FALL), 51
Forces populaires pour la démocratie au Congo (FPDC), 209, 212
Forces républicaines fédéralistes (FRF), 122
fragmentation, 93, 100–103; of political elites, 62–65; and Raia Mutomboki, 188–91
Francophonie Summit, 236
Frazier, Jendayi, 251–52
Freeport McMoran, 241
Front de libération du Congo (FLC), 202
Front des nationalistes et intégrationnistes (FNI), 209
Front for the Liberation of the Enclave of Cabinda (FLEC), 114
Front pour l'integration et paix en Ituri (FIPI), 209

Gasana, Guillaume, 148, 155
Gbenye, Christophe, 26
Geertz, Clifford, 72, 104
Geffray, Christian, 100
Gegere, 197
General Property Law of 1973, 197
genocidaires, 130
genocide ideology, 81–82
geography, variation of, 6
Gertler, Dan, 239, 249
Gihanga, Smith, 133, 135
Gishuba, Mayanga wa, 137
Glencore PLC, 239, 242
glissement (slippage), 53
Global and Inclusive Agreement, 4, 6, 228; donors, 39; enticing belligerents, 39–40; political conflicts created by, 38–49
Goetz, Alain, 85
Goldstone, Jack A., 58
Goma Peace Conference, 1–2, 138; affecting Congolese conflict, 37–56; recruitment during, 2–3; run-up to, 103

Gom: fall of, 145–46; key administrative positions in, 44
grants, 40
groupements, 179
Guerre de Masisi, 30
Guinea-Bissau, 115

Habarugira, Bonané, 160
Habyarimana, Juvénal, 32, 123–24
Hagmann, Tobias, 117–18
Harvard Humanitarian Initiative, 100
Heart of Darkness (Conrad), 9
Hege, Steve, 251
Hima Empire, 76
Hollande, François, 236
hostilities, outbreak of, 131–33
Human ights Due Diligence Policy, 234
Human Rights Watch, 69, 208
Hummers, 39
Hunde, 30, 179

independents, amount of territory controlled by, 42
Inspection de l'armée, 99
Interim Emergency Multinational Force (IEMF), 210–11
internal displacement in, 4–6
international actors, 117–18
international community, intervention from, 220–24
International Conference for the Great Lakes Region (ICGLR), 145
International Criminal Court, 143, 205, 216, 222
international media, 109–10
International Monetary Fund, 227, 240–41
International Security and Stabilization Support Strategy (I4S), 232
International Tin Research Institute (ITRI), 245
involution, 11–12, 93–94; ideational contours of, 107–13; material determinants of, 106–7; term, 104; theory application, 113–20

Iraq, 110

Ituri Pacification Commission (IPC), 209

Ituri, 194–96; alliances in, 207–8; escalating violence in, 207–8; ethnicity, 196–97; factors involved in conflict in, 213–18; FLC merger, 202–3; Hema self-defense group formation, 198–99; historical backdrop, 196–98; international community intervention, 220–24; outside actor dominance, 218–20; power struggle in, 203–6; UPC existence in, 214–18

Jackson, Stephen, 104

Kabarebe, James, 151

Kabika, Dieudonné, 148

Kabila, Joseph, 7–8, 34, 52, 59, 63, 66, 68, 71, 126, 157, 203, 205, 229, 240; informal networks of, 42–43; Kabila regime, 130; peace deals flaws, 228–29

Kabila, Laurent, 126, 159

Kabila, Laurent-Désiré, 4, 26, 32–33, 45

Kabundi, Innocent, 175

kadogo (child soldiers), 32, 73

Kagame, Paul, 68, 253

Kahuzi-Biéga National Park, 127, 173

Kaina, Innocent, 212

Kakwavu, Jerome, 209–10

Kamanzi, Emmanuel, 147, 155

Kambale, Moses, 148

Kamitau, Cleophas, 25

Kamoto Copper Company, 239

Kampala, 49, 200, 202, 205, 209, 215, 219–21

Kananura, Stanislas, 148

Kanganga, Limenzi "Bridge-Cutter," 179

Kangela, Musolwa, 175

Kapfere, Bruce, 111

Karegeya, Patrick, 79, 151

Karim, Peter, 219

Kasaï province, 84

Kasavubu, Joseph, 25–26

Kasikila, Shé, 131

Kasongo, Joseph, 126

Kataka, Janvier, 204

Katanga Mining Ltd., 239

Katanga province, 29, 84

Katoto, Katebe, 154

Kazini, James, 199

KBD, amount of territory controlled by, 42

Keen, David, 94

Khawa, Chief, 205

Kiir, Salva, 114

Kijege, Malik, 160

Kilalo, Mai-Mai, 53

Kimia II, 140–41

Kinshasa, 11, 33, 34, 37, 39, 43, 53–54, 64, 68, 92, 97, 106, 109, 121, 124, 134–35, 137–44, 148, 167–70, 204–6, 211–13, 241

Kivu Tutsi, 160, 162

Kisembo, Floribert, 204, 206–7, 211–12, 216, 219

Kyoka massacre, 168

Kzini, Brigade, 200

La Prospérité, 109

la rwandophonie, 129

Lambi, Djokaba, 212

le Grand Nord, 43

Le Potentiel, 109, 241

Lenge, Eric, 70

liberation insurgencies, 113

Liberia, civil war in, 117

Local Defense Forces (LDF), 158

local turn, 7

Lompondo, Jean-Pierre Molondo, 204

Lotsove, Adèle, 201

loyalists, 70

Luanda Agreement, 209, 229

Lubanga, Thomas, 143, 201–13, 216–18

Lubero, 27, 46, 49, 53–54, 76, 123, 158

LUCHA, 69

Lumbala, Roger, 202

Lumumba, Patrice, 25–27

Lundimu, Ngandu, 175

Lusaka Agreement, 228

lutende, 183

MacAdams, Dominique, 212
Machar, Riek, 114
Machel, Samora, 96
magic. *See dawa*; Raia Mutomboki: magical amulet
Mai-Mai Kifuafua, 173
Mai-Mai Mahoro, 103
Mai-Mai Ruwenzori, 103
Mai-Mai Shikito, 103
Mai-Mai: emergence of, 45–49; fragmentation of, 48; name origins, 263n16; and Raia Mutomboki, 167
Makenga, Sultani, 141, 144
maladie auto-immune (autoimmune disease), 49
Mali, democratization in, 116–17
Mamdani, Mahmood, 26, 155
Mandevu (FDLR commander), 89
Maniema province, 84
Mao Zedong, 138
Marandura, Musa, 26
Masisi, ethnic violence in, 178–82
Masudi, Pierre, 91
Masunzu, Pacifique, 160
Mathématiques congolaises (Bofane), 67
Mbaenda Delphin, 180
Mbuna, Dieudonné, 206
media, portraying conflicts in, 109
Meshe, Daniel, 176, 186
métier, 114
Micho, Claude, 88
middle peasantry, 96
militarized politics, democratization of, 102
military, estimates of, 97
minerals, 111, 243–44
mining, 83, 117–18, 140, 154, 173, 244, 253–54; artisanal, 32, 117, 230, 244–46; investments in, 69–70
Mirindi, Déo, 126
Mirindi, Séraphin, 138
Mission d'immigration des Banyarwanda (MiB), 27
mixage, 136–37
MNC-Lumumba, 28

Mobutu, Joseph-Désiré, 28; conflict incited by, 29–30
modern state, defining, 119
money, 92
MONUC, 210, 228
MONUSCO, 38, 233–37
Mouvement de libération du Congo (MLC), 33, 202, 204, 16
Mouvement du 23 Mars (M23), 10, 52–56, 61–62, 80–81, 85–89, 121–23, 250–55; decline of, 145–46; interests behind, 157–63
Mouvement national congolais-Lumumba (MNC-L), 26
Mouvement populaire de la révolution (MPR), 28
Mouvement révolutionnaire congolais (MRC), 213
Movement of Democratic Forces of Casamance (MFDC), 114
Mozambican National Resistance (Renamo), 100
mtu matata, 5
M23. *See* Mouvement du 23 Mars
Muba, Mutima, 173–74
Mubarak, Mugangu, 81
Mudundu 40, 103
muganga, 168, 176
Mugugu, Eyadema, 174–75
Muhima, Jeannot, 2
Muhindo, Faustin, 88
Mulele, Pierre, 26
Mulengwa, Jemsi, 49
multiparty democracy, introduction, 116
Murekezi (AFDL commander), 88
Museveni, Yoweri, 96, 113, 200–201
Mushikiwabo, Louise, 87
Musumbu, 168, 170
Mutebutsi, Jules, 126–27
Mutomboki, Raia, 51
mutuelle, 175
mwami (customary chief), 51
Mwanke, Augustin Katumba, 60
Mwendanga, Patient, 148

Nabyolwa, Prosper, 47–48, 126
national demobilization program, 49
National Resistance Army, 113
national revenues, 40
natural resources, violence tied to, 106–7
New York Times, 5, 139, 145
Ngalamira, Jean-Claude Musikami, 185
Ngaruye, Baudouin, 88
Ngbanda, Honoré, 68
Ngeve, Kambasu, 138, 148
Ngezayo, Victor, 154
NGOs, 1, 65, 99, 243
Ngoy, Kisula, 48
Niger Delta, 106
Niger, US support in, 118
Nkunda, Laurent, 44–45, 50, 123–25; ethnicity
   of, 111
No Nkunda No Job, 3
normalization, 108–9
North Kivu, 32, 45, 70, 87, 112, 122–27, 130, 134,
   143, 146, 149, 151, 158, 200; identification
   of citizenship" census in, 30; immigration
   to, 27–30; key armed groups in, 20–22;
   Mai-Mai groups in, 46; mining in, 244–45;
   nationalization campaign, 29; strongmen
   in, 49
notables, 182
nouveaux riches, 39
Nsengiyumva, Wilson, 88
Ntaganda, Bosco, 89, 134, 139, 141–42, 152,
   206, 212
Ntulumamba, 168
Numbi, John, 70, 135
nuns, 103
Nyamwasa, Kayumba, 79
Nyamwisi, Antipas Mbusa (Mbusa), 49,
   52–53, 200–211, 215–16
Nyanga, 30, 131, 234
Nyiragongo Volcano, 1
Nzabirinda, Déogratias, 147

Och-Ziff, 249
OC Muungano club, 171

OKIMO, 200
Olenga, Nicholas, 26
Olomide, Koffi, 3
Omari, Donat Kengwa, 175–76
Omasombo, Jean, 71
on contrôle tout, on ne contrôle rien, 64–65
Onana, Charles, 68
oncasseurs, 100
Ondekane, Jean-Pierre, 83
one percent doctrine, 83
Operation Artemis, 221–22
operation retour (return operation),
   47, 60
Organisation for Economic Cooperation
   and Development (OECD), 243
Orientale province, 84
Oriente Province, Cuba, 24
Ottoman Empire, 107

Padiri, Bulenda, 46, 48, 102–3, 175, 177, 185
Padiri Mai-Mai, 177
PARECO, 46, 112- 13, 137, 142, 172, 175
Parti pour l'unité et la sauvegarde de l'intégrité
   du Congo (PUSCI), 209
Pascal, Wangozi, 176
Pathways to Peace (report), 246
Pax Mobutuensis, 35
Pay-Pay, Christian, 88, 260
peace, structural impediments to, 95–103
peacebuilding: alternative realities, 246–49;
   core flaw in failure of, 247; flaws in logic
   of, 228–29; flaws in, 225–27; international
   economic stakes in, 238–46; lack of
   success in, 236; primary mistakes in
   approaching, 225; technocratic approach
   to, 227; technocratic solutions to,
   231–38; transforming Congolese state,
   230–49
peace process: arrangements put into practice,
   42; core of, 41
People's Redemption Army (PRA), 208
Petit Nord, 127
Pinaud, Clemence, 98

political agitation, rise of, 25–28

political compromise, 41

political elites, fragmentation of, 62–64

political problems, technocratic solutions to, 231–38

political settlement analysis, 246–47

pompier-pyromane (firefighter-pyromaniac), 49, 66, 255

population, abusing, 112

Pottier, Johan, 197

Poverty Reduction Strategy Papers, 249

power, informalization of, 59–62

Prendergast, John, 154

Pretoria Agreement, 228

prime de commandement, 71

Raia Mutomboki, 53; analysis, 182; clashing with FARDC, 176–82; developments leading to emergence of, 164–65; expanding into Kalehe, 176–82; expansion of, 172–76; first group, 172–73; first wave mobilization, 169; fragmentation, 188–91; and Goma Peace Conference, 170–71; groups (2012–2020), 189–90; historical backdrop to, 167–72; ideology of, 181; interests of, 191–93; leaders (2011–2014), 187; magical amulet, 168–69; numbers of groups, 181–82; and Rega, 169–70; representing society, 186; second group, 173–74; social constituency involving, 182–88; third group, 175–76

rapportage ("bringing in"), 60

Rassemblement congolais pour la démocratie (RCD), 8; amount of territory controlled by, 42; growing splits within, 128–31; internal divisions in, 43–44; losing power, 41; marginalization felt by, 41; vulnerability, 43

RCD-National (RCD-N), 202

Realpolitik, 130

rebellion, social nature of, 11–12

receptacles of collective action, 95

reform insurgencies, 113

reform projects, 241, 248

Rega: society of, 183; traditional society structure, 169–70

régimentation, 51, 142

Reno, William, 94, 115

repeat civil wars, 114

Rice, Susan, 11

Richards, Paul, 111

Ruberwa, Azarias, 41–42, 125, 128

Rugayi, David, 133

Rutshuru territory, conflict in, 131–33

Ruwenzori Mountains, 28, 31

Rwakabuba, Cyprien, 155

Rwanda: backing CNDP, 149–53; brigades, 125–26; development aid to, 251; different approach to, 253–58; economic interests, 83–87; ethnic solidarity, 87–90; foreign direct investment in, 227; government, 43–45, 76–89, 125–29, 149–53; interests of, 80–90; involvement in neighbor affairs, 86; Ituri objective, 219–20; mineral sector, 85; overseas development aid to, 226; peacebuilding interference, 249–58; Rwandan aggression, 122; security threats, 80–83; structure of, 77–89

Rwandan Democratic Forces for the Liberation of Rwanda (FDLR)

Rwandan Patriotic Front (RPF), 10, 31–32, 77–82, 86–88, 149–50; national security, 43; perceptions on, 252

Rwandan state. *See* Rwanda

Rwibasira, Obed, 160

Saba, Aimable Rafiki, 207

Sadiki Kangalaba Devos, 171

Sake, conflict in, 135–37

Saleh, Salim, 200

Salumu Kaseke, 171

Sanderson, Melissa, 241–42

Schmitt, Carl, 58

Second Congo War, 5; end of, 34–35; senior officer anecdote, 47; trend confluence, 29–36

Seko, Mobutu Sese, 4, 25
self-defense, label, 199
Semadwinga, Denis Ntare, 147
Sendwe, Jason, 25
Seninga, Robert, 49, 130
separatist insurgencies, 113
Serious Fraud Office, 248
Serufuli, Eugène, 43, 49, 84, 127, 129, 152, 159
Shabunda, 112, 167–76, 178, 180–86
Shadary, Ramazani, 237
Al-Shabaab, 113
Shannon, Lisa, 243
Sierra Leone, 106, 117
Somalia, 110
SOMINKI, 83
Soriano, Raphael, 154
Soumialot, Gaston, 26
South Kivu, 1; conflict erupting in, 27–28;
    Mai-Mai groups in, 46; mining in, 244–45;
    strongmen in, 49. See also Shabunda
Southern African Development Community
    (SADC), 146, 153
stabilization framework, transition to, 232
Stanley, Henry Morton, 197
state bourgeoisie, concept, 98
state power, limits of, 64–67
Stedman, Stephen, 57
structural adjustment program, 62–63, 117
Sudan People's Liberation Army (SPLA), 98
Sudan People's Liberation Movement
    (SPLM), 98
Sudan, political changes in, 114
Swedy, Kosco, 48
symbiosis, 105–6
syndicats, 156
Synergie, 123–26
Syria, 110
système ya lifelo, 3–4

Tembo, 30, 175, 178–83
Tenke Fungurume, 241
Third Republic, 35, 39, 228; reforms under,
    235–36

Thousand Sisters, 243
Tibasima, John, 200–203, 211, 215–16
Tinanzabo, John, 212
Torheim, Liv Elin, 114
Toynbee, Arnold J., 94
transitional government, 4, 6, 34, 39, 45–46,
    49, 68, 84, 118, 123–25, 127–28, 138, 148, 151,
    157–60, 193, 196, 203, 211–12, 217, 228–29,
    233, 239, 272n15
transitional government, forming, 34–35
Tshanzu, training camp in, 144–45
Tshisekedi, Félix, 231, 233
Tutsi, 30–33, 43, 75, 82, 87–89, 112, 122–23,
    128, 134, 152, 158–62, 191, 207
2002 mining law, 239
2011 elections, run-up to, 236
2018 elections, run-up to, 236–37
tyranny, intimacy of, 115

Ufamandu I, 179
Ufamandu II, 179
Uganda People's Defense Force (UPDF), 201:
    creation of, 198
Ugandan Alliance of Democratic Forces
    (ADF)
Umoja Wetu (Our Unity), 140, 172
umuryango, 156
umusabane, 156
UN Group of Experts, 69
Union des forces révolutionnaires du Congo
    (UFRC), 52
Union des jeunes patriotes sacrifiés (UJPS),
    103
Union des patriotes congolais (UPC), 134,
    199; cease-fire, 210; creation of, 200–202;
    decline of, 208–13; escalating violence,
    206–7; international community interven-
    tion, 220–24; outside actor dominance,
    218–20; shallowness of, 214–18; six-
    month movement, 206–7
United Nations Group of Experts, 97, 139
United Nations High Commission for
    Human Rights, 69

United Nations High Commission for
Refugees (UNHCR), 32
United Nations: civilian protection by,
233–34; on Ituri violence, 214–15; peace-
keeping mission of, 233; peacemaking
doctrine of, 228
UPC-Kisembo (UPC-K), 211
UPC-Lubanga (UPC-L), 211

variables, 7
Vigh, Henrik, 115
violence, 75; escalation, 139–40; media on,
111; peaks of, 6; understanding meaning
of, 108–9
violent kleptocracy, 66
Virunga National Park, 89

Waal, Alex de, 106, 118
Wakenge, Raphael, 5

Walendu-Pitsi
Walikale, 27, 30, 127, 154, 169, 176–81, 184,
190–92
Wamba, Ernest Wamba dia, 128, 197, 199
"war is not what it is," refrain, 91
warlord insurgencies, 113
Weber, Max, 119
Weinstein, Jeremy, 190
Wendt, Alexander, 11
Wolpe, Howard, 228
World Bank, 8–9, 39, 62, 76, 86, 226
World Cup, 79
World Development Report, 246

Yakutumba, William Amuri, 233
yando, 183

Zenawi, Meles, 96
Zulaika, Joseba, 111

A NOTE ON THE TYPE

This book has been composed in Arno, an Old-style serif typeface in the classic Venetian tradition, designed by Robert Slimbach at Adobe.

www.ingramcontent.com/pod-product-compliance
Ingram Content Group UK Ltd.
Pitfield, Milton Keynes, MK11 3LW, UK
UKHW040137060325
455863UK00003B/5